CAPITOL
HILL
IN
BLACK
AND
WHITE

*   *

CAPITOL HILL IN BLACK AND WHITE

by

ROBERT PARKER

with

Richard Rashke

DODD, MEAD & COMPANY
New York

To My Father
Robert Parker, Sr.

Published by Dodd, Mead & Company, Inc.
71 Fifth Avenue, New York, N.Y. 10003
Distributed in Canada by
McClelland and Stewart Limited, Toronto
Manufactured in the United States of America
Designed by Jeremiah B. Lighter

Library of Congress Cataloging-in-Publication Data
Parker, Robert, 1921–
    Capitol Hill in Black and White.

    Includes index.
    1. Washington (D.C.)—Politics and government.
2. Washington (D.C.)—Social life and customs—
1951–   . 3. Johnson, Lyndon B. (Lyndon Baines),
1908–1973.   4. Afro-Americans—Civil rights.
5. Parker, Robert, 1921–   . 6. Afro-Americans
Civil Rights.   5. Parker, Robert, 1921–
6. Afro-Americans—(D.C.)—Biography.
I. Rashke, Richard L.   II. Title.
F200.P37   1986   975.3′ 00496073   85-29917
ISBN 0-396-08670-5

    5   6   7   8   9   10

PREFACE

As I paid my last respects to Lyndon Baines Johnson, I was swirling with mixed emotions. He had given me a job when no one else would, had taught me all the politics I knew, and had helped create a new future for my grandchildren. I had worked on Capitol Hill for more than twenty years. Using what I had learned from him, I played the game his way and won. I was proud of my civil rights victories, and I loved the Lyndon Johnson who made them possible.

Yet for years, he called me "boy," "nigger," or "chief," never by my name. I remembered the morning I drove him from his home in northwest Washington to his office in the Senate. He was in the back seat, reading *The Washington Post,* as usual. Suddenly, he lowered the newspaper and leaned forward. "Chief," he said, "does it bother you when people don't call you by name?"

I answered cautiously but honestly. "Well, sir, I do wonder. My name *is* Robert Parker."

Johnson slammed the paper onto the seat as if he were slapping my face. He leaned close to my ear. "Let me tell you one thing, nigger," he shouted. "As long as you are black, and you're gonna be black till the day you die, no one's gonna call you by your goddamn name. So no matter what you are called, nigger, you just let it roll off your back like water, and you'll make it. Just pretend you're a goddamn piece of furniture."

I hated *that* Lyndon Johnson. And his words stuck in my belly like a fishhook for thirty years until I almost believed them.

Then I thought of the 1963 March on Washington, and in my

mind's eye I could see thousands of blacks carrying signs that screamed at me, "I am a Man." As I stood in that Texas graveyard, I knew that the "piece of furniture" was being buried there with Lyndon Johnson, and that I too could now say, "I am a Man." Because of what Johnson did for civil rights, I owed that freedom to him as well.

I watched his coffin being lowered into the Texas earth and felt more than a great sense of loss. It was as if a part of my life were being sealed up, like rooms in an old house, the drapes drawn and the doors bolted against intruders. One remembers those rooms with longing, perhaps with fear, and maybe one even counts the memories entombed there. But one can never enter them again.

I lifted my eyes from the mound of earth next to the grave and scanned the crowd of two hundred people tightly packed around the spot where the coffin had sat just a few minutes before. There were cronies from Lyndon's early days in Texas politics, New Dealers from the Roosevelt years, old colleagues from the House, scores of senators, former and present members of the Cabinet, and an army of White House staffers—all the people I would have expected to pay a last tribute. Most of them respected Johnson and would miss him. Some hated him and would not breathe easy until the last shovelful of dirt fell on his remains, almost as if they were afraid he'd leap from his grave to bellow at them.

At my side stood Zephra Wright, LBJ's personal cook, whom the Johnson family had asked me to escort from Washington. Quiet, unforced tears were rolling down the creases in her leathery face. They seemed to me to sum up the weariness and the trials of generations of blacks like my great-grandfather, who was a slave, my grandfather and father, who were sharecroppers as poor as the Texas sand and clay they tilled, and my sister, who had been robbed of her pride so early in life. I thought not only of them but also of Lyndon Baines Johnson, that tall Texan who was warm-hearted and caring, and vulgar and mean. I looked at the other fifty or so black men and women around the grave who were also weeping, and I realized for the first time how deeply black attitudes about Lyndon Johnson had changed in the decade since he had become president after the assassination of John F. Kennedy.

At first, blacks had refused to acknowledge Lyndon Johnson as their president because they considered him a southern white bigot.

To symbolize what millions of blacks were feeling but not saying when Johnson became president, several dozen of them lay on the streetcar tracks on Pennsylvania Avenue near the White House in protest. I myself had worked for Johnson for nineteen years on Capitol Hill, since 1944. I had watched him roar and whisper, had heard him whistle Dixie to southerners and Yankee Doodle to liberal northerners in the same breath. And on the day he so hastily took his oath of office on the Bible amid the shocked and weary witnesses on Air Force One, even I didn't know how much good Johnson would do for blacks in his five years in the White House.

But the Bible was right when it said, "This too shall pass." Soon Lyndon Johnson was sweet-talking and bullying through Congress the most important civil rights laws this country has ever seen or dreamed possible.

Now, ten years later, instead of wearing black armbands of protest against the "fox in the chicken coop," blacks were standing at his grave weeping. It was a fitting tribute.

It took the passing of that great man, as flawed and as difficult to grasp as Texas itself, to make me realize how much I owed him. In a strange way, it was his funeral that inspired this book. It made me re-examine my life as a black man, particularly the influence my long years with Lyndon Johnson had had on the kind of man I became.

I know that other men and women have experienced terrible hardships in their lives, too. Maybe my story will help them understand themselves better and give them a bit more hope for the future.

ACKNOWLEDGMENTS

I want to express my appreciation to several persons who assisted me during the five years it took to complete my manuscript. Barbara Shorter helped me to organize my materials, and she spent many hours transcribing my tapes and deciphering my handwriting. Fred Walters performed much of the initial research. Associate Professor Richard Duncan of Georgetown University reviewed my manuscript for historical accuracy.

Then there were those who "kept the faith" and encouraged me. My brothers and sisters and my dear Aunt Rebecca. Their faith in "Sonny" never wavered. My friends, Jane and Marvin Roth and Jerry Sisk, gave me much more than moral support. Many of my acquaintances and co-workers from the Hill provided me with details and "thumbs up" support. Alex Hewes, friend and legal adviser, always took time to listen and provide guidance.

In the moments when I contemplated quitting, my children and grandchildren inspired me. An understanding of the past is part of my insurance for their future.

CAPITOL
HILL
IN
BLACK
AND
WHITE

*   *

CHAPTER

1

The empty wagon creaked as we drove home down the clay and sand road. It was dusk, and night falls quickly in east Texas in the last days of October. All I could think of was the hot stew and cornbread my mother would be keeping warm on the wood stove in our tar-papered house. Held together with unfinished pine boards, it sat on seventy-five acres that grudgingly gave us the corn, cotton, peanuts, and sugarcane that we sold each year.

We were about a mile and a half from home, and it was getting chilly. My father, my sister Rebecca, and I were exhausted from cutting oak trees to clear more land for spring seeding. It had been raining for several days all over Montgomery County, and the fields were too muddy to work, so my daddy had decided to catch up on chopping wood. A thin, wiry man with a rich baritone voice, he always seemed to be wrapped in a blanket of inner peace, and he brooked no arguing or fighting in our home. Besides sharecropping, he sold firewood to our landlord and to other white folks around Magnolia, and my mother took in washing and ironing.

Our wagon was empty because we were too tired to load it with the wood we had just split for our landlord, Mr. Yawn, who owned the general store in Magnolia where we bought everything from cornmeal to overalls. While our mules, Nelly and Jack, hauled us home through the almost-bare woods, Rebecca and I sat up front with my father humming his favorite song, "I'm So Glad I Got My Religion in Time." Like his own father, my daddy was a Baptist minister, although he had never gone to school. And we were a religious family, gathering at night around an old pipe organ in our four-room house to sing hymns or spirituals.

It was 1932. I was eleven and Rebecca fifteen, but we weren't in school like the white children. We went to Tom Felder's one-room schoolhouse in Pinehurst, seven miles away, from November

1

until he closed it in April, when Negro children had to join their daddies in the fields. Most of the boys never finished all eight grades but the girls did, and there was no high school for Negroes in the area.

I heard his horse crunching the oak leaves in the woods even before he jumped through the pines along the edge of the road right in front of us. My daddy had to "whoa" the mules so the wagon wouldn't bump him or his horse. We skidded to a halt, and the steel rim of the wagon wheels screeched over a rock buried in the clay and covered with sand.

Mr. Yawn had always frightened me, from as far back as I can remember. He wasn't tall, under six feet, as I recall; but sitting on Prince, his red horse that had a cotton-white blaze running down its nose, and with a Texan hat hiding his bald head, black knee-high boots, and a belt with a buckle the size of a tin-can top, he looked like a white giant to me. Curled around his saddlehorn was a black leather whip. I had never seen him use it, but I had heard tell how he'd peel black skin with it every now and then. He used to make me and a much bigger neighbor boy fight each other like two cocks, and he'd give a nickel to the winner. Small for my age, I always lost. It got so that every time I saw the other boy, I'd run and hide. Mr. Yawn thought that was so funny, he took to calling me "Poor Boy." I resented the nickname almost as much as I did him.

Mr. Yawn was the most powerful white man in Magnolia, forty miles north of Houston, and in all of Montgomery County as well. Besides my daddy, Mr. Yawn worked forty other sharecroppers, each tilling seventy-five to a hundred acres. For the seed and tools he gave us, he kept two-thirds of the cash crop. And besides the land we worked for him, Mr. Yawn owned a huge cattle ranch and a sugarcane plantation along the Brazos River to the west, where the soil was black and fertile, unlike ours. He even had his own sugar mill, and in the winter months I used to lead the mules that turned the cane grinder.

Mr. Yawn was also the Grand Dragon of the Montgomery County Ku Klux Klan. I used to think the Klan was fascinating when I was little. A friend and I had heard about their secret meetings in the woods not far from my house. We used to slither on our bellies to the edge of the clearing where they met and, wide-eyed, watch the burning crosses and white hooded forms glowing pink and orange in the firelight. We didn't understand what they were so excited about, but as two Negro boys at the edge of the white man's mysterious world, we figured they'd be plenty sore if they caught us spying on them.

It didn't take me long to lose my fascination with the Klan. One night a posse of white robes carrying torches stopped at our house and shouted for my daddy to come out. I could almost smell his fear. I watched through the open door, and I can well imagine my mouth was hanging down to my belt. The horses were pawing the ground and prancing nervously, the flickering flames were casting shadows around the yard, and a mean voice was shouting from inside a white hood, "Nigger, you see so and so? We're looking for him. He killed a white man up in Conroe." My daddy said, "No, suh," nice and polite, and the posse thundered off to the next Negro home. I didn't know yet what that encounter in the night was all about, but I was sure it had nothing to do with a Sunday picnic.

My real introduction to the Klan was in every way the brutal experience it was meant to be. One morning, a truck came down the dirt road next to our house raising a cloud of dust. Two white men sat in the cab and one of them was shouting through a bull-horn, "Take a good look at this, niggers, and don't ever forget it." Tied by his feet with a long rope dragging in the dirt was a boy I had known. He had been tarred, feathered, and lynched for alleg-edly casting a lustful glance at a white girl. My mother tried to hide the hideous scene from me, but before she could get me into the house, I had seen and heard everything the white folks wanted me to. From that moment on, I lost all my fascination with the Klan, and it was no longer a mystery to me.

"Where you been, nigger?" Mr. Yawn demanded of my daddy as he leaned over Prince to peer down at us.

"Back yonder, suh," my father said.

"What you been doing?"

"We be cuttin' wood."

"Then why you going down this road with an empty wagon? Why don't you niggers think for once in your life? You could have loaded it with wood and then unloaded it at my house or yours, and not waste all that time. Turn that wagon around, you dumb nigger, and go back and fill it up."

"Yes, suh," my father said, and he seemed older and more bent when he said it. I hated Mr. Yawn more than I feared him when he talked to my father like that, and I was always disappointed when my daddy never spoke up to defend himself. I couldn't understand, with the great wisdom of an eleven-year-old, why he didn't just tell the white man that we had been cutting wood all day and were too tired to load and unload the wagon one more time. I thought my father was playing coward, and I didn't like it one bit.

Mr. Yawn looked at Rebecca, huddled close to me against the evening chill, dressed in a cotton shift and sweater. She was a quiet, obedient girl with wide, bright eyes, and she was such a hard worker that my daddy used to bring her to the fields to help us instead of our mother.

"Gal," Mr. Yawn told her, "you get off that wagon and sit here and talk to me."

My father spoke up quickly. "Us needs her."

"I want her to stay here with me, nigger," Mr. Yawn shouted.

Rebecca climbed off the wagon, and I could see she was scared. Why would this white man want to talk to her? What did she have to say? I was frightened too, because I feared something bad was going to happen. I waited for my daddy to order Rebecca back onto the wagon, but he didn't say a word. He must have sensed that I was about to do something foolish, for I heard him threaten under his breath, "You stay put, boy!"

My father turned the wagon around and headed back to the woodpile. I looked at his face, hoping to meet his eyes. I could see the muscles in his jaw working hard, but he kept his eyes down as if he were watching for potholes in the road. Every now and then, he pulled a red handkerchief from his hip pocket, pretending to blow his nose. But I could see him dabbing his eyes.

I didn't break the silence because I was afraid my father would hit me. He was a strict, religious man who stood for no sass from his sons. But I was more angry at him than I had ever been at anyone. If he had stood up to Mr. Yawn, I reasoned, the most the white man would have done would have been to yell at him or maybe hit him a few times with that snake of a whip curled around his saddlehorn. That would have been a small price to pay to protect his own daughter. I was just too young to understand. I couldn't read the helplessness in my father's face as I can now, the humiliation in his bent shoulders as he tapped the mules with the reins trying to make them hurry, or the anger boiling in his stomach like a sulphur spring. I couldn't see beyond my own boyish rage, and I didn't understand, as he did, what it meant to be a Negro in east Texas.

Forgetting how tired I was, I pitched split oak and pine logs faster than I had ever done before, until sweat dripped from my face and my arms ached, and when the wagon was full we drove as fast as Jack and Nelly could drag us back to the lonely spot in the road where we had left Rebecca. The wagon groaned under the weight. It seemed to be crawling to the crack of the whip and the "giddy up" that echoed in my ears.

I saw her from a distance, sitting still at the side of the road hugging her sweater, and I had to stop myself from leaping off the wagon and running to her. When my daddy finally halted the wagon, she climbed aboard but didn't say a word. "What's wrong?" I asked. My sister and I were very close. "What happened? Why you crying?"

Robbie, as I called her, said nothing, but hung her head as if she were ashamed to look me in the face, and the tears rolled quietly down her cheeks like dewdrops on a flower. My daddy didn't say anything either. What could he say to his fifteen-year-old daughter whom he had just sent to a white man to be raped?

We were silent the rest of the way home. We didn't hum "I'm So Glad I Got My Religion in Time." I didn't think God was with us, and I wasn't hungry anymore.

Our house had three bedrooms and a kitchen. My father and mother slept in one bedroom, I and my two brothers in another, and my three sisters in the third. I was too angry and confused to sleep that night, and even though I was only eleven, I could feel the tension between my father and my mother, who was part Cherokee Indian from Oklahoma. She was a proud woman with straight black hair that hung to her knees and mysterious brown eyes that danced when she was angry. All she had to do was look at me, and I knew the fear of the Lord.

Ours was a peaceful home, with praying and Bible-reading and neighbors coming in for weekday religious services with my father, who could pray like no one I've ever heard. But that night my mother's eyes were filled with fire. "Why you do it?" she shouted at my father. "Why you leave her?" No matter what my father said to defend himself, it sounded so weak and sniveling to me that I can't even remember it to this day. My mother had dared to ask the questions I couldn't. And like her, I was not satisfied with the answers.

Several days later, after relentless pestering, Robbie told me that Mr. Yawn had taken his pleasure with her, not that I hadn't suspected it all along. Knowing about sex comes early when you live with as little privacy as we did, and where the walls were cardboard thin.

"What he say?" I pressed Robbie.

"He say, 'You supposed to do this, gal. You owe it. If you fight me, I'll put this whip to you, gal.' "

I cried myself to sleep many a night after Robbie told me what happened, and as the days grew into weeks and months, so did my hatred of Mr. Yawn. Robbie was never the same again. The white man had stolen her dignity and dirtied a precious corner of her self when he had taken her, at dusk, on the leaves in the woods. She couldn't look at the world anymore with the bright, childlike eyes she used to have, full of wonder and delight. The sparkle had died, and in its place, it seemed to me then, there was sadness, maybe guilt, certainly disappointment in her daddy.

We swore to get even with Mr. Yawn, Robbie and I. My vow was like a worm in my stomach that gnawed from daylight until I fell asleep at night. Sometimes it even ate into my dreams. With each passing year, I grew angrier at my father and more full of hate for our landlord. As happens when one matures, I began asking more and more questions and found fewer and fewer answers. Like every Negro boy I knew, I began to see that there were two worlds, one black and one white, and I came to accept the fact that it would always be that way. What I wanted to know was why, because it wasn't right.

Why couldn't I go to a movie when the white children could? Why couldn't I swim in the same places white children did on simmering summer days? Why did the KKK always pick on Negroes? Why didn't the police protect us like they did the white folks? Why did the sign outside Conroe say, "Nigger, Don't Let the Sun Go Down Upon You in This Town"?

6

I remembered the time a friend and I were walking back home down the "big road" and two white men in a pickup stopped us.

"You nigger boys want a ride?" they asked.

"Yes, suh," we said.

We climbed aboard, and as we neared the side road where we lived, we pounded on the roof of the cab. "Here's where we go," we said.

"If you niggers want to get off," one of the white men shouted against the wind as the truck picked up speed, "you gotta jump."

We did. My friend broke his back and has been in a wheelchair ever since, paralyzed from the waist down. I told myself then, "If this is the way it is gonna be, I'll learn to live with it. But I won't stop asking why."

To me, that was the biggest question in the world, and I couldn't help asking it even if no one could give me an answer.

In my own childish way, I kept my promise to get even with Mr. Yawn. At first, I'd creep at night up to the white house where he lived with his wife and daughter. It was the biggest house in Montgomery County, as far as I could tell, with tall pillars standing guard along the porch and a tin roof to catch rainwater. I'd wait until it was quiet and then pitch rocks onto the roof. As I ran away, I could hear them hit with a thud and roll down to the gutter. I never gave a thought to what would happen if Mr. Yawn ever caught me.

Before long, I graduated from rock-throwing to nail-tossing. I'd spread nails all over Mr. Yawn's road, hoping one would sink into a tire on his blue four-door Chevrolet. A couple of times, I even pounded nails into the tires when Mr. Yawn left his car parked beside a field and was out of sight. As I grew older, my plots and plans became more ambitious.

One day, Robbie came up with the idea of sneaking up behind Mr. Yawn as he drew water from the field well near our house. Next to the well was a long trough, which I had to keep filled for Prince, and whenever Mr. Yawn stopped there to water the horse, he would lower the wooden bucket and take a drink of the cool water himself. Robbie wanted to push him in and then listen to him drown in the dark hole. But I talked her out of it. "Supposin' he gets hold of you and pulls you in there with him?" I asked her. The thought of

7

thrashing about in the water with Mr. Yawn was enough to chase the notion right out of her head.

Then one day in 1936, when I was fifteen years old, I found a rattlesnake in a potato sack in our shed. I tied the end of the burlap bag closed and hung it in a tree. A day or so later, my brother Richard caught a copperhead in a field and gave it to me in a box. He watched me put it into the sack with the rattler. Although I didn't tell Richard, I knew exactly what I was going to do. Mr. Yawn's empire was so large that he used to travel it every day by car and by horse. Pulling his horse trailer, he'd drive the Chevy as close as he could to the fields he wanted to inspect. Then he'd leave the car parked by the side of the road and ride off on Prince. I made up my mind to watch for the blue car and then put the two snakes inside. If I was lucky, they would kill him. If I wasn't, Mr. Yawn would be one hell of a scared or sick white man. I talked it over with Robbie, and she agreed to be in on the plot.

My mother found out before we could plant the snakes. I'm not certain, but I think Richard told her I was collecting them in a sack. She sat me down and lectured me good. "Don't you know, boy," she said, "that the Bible says 'Thou shalt not kill'? You let those snakes be."

That night she told my father, and he came after me with a razor strap. It was the worst beating he ever gave me, and I couldn't forgive him. I was the only one who was man enough to stand up to Mr. Yawn, and it was me who was being punished. My father had the courage to beat his fifteen-year-old boy, but couldn't even speak up to the white man who had raped his own daughter. It just wasn't right.

My mother had the sense to see the bitterness growing in me, and she knew that my hatred for Mr. Yawn was spilling over onto my own father. I was heading for certain trouble if I stayed in Magnolia. At worst, I would be lynched. At best, I'd have my tongue cut out, or I'd be castrated as others had been or I'd be whipped until I was broken and crippled. So in 1936 she packed me up and sent me to live with my aunt in Wichita Falls, where I would soon meet Lyndon Baines Johnson.

My mother did the right thing, and I knew it at the time. I've never held it against her. She died at the age of thirty-eight, worn out from bearing too many children too fast with no proper medical

8

care, and too much worry. Robbie died at the age of twenty-one. I can't be sure, but I've always felt that, along with her virginity, Mr. Yawn took her will to live. My one regret is that she died before forgiving our father for leaving her alone that day.

For my part, I wouldn't see or forgive my father for thirty-six years. Only after I had worked in Washington for Lyndon Johnson did I come to recognize that blacks had no rights under the law in places like Magnolia, Texas—none. My daddy had done the right thing, for he had no real choice. Had he stood up to Mr. Yawn the way I had expected and hoped he would, Robbie would have been raped anyway and perhaps physically battered and beaten as well, my daddy would have been whipped and probably lynched, and our house would have been burned to the ground. My mother might have been raped for good measure, and I and my brothers might have been castrated. I finally came to realize that if all that had happened, there would not have been one single thing he could have done about it. It took me twenty-seven years to learn what my daddy had known all along.

The aunt and uncle my mother sent me to live with were prominent in the Wichita Falls colored community. Aunt Rebecca was the only black beautician there that white women allowed to curl their hair. Uncle Curtis was a real estate investor who owned twenty-five or thirty homes. I enrolled in Booker T. Washington High School in 1936 and got a part-time job as a busboy at the segregated Wichita Falls Club, where my older brother George was headwaiter. I was angry and lonely during my high school years. Fortunately, there was football, and I soon became BTW's star fullback. Jackie Robinson, the most versatile athlete in the country, became my idol. He was a star at every sport he tried at UCLA—football, baseball, basketball, track, and tennis, even Ping-Pong and bowling. He was bright and famous—everything I wanted to be. Like him, I planned to go to college and earn my reputation on the gridiron.

My aunt and uncle tried to help me live with my bitterness, for they knew what I hadn't learned yet: To survive in Magnolia or Wichita Falls—and there wasn't much difference between the two—black people had to swallow their bitterness. If they didn't, it would either eat away at them until there was nothing left, or it would drive them to dangerous heroics.

George knew I was interested in people. One day in 1939, when Lyndon Johnson came to the club for lunch, George asked me if I wanted to meet the congressman. He had seen me eyeing the club's prominent guests as I cleaned up the dishes. He knew them all and, like good headwaiters everywhere, had developed the knack of making them feel that he was there just to serve them.

I was eager to meet Lyndon Johnson, for, although he was not yet a senator, everyone in Texas knew he would be someday. Wichita Falls had been little more than an old oil town before Senator

10

Morse Sheppard dipped into the pork barrel and came up with Sheppard Air Force Base, just outside of town. Now Wichita Falls was a key city in the congressional district, and since Johnson was widening his political base, he and his chief aide, Walter Jenkins, were frequent visitors at the local club.

"This is my little brother," George said to Congressman Johnson. "He's a star football player at Booker T. Washington."

Johnson shook my hand. I was impressed by how tall and skinny he was, and I kept my eye out for him over the next several months. He'd always say hello to me. It made me feel good that important people were beginning to recognize me, for already as a teenager I sensed that meeting the powerful would be my way out of poverty.

After that, I watched Johnson closely whenever he came into the club. My mother had told me that I could learn more about people by watching them than by hearing what they were saying. Johnson impressed me as a careful, cautious, and determined man, preoccupied with something bigger than just his steak, his friends, and Wichita Falls. As he listened to the politicians and contributors he met at the club, he seemed to be making mental notes. When I heard him speak, his voice was soft and persuasive. There was none of the raucous bellowing that I would hear later when I worked for him.

I was graduated from high school in 1940. But before I could be drafted, I joined the army. In August 1941, I entered Fort Leonard Wood, Missouri, for my basic training. I hated army life. Most of the black soldiers were old, uneducated, and mean; the officers were young, white, and filled with contempt. It was hard to find a drop of human kindness.

After three months of basic training, the army offered me four limited choices: work in the supply room, at a typewriter, as a Military Policeman, or in the kitchen. I saw no future in sorting uniforms in the supply room or in guarding fences in the Military Police. Not knowing how to type and not especially interested in learning, I chose the kitchen, where at least I could eat well. It was a decision that influenced the entire course of my life.

The army sent me to cooking school. Before long, I was promoted to mess sergeant. When there was an opening for a mess sergeant in the all-white officers' club at Fort Leonard Wood, I applied. By the fall of 1941, I was a master sergeant. About that time, I met Modean Jones at a USO dance. A student at the Homer G. Phillips Nursing School in St. Louis, she was a stunning woman, vivacious and warm, with big black eyes and a baby voice. Mo, as I called her, weighed just over a hundred pounds and was my first real date. After courting for six months, we married.

Once the Japanese invaded Pearl Harbor, the army decided it needed Negro officers to command its Negro fighting men. I took an exam for the officers' training school at Fort Belvoir, Virginia, and passed. Modean answered the government's urgent call for help and took a job as a War Department secretary in Washington for $1,040 a year, so we could be together. Before I could be admitted to Fort Belvoir, I had to complete combat training at Fort Leonard Wood. Unfortunately, I was severely injured in a fall, breaking my right shoulder and leg in several places and twisting my neck. Doctors had to use pins and plates to put me back together again. I would never make it to Fort Belvoir. In the fall of 1943, I received a medical discharge and left Missouri to join Modean. I had big dreams.

The army had opened my eyes, as it did for hundreds of thousands of black boys and men, to a world much bigger than Magnolia and Wichita Falls. Although I tasted a bellyful of prejudice in the army, I saw enough to convince me that a black man might be able to achieve something if he had courage and managed to find a decent job.

With more hopes and dreams than were good for me, I boarded the train from Fort Leonard Wood for the nation's capital in October 1943. That's where the power to change the world lay, I innocently thought. A city on a hill, where good laws were made and bad ones repealed, where educated men and women worked together to create a just world for blacks and whites alike, where petty differences and regionalism were buried for the good of all. If any city could be free of racial hatred, it had to be Washington. If a black man didn't have a chance there, he wouldn't find one anywhere.

I dreamed a bright dream on the train north. I dreamed I would get a job and work my way into some important position. I would go to college at night, if that would help. I would buy a fine home. No more tar-papered shacks for me. Modean's and my children would go to the best schools. No one would control my family as Mr. Yawn had my father's. I was going to be treated like the first-class citizen I knew I was, even though the whole white world, and much of the colored one, seemed to be telling me different.

Somewhere in the Shenandoah Valley surrounded by the hazy Blue Ridge Mountains, the train rumbled to an unscheduled stop. Three military police led eight handcuffed German prisoners of war into my car and told them to sit down behind me in the colored section. The prisoners had been working on a farm in the valley and were being taken back to their prison camp. Soon after the POWS had settled into their seats, the white train conductor burst into the car. He yanked down the COLORED sign and moved it behind the last German prisoner.

"Get up, nigger," he snarled at me as if I were an animal. "Move behind the sign!"

My heart began to hammer, and I was choking with rage and humiliation. I had served my country with pride and had just returned to civilian life with an injury. Now I had to sit behind the "enemy" because I was black and the conductor hated me. I was ready to tear the seats apart, smash the COLORED sign, strangle the conductor.

But I had learned my Jim Crow lessons as a black child. I recognized that I was angry at my own helplessness more than I was at the conductor. And I knew I couldn't change him or take down the offensive sign. Choking on my pride, I moved behind the sign, dreaming once again of the better life ahead in Washington.

The first place I went for a job in the capital, after Modean and I had settled into our one-bedroom apartment on S Street in northwest Washington, was to Lyndon Johnson. I visited his office at least once a week but couldn't get past his receptionist and aides. "He's out of town," they'd say. "Away from his desk. Not in." They wouldn't tell me when he would be available or let me make an appointment to see him. But I kept coming back.

My determination paid off. One morning, late in 1943, the receptionist told me Congressman Johnson would see me. I was naïvely counting on him remembering me. "I'm Robert Parker," I told him. "I met you several times at the Wichita Falls Club." When his eyes showed no recognition, my heart sank. I began dropping names of mutual acquaintances. He remembered them, but not me.

13

As a last resort, I described how I used to wait on him. There was a flicker of recognition and a little smile on his face. He didn't know Robert Parker, but he knew the "boy" who had served him so often with obvious admiration and eagerness to please.

My mouth felt like cotton when I realized that this was my *one* chance to land a decent job. If I failed in the next sixty seconds, I'd probably never find work.

"What can I do for you, boy?" Johnson asked quietly.

"I need a job, sir," I managed to say.

"What kind of job, boy? What can you do? Would you like to work in the post office, boy?"

I couldn't even stammer an answer. Johnson grabbed the phone and dialed the city post office director. "I wanna sponsor this boy," he said.

At that moment, I stood in awe of Lyndon Johnson. I had never seen such power. With one phone call, I not only had a job, but I had a *career* civil service position, without even taking an examination. Little did I realize then how simple the whole thing was, for Johnson had developed contacts all over Washington who owed him favors. What I did realize, however, was that now that Johnson had sponsored me, I owed him. And if I didn't pay, I could have my "career" job jerked away as fast as it had been granted. It was a polite form of slavery, but a small price to pay for a good job that, I sensed, had opportunities for a black man. That civil service rating turned out to be extremely important, for twenty years later I would use it to win better working conditions for the blacks who worked in the Senate Dining Room.

I began working as substitute mail carrier in late 1943 for $1,200 a year on the Cleveland Park route where Lyndon Johnson, Vice President Harry Truman, FBI Director J. Edgar Hoover, and other powerful and important people lived. I was twenty-three years old. The job was a real education, for it gave me a chance to see two Washingtons. The Post Office paid my salary but I considered LBJ my employer, and he remained my employer till 1961.

The nation's capital had a split personality in 1944. One Washington was a town without power, peopled mostly with southern blacks who had come north searching for opportunity, only to end up doing what they had always done—serve white people.

The other Washington was beautiful and powerful, from the

14

polished white marble of the Capitol, to the all-white law offices that clung to the government like barnacles, to the white lobbyists who roamed the halls of Congress, to the brick row houses on the Hill and the white frame homes of northwest Washington, painted, gardened, and cleaned by blacks.

I had seen all that before as the son of a sharecropper, as a high school student in Wichita Falls, and as a soldier at Fort Leonard Wood. But what I found in the District of Columbia post office shocked me. I carried mail side by side with young black lawyers—several of whom later became judges when the U.S. courts were shamed into integration—who couldn't find work on the Hill or in the white law firms that fed off the government. Those black lawyers shattered a precious myth of mine: that if blacks managed to get an education, doors would open. That myth was a lie in the capital city in 1944.

In the post office, I learned an important survival lesson: At most, education could only *help* get me somewhere. What I really needed was power, the kind that comes from money, friends, and inside information. I took stock. I had no experience and only a high school education, yet I was sorting and delivering mail next to attorneys, making the same kind of money and lifting the same kind of bags, because I knew someone with power and had gone to him for help.

Rightly or wrongly, I decided early in my post office job that a college education would not help me survive in Washington, although it might work for other young black men. I saw the world as a jungle, and I knew I needed to learn quickly who had the power and how I could get some.

I got what I thought was a break several months after I became a mail carrier. Johnson's office called to tell me that the congressman needed a driver at six o'clock in the evening to take him and Mrs. Johnson to dinner at the Congressional Country Club, one of his favorite haunts. I was told to dress like a chauffeur, black hat and all, and that if I didn't have a uniform, to buy one. Lyndon Johnson, who did not have either a limousine or a regular driver, was beginning to collect on my debt.

I became such a good unpaid chauffeur that Johnson called on me at least once a week to drive him around town and to the Naval Academy in Annapolis on every Saturday that the Navy football

15

team played at home. Johnson was on the Naval Affairs Committee and got free tickets. I hated those Saturday trips. I'd pick up LBJ at ten in the morning. Usually he had invited Virginia Senator Harry Byrd and Georgia Senator Richard Russell to ride with him. Both were also on the Naval Affairs Committee, and the free ride was just one more way for Johnson to extend his power base in Congress.

Annapolis had been one of the biggest slave markets on the East Coast, and in the mid-1940s its attitude toward blacks was just as hostile as it had been before emancipation. I would drive Johnson and his party up to the front gate of the Navy stadium with instructions to be waiting there when they walked out after the game. Whenever I was late, no matter what the reason, Johnson called me a lazy, good-for-nothing nigger. He especially liked to call me nigger in front of southerners and racists like Richard Russell. It was, I soon learned, LBJ's way of being one of the boys.

After I dropped Johnson off at the stadium, I had no place to go. Annapolis had posted "whites only" signs all over town. There were no bathrooms for blacks, no restaurants or sandwich shops. There were no drinking fountains, and the police wouldn't let a colored park within miles of the stadium. Needless to say, there were no black spectators at the games. Since I couldn't prove that I was Congressman Johnson's chauffeur, the officers just kept saying "Move it nigger" until I was out of town. I would spend the hours listening to the game on the radio until it was almost over, then try to get back to the academy just in time to meet Johnson as he stepped out of the stadium. If I got there too early, the police forced me to keep moving. When they did, I would circle back and make another pass at the entrance. Before long, my timing was nearly perfect.

One Saturday afternoon, I arrived too early. The police moved me on, and I got caught in traffic. When I got back, Johnson was waiting, livid with anger. For him to wait five minutes was a major crisis, and he had been standing there for at least fifteen. "Goddamn nigger!" he shouted. "Can't you get here on time?" When I tried to explain, he cut me off. "I don't want to hear that horseshit!"

When we were alone later, Johnson softened a bit. "I can't be too easy with you," he told me. "I don't want to be called a nigger-lover."

Around six o'clock one Saturday morning before a Navy game,

16

I almost lost my job. I got caught in a raid at Puddn'head Jones, an after-hours club. Washington was famous on the East Coast for its after-hours clubs, which were all clustered around Sixteenth Street and Georgia Avenue. In many ways, they were the heart of the black community.

There weren't many places for Washington's blacks to meet and relax in the 1940s. We had a few theaters, like the famous Howard, and restaurants and bars, but nothing much happened until after two o'clock, when white Washington went to bed. Then black Washington began jiving in clubs like Gracie's and Linsey's and Billy Simpson's, whose soul food sandwich, the 652, named after the club's address, 652 Newton Street, was the most famous in town. The clubs were in private homes, and you couldn't get in unless the doorman, who peeped through a hole, knew you.

Most of the after-hours clubs were classy places, with some gambling but no open prostitution, although if you had money and the proprietor was a friend, you could get a room upstairs. The clubs were a necessary part of black life because they gave cooks, bartenders, doormen, bellhops, waiters, busboys, cab drivers, entertainers, and all the other black service people a place to eat and relax after white Washington no longer needed them. Insulated from the contempt and hatred of the city, the clubs were the place to be seen and meet people.

The after-hours clubs offered no special entertainment, but there was always a piano and someone playing it. I heard most of the famous black musicians of the 1940s in jam sessions at the clubs: Billie Holiday, Count Basie, Nat King Cole, Duke Ellington, Ella Fitzgerald. Sometimes they would come to Linsey's or Gracie's for steak and eggs, cornbread and beans, barbecued ribs or ham and grits, after performing for white audiences in the downtown nightclubs. Sometimes they were just in town visiting. And they never could resist making music. At the clubs, they sang and played their hearts out for their own people. That was part of the excitement of the after-hours places. You never knew who would be there, tinkling the ivories or shaking the rafters.

Occasionally, a few whites would be allowed in the clubs, but they had to be famous—I saw Frank Sinatra and George Raft in one—or they had to be guests of famous blacks. Congressman Adam Clayton Powell, whom every black in Washington knew, liked to bring whites with him. Naturally, the police were on the take and generally left the clubs alone. Even during an occasional raid for the books, the club owners' close friends were seldom arrested or even fined. But when white women entered a club, the police played for keeps. Every after-hours doorman tried to discourage famous customers from bringing white women, because they were a sure invitation to a raid. It drove the police, who were always watching to see who was coming and going, insane to see white women in an all-black club. It was the one thing they simply wouldn't tolerate.

Puddn'head Jones was not a typical, classy after-hours place. The club was a casino—craps, mostly—and the city's black numbers bosses, pimps, and petty thieves hung out there. Even though the police were on the take, they raided it more frequently than all the other clubs put together. When they charged through the door blowing whistles early one Saturday morning, I happened to be there, even though I was too broke to do any gambling. The police shoved me into a paddy wagon along with the gamblers and took me to the station. When I didn't have five dollars to pay the fine, they tossed me into the holding tank. I started to panic. In a few hours, I had to be at LBJ's home to drive him and his friends to the William and Mary game in Annapolis.

"I got to get out," I told the guard. "I drive for Congressman Johnson. Call his office if you don't believe me."

I could hear the guard talking to his superior. "Captain, we got a nigger back there who says he drives for Congressman Johnson. What should I do?"

The captain called Johnson's office after nine o'clock, and luckily someone was there who could vouch for me. The captain sprang me on the promise that I'd pay my fine later, which I did.

Johnson never brought up the incident, so I assume he didn't know about it. I got caught in at least a dozen more raids, but I never had to go to jail or pay a fine again. The first couple of times, vice squad officers hauled me in like everyone else, then let me go after the captain told them I was "Johnson's boy." Soon I would just walk out of the club to the paddy wagon with everyone else. The officer loading the disorderly into it would nod and I would keep walking.

I was beginning to feel a sense of power. I was somebody, because I drove for Lyndon Johnson. Today, I know that makes me sound like an Uncle Tom, but in the mid-1940s it was one of the few kinds of power for a black man. And I was proud because I was surviving, and doing it honestly and better than most. One evening while I was driving Lyndon and Lady Bird Johnson to the Congressional Country Club for dinner, I asked Johnson if he could get me a job there. "You want to work, boy?" he asked, not waiting for an answer. "Why not serve at my parties and my friends'?"

A new life opened up for me.

CHAPTER

* 3 *

Serving Lyndon Johnson's parties from the mid- to the late 1940s was more than just an opportunity for me to see important people and make pocket money. I was an intern, getting an education and an introduction into power politics. White Washington was a narrow-minded and pompous place in the mid- to late 1940s, and it measured influence by who and how many came to dinner and by the elegance of the party. As he did most things, Johnson used the dinner party superbly to gain power, win friends, and appear to be more prominent than he actually was.

Johnson's parties were usually small affairs for half a dozen politicians and their wives. Sam Rayburn, who was unmarried, was always there. Vice President Truman came sometimes. So did Henry Stimson, the secretary of war. Then there were Senators Richard Russell of Georgia, Alben Barkley of Kentucky, Theodore Bilbo of Mississippi, Tom Connally of Texas, Olin Johnston of South Carolina, and John McClellan of Arkansas. Given Johnson's political ambitions, it was a powerful group. Rayburn was Speaker of the House; Barkley, majority leader in the Senate. Truman would become president the following year, 1945, after Roosevelt died; Barkley, Truman's vice president in 1949. Senator Connally was chairman of the Foreign Relations Committee and a power in Texas politics. Russell, Bilbo, Johnston, and McClellan were white supremacists and leaders of the Democratic southern bloc that, most observers agree, controlled Washington at that time.

I began taking notes on who drank what and when. Soon I was passing out the right drinks before I was asked. Truman liked Old Fitzgerald with branch water; LBJ, Scotch and water; Rayburn, who didn't drink much in public, sour mash and ginger ale; and Olin Johnston's wife, ginger ale and whiskey without ice. Before long, even bigots like Bilbo were asking Johnson, "Where did you get this nice colored boy? We'd like to use him, too." They gave me their private phone numbers, and I began moonlighting several nights a week. I had become a status symbol. "If you want a successful party," the word went, "you must have that nice colored boy."

With back doors opening all over town, life became so hectic that I bought an engagement book to keep track of where I was supposed to be and when. I carefully wrote down the private phone numbers of all my employers, the personal touches they required, and a list of their usual guests and their likes and dislikes. Soon I was inside the homes of Cabinet members as well. I served the parties of socialite Perle Mesta, "the hostess with the mostest," as she became known around town. Harry Truman always seemed to be at her parties, pounding the piano keys and belting out songs. Her well-planned dinners were so informal and so much fun that they didn't seem as lavish as they really were. She'd have three in one week, then go for three weeks and only have one, just to keep other socialites like Gwen Cafritz, whose extravagant parties I also served, guessing. Cafritz and the other wealthy women addicted to throwing formal parties for the powerful were so jealous of Mesta that they referred to her as "Mrs. Thing."

I was even doing double-headers—an early cocktail party here and a late dinner there. I had to buy a tuxedo, because most of the wives insisted that I dress in black, as Negro servants did in the movies.

During the next few years, Johnson loaned me to his friends for a variety of jobs as a means of extending his power base. I regularly drove Olin Johnston, Tennessee Congressman Estes Kefauver, and Oklahoma Congressman Carl Albert around town. I'd take them to the airport in LBJ's car and drive them to apartments and hotels at night. I'd sit in the car, struggling to stay awake, until one or two o'clock in the morning, sometimes all night. When I worked exceptionally late, Johnson or an aide would call the post office and get me the next day off.

The spot LBJ, Kefauver, Johnston, and Albert seemed to like to visit the most was the Rhode Island Avenue Plaza, a luxurious apartment house for blacks in northeast Washington. In the 1940s, successful, professional blacks couldn't rent apartments or buy homes in the nicer parts of the city. Most drifted to the Plaza, which housed more talent and ambition than any building in Washington, including the Capitol.

I'd drop the congressmen or LBJ's constituents off at a side door at the Plaza and wait until the wee hours of the morning. I remember driving Kefauver there one night. As we turned the corner, he saw Carl Albert coming out the side door. "Keep driving," Kefauver ordered as he slid down in the back seat. "Go around the block." He didn't want Albert to know he had a colored "friend" there, too. I never did find out which women they visited, but I know that one or two who lived there eventually broke into politics.

Johnson never paid me for the boring night duty, and I understood this was how he expected me to earn his patronage. But when I didn't bring money home, Modean thought I was cheating on her. There she was, sitting at home with our baby, Barbara Ann, who was born in the spring of 1945, while I was out on the town. How was I to convince her that I wasn't the one who was out at night with a woman? The moonlighting and late hours brought a terrible strain to our marriage.

It also got me to the Army-Navy game. Though I had to stand in the end zone bleachers, I think I was the only black in the stadium. The reason I got in was because Lyndon Johnson asked me to work the cocktail lounge in the congressional car on the Army-Navy Special, which carried Washingtonians from Union Station to the game in Philadelphia. President Truman came along in 1945 and 1946, riding in the presidential car. The congressional car had a piano, and President Truman, who loved to mingle with the boys, used to come in to play, his Old Fitzgerald and branch water sitting on the piano next to him. The car would rock as the president and the congressmen sang.

The Army-Navy games always left me emotionally confused. I felt privileged to be the only black at the game but ashamed that I felt privileged instead of outraged. Back in Washington, the feeling became more intense. I was a hero in the black community. I had ridden in the congressional car and served President Truman his bourbon. I had actually stood inside the stadium to watch one of America's traditional spectacles, all-white Army playing all-white Navy. Though I couldn't resolve the conflict I felt at the time—I was only in my mid-twenties—at least I recognized the feelings warring inside me.

As pleased as I was with the exposure I was getting and the extra money I was making, working for Johnson during the 1940s in Washington was a painful experience. Although I was grateful to him for getting me a job with the post office and for giving me other opportunities, I was afraid of him because of the pain and humiliation he could inflict at a moment's notice. I thought I had learned to fight my bitterness and anger one day at a time, the way my mother had taught me, with kindness. But Johnson made it hard to keep the waves of bitterness inside. I would like him one minute and hate him the next. But I had to swallow or quit. If I quit, how would I support my family?

I chose survival and learned to swallow with a smile. It's what most black men did in Washington in the 1940s, before the civil rights movement was even a dream. As young as I was, I knew that before I could fight racism, I needed power. To get it, I had to survive. And that was a lonely, full-time job.

In front of his guests, Johnson would often shout "nigger" at me. He especially liked to put on a show for Senator Bilbo, who used to lecture, "The only way to treat a nigger is to kick him." The abuse got so bad that I used to dread being around Johnson when Bilbo was present, because I knew it meant that Johnson would play racist. That was the Lyndon Johnson I hated.

Privately, he was a different man as long as I didn't do anything to make him angry. He'd call me "boy" almost affectionately. Sometimes I felt that he was treating me almost as an equal. And then he'd tell me that I was a credit to my race—a "compliment" I soon came to detest.

Although I never heard him speak publicly about black men without saying "nigger," I never heard him say "nigger woman." In fact, he always used to call his black cook, Zephra Wright, a college graduate who couldn't find any other work, "Miss Wright" or "sweetheart."

My life during this time confused me as much as it angered me. In the kitchen, I was somebody; in the dining room, nobody. In the white community, I was a "nigger man"; in the black community, Robert Parker, because I drove or poured drinks for Lyndon Baines Johnson and his friends. I had come to Washington believing that the capital's heart was open to blacks. Whites in Magnolia and Wichita Falls had limited education and small vision. They were

23

farmers and laborers and drifters. In Washington sat educated lawmakers who had sworn to uphold the Constitution. But what I heard at the private parties where I served was depressing beyond words. Senators like Bilbo, Johnston, Russell, and McClellan bragged from one dinner party to the next, "There will never be integration. Never!"

Bilbo had been a member of the Ku Klux Klan while he was governor of Mississippi. In his twelve years in the Senate, he spoke openly on the floor about white supremacy over Negroes. He led a filibuster against the Fair Employment Practices Act, which was drafted to give protection to black workers. After the Supreme Court upheld the right of Negroes to vote in party primaries, he defied the law, announcing back in Mississippi, "I'm calling on every red-blooded American who believes in the supremacy and integrity of the white race to get out and see that no nigger votes. And the best time to do it is the night before."

As governor of South Carolina, Olin Johnston had also defied the Supreme Court by calling a special session of the state legislature, where he pushed through a bill repealing the state's primary laws. "Keep our white Democratic primaries pure," he urged South Carolina lawmakers. Senators Connally and McClellan also opposed every piece of civil rights legislation, including an antilynching law.

The shocking thing to me was that each one of those southern racists was an attorney. In my political innocence, I couldn't understand how one could be a student of the law, swear to uphold it before God, have the power to make it just, and then spend one's energy subverting it. Lyndon Johnson used to smile and nod when Bilbo and his friends vowed to fight integration, but to his credit I never heard him say "never."

I used to go home numb after those parties, with "never—never—never" echoing in my ears. Things got so bad during 1945 and 1946 that I reached a point where I half-believed that God meant there to be two worlds, a black one to serve a white one. If it couldn't be different on the Hill, I thought, then where?

Then I heard the honest and direct voice of President Harry Truman. Deeply disturbed about the rise of Klan terrorism, Truman recognized that only legislation could end "un-American practices," as he called them. To get the facts on racial discrimination and to publicize the need for civil rights laws, President Truman created the President's Committee on Civil Rights. When the fifteen members of the committee met at the White House in January 1947, he told them, "I want our Bill of Rights implemented in fact. We have been trying to do this for 150 years. We are making progress, but we are not making progress fast enough. This country could very easily be faced with a situation similar to the one which it faced in 1922." Truman was referring to the wave of Klan lynchings in that year.

Today, the creation of a commission to study a problem sounds like a cop-out. But in 1946, it was an extremely courageous act, one for which I believe President Truman has never received enough credit in civil rights history. The committee report, made public in October 1947, stands even today as one of the clearest and most honest civil rights documents ever written.

From where I stood, surrounded by the racist friends of Lyndon Johnson, Truman's call for racial justice sounded heroic but weak. The president seemed to be standing on the edge of a cliff, where one gust of wind from the South could blow him off. Curious lawmakers watched in silence from a distance, some sympathetic, some hostile, most just waiting to see what would happen.

Somewhat hopeful, I began listening with both ears from that day on. In one, I heard the bigot's thunder of "never" all around me, and in the other, Harry Truman's quiet but clear whisper promising equal rights.

CHAPTER

One night in early November 1947, I was serving a party at Leslie Biffle's home in Georgetown. "Biff" was a close friend of President Truman. As secretary of the Senate, with a thousand parliamentarians, librarians, clerks, bookkeepers, and pages under him, Biffle was a powerful man on the Hill and Truman's liaison. Short and always impeccably dressed, he had taught himself how to whisper without moving his lips. He had his own private dining room in the Capitol, where Truman frequently ate chicken and chatted with his friends. I liked Biffle, even though he was a racist from Arkansas and a close friend of Senator McClellan. His lively parties attracted some of the most powerful men in Washington. He was also a good tipper.

Most of the conversation at Biffle's party that November evening centered on the Freedom Train, the brainchild of Attorney General Tom Clark, who was facing two menacing postwar law-and-order problems. There was the "Red Scare" of the Cold War, which almost paralyzed the Justice Department and the FBI, and there was the racial unrest stirred by the growing boldness of the KKK. Blacks returning from the war were not as docile as they had been in the cotton fields and ghettos. A lot of whites felt forced to defend the white supremacy that they had always taken for granted. There was tension everywhere. Whites were demonstrating against school integration in Gary, Chicago, and other northern cities. (School integration would become mandatory in 1954.) Black soldiers were trying to integrate "white" officers' clubs in places like Freeman Field, Indiana. The KKK was lynching blacks like Jesse Payne of Madison County, Florida. There were race riots in Philadelphia, in Columbia, Tennessee, and in Athens, Alabama. James Farmer, cofounder of CORE, and a group of blacks were making the first tentative Freedom Rides south.

Attorney General Clark knew he was watching the ripple before the tidal wave. Supportive of President Truman's strong stand on civil rights, he cooked up the idea of sending a train full of freedom documents into every major city in the country to instill national pride and to demonstrate that the nation was built on the principles of equality. Truman, of course, backed the idea. So that no one could accuse the Truman administration of using the Freedom Train as an election gimmick or as a ruse to force integration, Clark had the Justice Department sponsor the train and a group of private citizens raise money, set policy, plan, and promote. Under the leadership of Winthrop W. Aldrich, chairman of the Chase National Bank, the group called itself the American Heritage Foundation, or AHF.

Clark called a White House meeting in May 1947 to explain the Freedom Train to a cross-section of business, religious, labor, and communications leaders, as well as to groups like the American Legion, the Daughters of the American Revolution, and the Lions Club. Of the more than fifty organizations participating, only the NAACP represented blacks. Clark and the officers of the American Heritage Foundation carefully couched the equal rights issue behind broad goals, using language such as "reassert the emphatic advantages of American Democracy." It was almost as if Clark wanted to get the Freedom Train rolling before anyone realized that racial equality was one of its two major themes. Of the more than twenty speakers at the White House Conference, Walter White, executive secretary of the NAACP, was the only one to link the Freedom Train to racial equality.

White was angry when he took the microphone. An all-white jury in Greensboro, North Carolina, had just acquitted twenty-six white men who had confessed to murdering Willie Earle, a black accused of killing a white cab driver. They had admitted to dragging Earle from his jail cell, beating him mercilessly, and then blowing his head off with a .16-gauge shotgun. After the clerk read the not-guilty verdict, defense attorney Tom Wofford shouted in the courtroom, "I think this is a perfect example of proving that the Department of Justice, Walter Winchell and other people up north should keep their mouth out of the south's business."

White was clearly disturbed at how the meeting had been focused almost exclusively on the threat of communism. "I am not nearly so much worried about foreign ideologies," he told the audience at the Freedom Train meeting, "as I am about some of the native totalitarianism here in the USA which can lynch the laws as has been done in North Carolina and repeatedly with respect to minorities in other parts of the country. . . . I pledge you the unqualified support of 13 million American Negroes who desperately want to see Democracy have a living reality in our country."

Almost as if they were waiting for the right moment, Truman and Clark spoke out forcefully during the official sendoff of the Freedom Train from Philadelphia on September 16, the eve of the 160th anniversary of the signing of the Declaration of Independence. After reading a message from the president emphasizing that in freedom "without distinction because of race, creed or color, lies the world's greatest hope of lasting peace," Clark emphasized the racial theme. "Prejudice grows out of ignorance," he said. "When you find a man who is prejudiced against some certain group of Americans because of color, race or religion, you can set it down that he is an ignorant man." Those may sound like tame words today, but they were courageous and powerful in 1947.

Enthusiastic crowds greeted the Freedom Train up and down the Northeast. Among the hundred documents it carried were the Emancipation Proclamation, the Bill of Rights, and the charter of the United Nations. Most cities held a "Freedom Week," with school programs, newspaper articles, and radio ads, ending with the arrival of the Freedom Train itself. In a typical twelve-hour stopover, ten thousand people could pass through the three windowless exhibit cars, guarded by U.S. Marines, to view the documents displayed behind shatterproof glass inside cabinets bolted with security screws. Thousands were turned away because the viewing hours were too few.

The directors of the American Heritage Foundation knew that the Freedom Train would cause a stir in the Deep South, which was still ruled by Jim Crow laws. Already in July, four months before the Freedom Train dared to venture south, AHF quietly and unanimously passed a resolution: "No segregation of any individuals or groups of any kind on the basis of race or religion [will] be allowed at any exhibition of the Freedom Train held anywhere." The resolution would force segregated southern cities either to integrate the exhibits, breaking their own ordinances, or to have the train puff through town without stopping.

On the day I served Biffle's party, the Freedom Train was only three weeks away from its sweep of the South: North Carolina, Virginia, South Carolina, Georgia, Florida, Alabama, Tennessee, Mississippi, and Louisiana. Truman and Clark, as well as the American Heritage Foundation, were getting nervous. They knew there would be trouble, but they weren't sure where or from whom. Southern senators like Johnston, McClellan, and Russell were miffed that the AHF had dared to order the South to integrate. They viewed the Freedom Train as a Truman ploy to humiliate them. Furthermore, not realizing that the AHF had passed the resolution to block segregation on the train in the South, black leaders were convinced that the Jim Crow laws would be enforced. They pointed out that no blacks were on the board of the AHF and that all the Marines who guarded the Freedom Train, as well as the professional staff it carried, were white. Black writer Langston Hughes wrote a poem, "The Ballad of the Freedom Train," protesting the white version of freedom and democracy.

To set a good example for the South and to appease blacks, the AHF added three Pullman cars to the train and invited famous blacks to ride along with some famous whites. In effect, the Freedom Train would arrive in each southern city already integrated and hence in violation of Jim Crow laws. Naturally, the passengers would need black waiters. Always eager to score points with President Truman, Tom Clark, and Les Biffle, Lyndon Johnson offered my services to Biff for as long as he needed them. I don't think Biffle realized that LBJ was simply pulling me off my job at the post office.

During his party, Biffle asked me if I would ride the Freedom Train as a waiter. I told him that it would be an honor. Since Modean and I had just separated, I wouldn't be concerned about leaving a wife and daughter home alone. My moonlighting had strained our relationship and all but destroyed the trust Modean once had in me. I couldn't blame her for going to live with relatives in Chicago for a while to think things over.

When I first saw the Freedom Train in Washington's Union Station after Thanksgiving, 1947, I was impressed. A shiny new General Electric diesel, "The Spirit of '76," pulled three exhibit cars with red, white, and blue stripes racing down the sides, three of the best Pullman cars in the country, and one baggage car. There were twenty-eight armed Marines waiting to head south and a staff of twelve, including maintenance men, waiters and porters, a conductor, a document specialist from the National Archives, and a photographer.

It was clear to all of us that the ride would not be entirely smooth. The city councils of Memphis, Hattiesburg, and Selma had already refused to allow blacks and whites to view the exhibits together because, they said, they feared a race riot. They proposed to allow whites to visit the Freedom Train for the first six hours; blacks would have the next six. Birmingham proposed a face-saving compromise: Whites and blacks could mingle on the train itself, but they would have to wait their turns in two segregated lines. The compromise became known throughout the South as the "Birmingham Plan." Soon cities like Charleston, South Carolina, and Savannah and Brunswick, Georgia, were copying Birmingham in their preparations for the train's arrival.

To its credit, the AHF wouldn't back down. Though it kept a dialogue open with the cities that showed signs of softening, it scratched Memphis and Selma from the tour. Memphis was particularly touchy about the mingling of the races. It had one of the strictest movie censorship laws of any southern city. If a film showed black children sitting in a schoolroom with white children, for example, the scene had to be cut before the film could be shown there. More than fifteen years later, I wasn't especially surprised when blacks and whites demonstrating in Selma against discrimination were brutally beaten or that it was in Memphis that Dr. Martin Luther King was assassinated.

I can't remember which blacks joined the Freedom Train in which city or who got off where during the next six weeks because I was so busy serving. But I do remember their names: Walter White, educator Mary McLeod Bethune, boxing champion Joe Louis, Illinois Congressman William Dawson, Howard University Dean Charles Houston, actor Canada Lee, singer Marion Anderson, poet Langston Hughes, General Benjamin O. Davis, educator W.E.B. Du Bois, UN negotiator Dr. Ralph Bunche. I recall a few of the whites who rode with us as well: Eleanor Roosevelt, former boxing champ Max Baer, and D.C. Commissioner "Jiggs" Donahue, Washington's equivalent of a mayor.

Unknown to President Truman, Tom Clark, or the American Heritage Foundation, the Freedom Train itself was segregated. There was one sleeping car for blacks and one for whites. The white head conductor ordered me to serve the whites first in the dining car, then clear it so the blacks could eat. In fact, the only time whites and blacks were allowed to mix was when they got off the Freedom Train.

There was one minor exception to this rule. During the first week of the ride through the South, the blacks made their plans for visiting each city in their car, and the whites in theirs. I served as liaison, carrying messages back and forth. But planning became so awkward that both groups finally met together in the dining car, but with shades drawn and only between cities. When the conductor announced that the train was approaching a station, the blacks and whites separated.

I don't know who insisted on the segregation or why. The decision may have been inspired by the racial prejudice of the whites who rode the train, or it could have been forced by southern politicians like Senators Johnston, Russell, and McClellan. Whatever the reason, I was confused at first, then shocked and angry. The Freedom Train carried the Bill of Rights, but our rights were being denied. We rode with the Emancipation Proclamation, but were not emancipated. Behind glass for all to see was the UN charter guaranteeing U.S. support for world freedom, but we were not even free on the Freedom Train. Just as galling was the fact that every time we got off the train, a church or school choir would be singing the Freedom Train Song composed by Irving Berlin: "Inside the Freedom Train you'll find a precious freight. Those words of liberty. The documents that made us great."

The hypocrisy hit me full force when we entered South Carolina and Georgia, our first trouble spots after the smooth ride through North Carolina and Virginia. Charleston, Savannah, and Brunswick tried to sneak a compromise past the American Heritage Foundation. AHF rules permitted segregated lines up to the beginning of the train cars. At that point, however, they had to merge into one line. The three cities had decided on a modified Birmingham Plan: blacks and whites would stand in segregated lines up to the actual entrance to the exhibit car. Then, just before they got on the train, the lines would merge. Only days before the Freedom Train pulled into Charleston, the AHF got wind of the plan and sent a negotiator from Richmond. There would be no compromise. Reluctantly, the city councils agreed, but they were nervous. Black policemen were assigned to cover the black line; white police, the white line. National Guardsmen would be on hand to keep order. Senator Johnston was so angry that he wouldn't come down to welcome the train when it pulled into Charleston.

When the Freedom Train arrived in Charleston on December 15, 1947, it met the usual reception committee, the mayor and the chief of police, who read a prepared statement: "If whites and Negroes are going to mix on the train in this town, they will have to keep the window shades pulled down. This is the law of the State of South Carolina."

By today's standards, the scene in Charleston, Savannah, and Brunswick was more sad than shocking. On one side of the tracks, a white choir intoned the state song; on the other, a black Baptist choir sang spirituals. A white band played "Stars and Stripes Forever" in one corner of the trainyard; a black band played "When the Saints Go Marching In" in another. A white and black thread—the segregated lines—stretched for what seemed like a mile; then, with the help of black policemen on one side and white policemen on the other, they blended. Blacks and whites got off the Freedom Train together, only to separate quickly.

By the time we left Georgia for Florida, the blacks still on the Freedom Train were frustrated and angry. It seemed that their sole purpose in being aboard was to step off the train with whites so that southerners would think the Freedom Train was integrated. The blacks weren't even given a chance to speak to the crowds. At each stop, the mayor or governor did that. Tension between the blacks and the whites riding the train grew with each mile. Dr. Bunche became our spokesman. No stranger to discrimination, he had barely escaped a lynch mob in Alabama in 1938 while helping Swedish sociologist Gunnar Myrdal gather material for his classic book, *An American Dilemma*. And as UN negotiator, he still suffered segregation in hotels and restaurants, as he later would even after winning the Nobel Peace Prize for negotiating the 1949 accord between Israel and the Arab states.

Dr. Bunche told us how surprised he had been to find the nation's capital to be just another segregated southern town when he first moved there in the late 1920s to become president of Howard University. He had since learned, he said, that discrimination in the halls of government was alive and well. The Freedom Train proved that. If the government wanted to clean up the South, it should begin in its own backyard.

For some reason, the blacks decided not to make an issue of the segregation on the Freedom Train. One by one, they got off to go about their business, and the Freedom Train rolled on its segregated tour of the Deep South. Looking back, I suspect they felt that a protest would do more harm than good. It might even have sparked a race riot.

In spite of my anger at the hypocrisy, I found moments to enjoy myself on the Freedom Train. I met and talked to some of the most prominent blacks in the country, and it made me feel proud. I remember Mary McLeod Bethune talking about her warm relationship with President Roosevelt, who had appointed her to the National Youth Administration. She held the highest federal post ever given a black woman. One day, Roosevelt sent her to Hyde Park in the presidential train, but the black porter wouldn't let her on until she could prove that FDR had sent her. During another trip on the presidential train, a little white girl pointed at her. "Look! Mommy," she cried, "the maid is on the train." Mary Bethune laughed from her belly when she told these stories.

I also remember a conversation between W. E. B. Du Bois and Joe Louis. Du Bois was lecturing Louis about the importance of education for black men. "You are the greatest boxer in the world," Du Bois said, "but what else can you do?" He hastened to assure Louis that he wasn't faulting him but was making a point. Whites have programmed blacks to educate their daughters, Du Bois stressed, but to keep their sons home to work the fields or make money. It was a devious system to keep blacks powerless. I had to nod in agreement because that is exactly what had happened to me and my brothers. If my mother hadn't sent me to Wichita Falls, I would never have completed high school. "When you hang up your gloves," Du Bois asked the boxer, "what are your plans?"

Joe Louis didn't have any. He died penniless more than thirty years later. When I went to view his body, I thought of Du Bois's words.

Although the crowds that lined the tracks in North and South

Carolina, Virginia, and Georgia were enthusiastic and orderly without exception, the mobs in rural Florida were mean. I remember angry whites tossing rocks, bricks, eggs, and tomatoes at the Freedom Train. I also recall that the train refused to stop in one smaller Florida city because the mob was so angry. None of these disturbances made the news. But what happened in Birmingham did.

While we were in Florida, the American Heritage Foundation was still trying to force Birmingham's hand. At first, the city and county commissioners had tried to keep the Birmingham Plan secret so that public opinion could not make them back down. But the local NAACP office got wind of it and notified the AHF. On December 23, less than a week before the Freedom Train was to visit Birmingham, the AHF wired Cooper Green, president of the city commission: "We reiterate position that there can be no segregation on Freedom Train. We cannot agree to published proposal that separate lines be merged at entrance to Freedom Train. Single line leading into Freedom Train must be open to all and must extend length of train and throughout exhibition area."

Unable to reach an agreement with the city, the AHF canceled the stop. It was a good thing. Birmingham Police Commissioner Bull Connor had bragged that even if the AHF allowed segregated lines, he and his troops would uphold the law and refuse integration on the train itself. Fifteen years later, Connor turned loose firehoses and police dogs on antisegregation demonstrators.

The Freedom Train had its first rest in Mobile over the Christmas holidays. The city trimmed a tree, placed it in one of the cars, and sent home-cooked meals and cookies to the Marines and the staff who stayed on the train. I went home to Texas for Christmas and returned after the holiday to ride through the rest of Alabama, Tennessee, Mississippi (Hattiesburg changed its mind and allowed integration), Arkansas, and Louisiana. We had no more problems.

I especially remember New Orleans. A swarm of bombers and fighter planes escorted us into town, where Louis Armstrong greeted us with "When the Saints Go Marching In," and the Wings Over Jordan Choir sang "Roll, Jordan, Roll." I felt proud to be black and pleased that I had ridden the Freedom Train, which had completed 7,300 miles of its 33,000-mile journey by the time I left it to return to Washington and my job at the post office. The train had visited

34

eighty cities, and 870,000 blacks and whites had seen the exhibits—together.

Walter White awarded the American Heritage Foundation an NAACP scroll of merit for enforcing desegregation in forty-nine southern communities where Jim Crow was law. "I believe nothing comparable to the achievement of the American Heritage Foundation has been done before," he said.

I could not have agreed more. Looking back, I am amazed at how much the Freedom Train actually accomplished. It was at least five years ahead of its time. Most books on civil rights, however, do not even refer to it. I suspect that's because the Freedom Train had no effect on laws and attitudes that anyone can point to. I disagree. For the first time in history, blacks and whites mingled during a public function in segregated southern towns. I would not be surprised if some of the black and white civil rights activists of the 1960s had stood side by side on the Freedom Train of 1947–48.

I tip my hat to Harry Truman and Tom Clark. I think they knew exactly what they were doing when they created the Freedom Train.

In June 1948, I served a hush-hush cocktail and dinner party in the northwest Washington home of James F. Byrnes. It was a small affair, with only key southerners present—Senators Johnston, Connally, Russell, Bilbo, and Byrd, and Representative Estes Kefauver, among others.

Although Jimmy Byrnes was no longer in government, he was still a powerful man in Washington. As a former senator from South Carolina who had resigned to become a Supreme Court justice in 1941, he had many friends on the Hill. When FDR appointed him director of the War Mobilization Office in 1943, he soon became "assistant president" and, next to FDR himself, the most powerful man in Washington. When FDR died in April 1945, President Truman appointed Byrnes secretary of state. As one of Truman's most intimate advisers, Byrnes was a key in the decision to drop the A-bomb and in the peace negotiations after World War II.

Whether Byrnes voluntarily resigned as secretary of state in 1946 or whether Truman forced him out is still not clear. What is clear, however, is that Byrnes didn't like Truman. For one thing, he had expected FDR to select him as his running mate in 1944 instead of the haberdasher from Missouri. Furthermore, as a southern conservative, Byrnes felt that Truman was too soft on communism and too hard on civil rights. But Byrnes was too much of a politician to take a public stand against Truman before the 1948 Democratic Convention. He preferred to pull strings in the dark. Hence, the hush-hush party.

As I served drinks in the garden and food in the dining room, where all the politicians (without their wives) sat at Jimmy Byrnes's long table, I caught enough of the conversation to suspect what was happening. When General Dwight D. Eisenhower arrived for dinner, there was no doubt.

President Truman's election bid was in deep trouble. Southern Democrats couldn't accept his uncompromising stand on racial equality; old New Dealers felt he had turned soft on communism; and big city bosses like Chicago's Jake Arvey and Bronx County's Ed Flynn feared he couldn't win and was therefore a bad risk. South Carolina Governor J. Strom Thurmond had already threatened to bolt from the party and take a pack of southern Democrats with him. The three groups had one thing in common: They were all willing to rally around General Eisenhower, should he accept a nomination during the convention in Philadelphia in July.

General Eisenhower had made it plain in January, five months before Jimmy Byrnes's dinner party, that he wouldn't run against Truman on a Republican ticket because, he announced, professional soldiers should not seek high political office. Soon after that statement, however, Eisenhower resigned as army chief of staff and accepted a post as president of Columbia University. For the Democrats mounting a "stop-Truman" campaign under a "draft-Eisenhower" banner, it was a new war. No one knew for sure whether Eisenhower was a Democrat or a Republican, but he was no longer on active military duty, and he had never said he wouldn't run against Truman as a Democrat. The fact that he remained silent in the face of the Democrats-for-Eisenhower movement fanned the hope that he would at least accept the nomination should it be offered to him.

As far as civil rights were concerned, the racists at Byrnes's party knew they could count on Ike. He was firmly opposed to integrating the armed services and the schools. Some years later, I heard Senator John McClellan of Arkansas tell LBJ about a private meeting that Governor Orval Faubus had had with President Eisenhower in September 1957. Faubus had called out the Arkansas National Guard to prevent Little Rock Central High from integrating. That was the first time since the 1954 Supreme Court decision calling segregation in public schools unconstitutional that any governor had tried to prevent integration before violence had actually occurred. When a federal court ordered the U.S. attorney general to seek an injunction against Faubus, the governor asked President Eisenhower for a private conference. Ike invited him to the U.S. Naval Base in Newport, Rhode Island, where he was vacationing. During the conference, Eisenhower told Faubus, according to McClellan,

"I'm in full accord with your stand against integration. I've a strong belief in segregation. Integration weakened the armed forces. I'm sure it will do the same to schools."

Jimmy Byrnes and Olin Johnston, both from South Carolina, seemed to lead the strategy session in Byrnes's home. They told Ike that they knew he would not run as a Republican candidate against Truman, but would he accept a Democratic nomination if it were offered? General Eisenhower said he wouldn't, because he didn't think he could wrest the nomination from the president. The "dump-Truman" movement in the party was just not that strong.

Next, Byrnes and Johnston asked Ike if he would run on a fourth-party ticket against Democrats, Republicans, and the Progressives of Vice President Henry Wallace. They assured Ike that there were enough Democrats who disliked Truman and enough Republicans who liked Ike to send him to the White House. Eisenhower turned them down again. I heard him say that he was a Democrat and had been all his life. He wouldn't turn on the party now. "You don't want me," he said. "You want Douglas MacArthur."

Soon after Byrnes's dinner meeting and shortly before the July convention, Ike finally made his position clear: "I will not at this time identify myself with any political party and couldn't accept nomination for any public office or participate in partisan political contests."

A few weeks later, I was serving a cocktail party for thirty or forty people at Leslie Biffle's home. It was a preconvention planning party and, of course, Rhode Island Senator J. Howard McGrath, the national Democratic chairman and future U.S. attorney general, was there. Biffle suggested that McGrath take me along to the convention to serve in the Senatorial Hospitality Room, just as Biffle had suggested that I serve on the Freedom Train. McGrath agreed. Once again, Lyndon Johnson arranged for my release with pay from the post office for a few days.

It was my first convention, and I was excited. By the time I arrived in Philadelphia, it was clear that no group was strong enough to block Truman's nomination and that the issue that would heat the convention was: How strong would the Democratic civil rights platform be? Given the fact that blacks couldn't stay in the Roosevelt Hotel in the City of Brotherly Love where the convention was being held and where I would be working, the civil rights plank interested me immensely.

My job was to serve drinks, coffee, and doughnuts in the large room, with a bar set aside for big campaign contributors. A receptionist sat just inside the door to accept checks. Half a dozen smaller rooms opened off both sides of the main room, where contributors could talk privately with congressmen. At any given moment, there were at least eight to ten people, mostly men, drinking in the hospitality room. Hubert Horatio Humphrey was the big topic of conversation among southern senators.

As mayor of Minneapolis and a member of the platform committee, Humphrey had opposed the weak civil rights plank, identical to the one FDR had written in 1944, that party leaders and the White House supported. To the anger of the majority on the committee, Humphrey and Andrew Biemiller, a Wisconsin congressman, tried to add a strong final paragraph to the moderate plank. Today, that paragraph sounds tame, but in 1948 it was dynamite: "We call upon Congress to support our President in guaranteeing these basic and fundamental rights: (1) the right to full and equal political participation, (2) the right to equal opportunity of employment, (3) the right of security of person, and (4) the right of equal treatment in the service and defense of our nation."

Fearing a deeper split in the party and a large walkout of Governor Thurmond's Dixiecrats, the platform committee rejected the Humphrey-Biemiller paragraph. But Humphrey wouldn't compromise. He and Biemiller wrote a minority report. Then, Humphrey asked the convention chairman, Sam Rayburn, for permission to give a speech supporting the report. Rayburn was reluctant to do so because he didn't believe the delegates would accept the minority plank, and he knew it would cause division in the party.

Speaking with the authority of the White House, Howard McGrath tried to discourage Humphrey. "It will be the end of you," I heard McGrath tell Hubert. The stakes were high, and Humphrey began to waffle. He knew that if he gave the speech, if it further split the party, and if Truman lost the election, he, Hubert Humphrey, would be blamed.

Not long after overhearing McGrath's remark, I was bringing a tray of ham-and-cheese sandwiches and coffee to Senator Richard Russell's suite down the hall from the hospitality room. As I opened

Russell's door, I heard the senator asking, "Who the hell is that damned fool from Minneapolis who keeps talking about civil rights?"

Delegate Russell Long, who would be elected Louisiana senator in the fall and who knew Humphrey (they had both done graduate studies at LSU), warned Russell not to underestimate the mayor. Humphrey is a powerful speaker, Long said.

Russell and his friends discussed the pros and cons of allowing Humphrey to address the convention. Although the final decision to give Humphrey the podium was Rayburn's, they felt they could lean on Rayburn and block Humphrey if they wanted to. In the end, they decided to offer a states' rights minority plank and let Humphrey commit political suicide in public. "If he wants to make a damned fool of himself," I heard Russell say, "let him."

For me, Humphrey's civil rights speech was the highlight of the convention, even though I was not in the hall to hear it. I could feel anticipation and tension in the hospitality room. Would Humphrey actually deliver the speech? He could back out right up to the last minute. What would he say? What would the Dixiecrats do? Would a party split cost Truman the election?

Less than three hundred words, it was Humphrey's shortest, and some say the best, speech in his political career. It had a profound effect upon me when I read it in the newspaper the next day. Never had I heard a white politician say so many hopeful and powerful things in so few words.

"In spite of my desire for unanimous agreement on the platform," Humphrey said in part, "there are some matters which I think must be stated without qualification. There can be no hedging—no watering down.

"There are those who say to you—we are rushing this issue of civil rights. I say we are a hundred and seventy-two years late.

"There are those who say—this issue of civil rights is an infringement on states' rights. The time has arrived for the Democratic Party to get out of the shadow of states' rights and walk forthrightly into the bright sunshine of human rights.

"People—human beings—this is the issue of the twentieth century. People—all kinds and sorts of people—look to America for leadership—for help—for guidance.

"My friends—my fellow Democrats—I ask you for a calm consideration of our historic opportunity. Let us forget the evil passions, the blindness of the past. In these times of world economic, political, and spiritual—above all spiritual—crisis, we cannot—we must not—turn from the path so plainly before us.

"That path has already led us through many valleys of the shadow of death. Now is the time to recall those who were left on that path of American freedom.

"For all of us here, for the millions who have sent us, for the whole two billion members of the human family—our land is now more than ever, the last best hope on earth. I know that we can—I know that we shall—begin here the fuller and richer realization of that hope—that promise of a land where all men are free and equal, and each man uses his freedom wisely and well."

When Humphrey finished, Minnesota delegates jumped to their feet, and Illinois delegates led a parade. The demonstration lasted eight minutes. When the vote was taken, the southern states' rights plank was trounced; the Humphrey-Biemiller plank had won a majority. The auditorium shook with applause and cheers. Governor Thurmond and a paltry thirty-five southern delegates walked out. The convention nominated President Truman on the first ballot.

I left Philadelphia hopeful but skeptical. Was it all talk? Were the Democrats just using a liberal civil rights plank for some political purpose and playing with the hopes of blacks like me?

President Truman himself, however, left no doubt in my mind that, at long last, someone was doing more than commissioning reports, writing platform planks, and making speeches. A week after the convention, Truman issued two executive orders. One ordered the integration of the armed forces; the other, an end to discrimination in the civil branch of the federal government. Truman had hurled a thunderbolt into the Deep South. It was a reminder that he meant business.

Soon after Truman's executive orders, I served a party at Senator Olin Johnston's home in Chevy Chase, Maryland, just outside the District. It was a typical hot, humid August evening. Leslie Biffle had suggested the party in the hope of pulling men like Johnston away from Thurmond's Dixiecrats and toward Truman. As a southerner, Biffle felt at home with the southern racists; as a Truman confidant and supporter, he got along well with northern liberals. I can't remember all the politicians at Johnston's home that evening because I was too busy barbecuing steaks with LBJ's special sauce and serving drinks. But I do remember that former Governor Robert Kerr of Oklahoma, who was running for the Senate, was there with Oklahoma Senator Elmer Thomas, a bitter racist. (Governor Kerr had the steaks flown in from Oklahoma for the occasion.) So was Senator McClellan and Florida Senator Spessard Holland, a former Polk County judge whom blacks called "the Hangman" because he sentenced blacks to death every chance he got.

I heard Senator Johnston sounding off about Strom Thurmond in that oily voice of his. A reporter had asked the Dixiecrat why he was so upset with Truman, who was only finishing what Roosevelt had started. "Yes," Thurmond had said, "but Roosevelt was just playing. This haberdasher means business." Senator Johnston repeated what Thurmond had told him privately: "Truman's really serious about that civil rights bill. Why, ever since he dropped that bomb on Japan, he's been crazy."

I was excited and hopeful. Though I can't remember what else was said that evening, for the first time I sensed that equality for all *was* possible. Men like Truman and Humphrey were serious, and they had supporters on the Hill. It dawned on me that the President of the United States shared my dream of freedom, and what's more he had the power to begin to make that dream come true.

I remembered how my mother had wrapped her arms around me when she sent me off to live with my Aunt Rebecca in Wichita Falls. "Sonny," she had said, "class will tell." At fifteen, I hadn't understood her. Now I did. President Truman had the courage of his convictions. He was moved by what was right, not by what was expedient. He refused to buckle under pressure. He had class, and it showed. Hubert Humphrey was cut from the same honest bolt of cloth.

It struck me that, as a black man, I *did* have choices, even though they were limited. I could face the harsh real world with hope, or I could hide behind a wall of anger and self-pity. I would be a prisoner of my color only if I allowed my color to imprison me.

And a prisoner I was. When I got on the bus each morning, a white driver would shout at me, "Move to the back." In the Cleveland Park post office, recently integrated, I listened to insults all day long. If I had to go to the bathroom while delivering mail, I had to return to the post office, for there were no facilities for blacks in fashionable northwest Washington. If I forgot to bring a brown bag for lunch, I had to go to the service entrance of a restaurant to buy a sandwich. Policemen watched my every move, waiting for me to make a mistake so they could bark at me. After carrying mail all day long, I got back on the bus, only to hear the driver shout again, "Move to the back." All this, every single day. A continuous assault on my dignity and pride.

It was no different in Washington from the way it was in Magnolia, Wichita Falls, or Fort Leonard Wood. I was still a "nigger," even though I ate better. I had believed that I would always be one unless I freed myself, for there was no civil rights movement to fight with me and for me. I was surrounded by black men and women no better off than I was.

What I had to do became clear. Up until that party at Johnston's home, I had directed all my attention to economic survival. I was winning: I had a good job and was making decent money. Now I had to learn how to survive as a man, with dignity and pride. To do that, I knew, I had to solve two problems: find a way of keeping hope alive inside me, for I had seen how despair can kill a man; and learn to cope with the hatred and insults directed at me, or I would never be able to face the world.

My hope for a free society rested on the political system. For change to be real, it had to begin in Washington—on the Hill and in the courts. To keep my hope alive, I had to learn everything I could about how the political system worked, who the movers and shakers were, where the power lay, and what steps were necessary for change. If I could understand the system and its players, I would become sensitive to every inch of progress. I would then be able to watch the flower of civil rights open slowly, a petal at a time.

I decided to become the best waiter Washington had ever seen and in so doing learn as much as I could about politics and the people who make the laws. I would not risk my job, but I would train myself to make my work so mechanical that I could concentrate much of my energy on listening and watching. My knowledge, I believed, would still the voices of despair inside me.

Like most black men, I was so afraid of rejection and had been so hurt by the hatred, contempt, and neglect of whites that there were many things I would not even attempt. Why should I put my hand in the fire? But what I had heard and seen during the summer of 1948 gave me the courage to face the fire and to learn not to let it burn me. I resolved to build a wall of inner peace out of the blocks of belief in myself, in God, and in the system. I would allow nothing to enter the private world behind those walls, not the contemptible looks nor the insults nor the harsh words. My wall would be held together by an indestructible sense of dignity.

Finally, I concluded that if I wanted respect, I was going to have to earn it. I took stock of my assets. I had a certain charm and an optimistic personality. My strongest asset was my ability to respond to people no matter what their color or creed. I knew I was superior to those who hated me, for I didn't hate back. I would earn respect by doing my job well and trying to be open to people.

Realizing that knowledge was power, but not sure how I would ever use that power, I started to take notes on what I heard and saw, especially about civil rights. I was tentative at first, afraid that those whom I served would suspect I was scribbling down in the kitchen what they were saying in the dining room. Later, I studied my notes and tried to understand why people spoke and acted the way they did.

Looking back, my strategy worked. By being a good waiter, I made powerful friends who eventually helped me find a position on the Hill with influence. My years of observing people, especially Lyndon Johnson, taught me how to use that power for the powerless. But I am getting ahead of my story. . . .

CHAPTER

One mid-September evening in 1948, after finishing at the post office, I served a small cocktail party in Speaker Rayburn's office. President Truman was planning to whistle-stop through Texas; Sam Rayburn had agreed to ride the campaign train with the president and with Attorney General Tom Clark, who was from Dallas. As always, Lyndon Johnson was there. I heard Johnson tell Rayburn that he wanted to campaign with Truman, too. LBJ had just won the runoff Texas Democratic primary for the Senate by a mere eighty-seven votes and his election prospects were doubtful. Rayburn's reelection, on the other hand, was virtually guaranteed.

"It's political suicide," I heard Rayburn warn Johnson as I mixed LBJ's White Horse and water. "You can win if you're not seen with Truman."

Johnson didn't say much. I never heard him lecture Rayburn as he did everyone else. With Mr. Speaker, he was as quiet and respectful as a student with his teacher. I did hear Johnson say he'd take his chances. He hoped Truman would make a few car trips into the Texas countryside with him and that the president would invite him to join the campaign train through the rest of the South.

I had heard enough at the parties and dinners I served to know that LBJ's decision was a brave one. To campaign in the South with Truman was to stand on Truman's civil rights platform, which was as popular in Texas as Yankee Doodle. Even northern politicians tried to avoid being seen with Truman. Expecting him to lose to Thomas Dewey in November, most Democratic congressional and gubernatorial candidates either declined to whistle-stop with the president or agreed to do so with great reluctance.

Some years after the election, I overheard Senator Frank Lausche of Ohio tell about how he had tried to hide from Truman.

Campaigning for reelection as governor, Lausche had had little choice when Truman's train puffed into Ohio. Out of courtesy, he climbed aboard the presidential train, intending to hop off at Cincinnati. When the train pulled into the station, the largest campaign crowd Lausche had ever seen in Ohio was waiting. Lausche stood on the platform of the last car next to Truman, who spoke in simple language laced with earthy humor. The Republicans will give farmers and workers the little end of the stick again if they have the chance, Truman said. If voters are foolish enough to accept the *little* end again, well, they deserve it. Hardly an inspiring speech, and totally unrehearsed.

Sensing that he would look more foolish if he tried to sneak away, Lausche decided to stay with the president for one more stop. When the train pulled into the next station, there were even more people. In fact, they were lining the tracks just to wave at the speeding train. Impressed, Lausche hung in with Truman all day. After his last speech, the president invited Lausche to have a drink.

"Have all the crowds been this big?" Lausche asked.

"Hell," Truman said, "this is nothing compared to some we've had."

After Lausche told that story in a private Senate dining room, he pounded the table with his fist and bellowed. He had been campaigning for almost a year and never had he seen so many voters. He was reelected with ease.

A few days after Rayburn's cocktail party, Johnson's chief aide, Walter Jenkins, called me at the post office to say that LBJ had arranged my release with pay to drive his car to Texas. It was common for southern congressmen to have black chauffeurs drive their cars home while they traveled in comfort by train. Johnson was on his way to join Truman, who would be making twenty-three whistle stops in Texas between September 25 and September 28.

LBJ gave me the keys to his black Mercury and told me to meet him on the morning of September 24 in the lobby of the Rice Hotel in Houston. Jenkins gave me a map, eighty-nine dollars for the trip, and the name and address of a black family in Little Rock where I could rest or spend the night if I needed to. Excited and proud, I bragged to my friends how I was going to chauffeur the president and Congressman Johnson all over Texas once I got there.

* * *

I had met Harry Truman many times, both as vice president and president, and he knew me by name. When I didn't have a party to serve, I moonlighted at Harvey's Restaurant, next to the May-flower Hotel. The third floor of the restaurant was reserved for VIPs, and every evening twenty to twenty-five senators, congress-men, and other important people would be eating and drinking there. J. Edgar Hoover and his friend Clyde Tolson had their own table, number 32. Edward R. Murrow, whom I got to know well, was a regular. The Third Floor, as everyone called it, was quiet, private, and popular. Decorated simply with old tables and chairs, it had its own open charcoal grill, on which a black chef cooked steak, fish, and barbecued ribs. Close to the grill was a lob-ster tank and a butcher-shop meat counter, from which guests select-ed their own steaks and fish. In the middle of the black-and-white-tile floor hung a huge cast-iron caldron of soup, usually oyster or crab-meat gumbo. Next to the soup sat a mound of oyster crackers. The Third Floor had its own aroma of sizzling meat, browned barbecue sauce, fresh fish, and cigar smoke. To get there, you had to ride up in a dinky elevator. Most Harvey's diners didn't know the room ex-isted, and if they did, they had to get past Pooch Miller, the head-waiter who guarded the elevator like a black Samurai, to get in.

I got to talk to President Truman at least once a week, and the conversation was always the same. Truman would be bored at the White House or at Blair House, where he lived while the White House was being repaired. He'd call Pooch and ask who was up-stairs. Pooch would turn the president over to me, and I would scan the room and recite the names of everyone there. Of the southern-ers, Truman especially liked LBJ, Russell Long, and Estes Kefauver. "Cut me up a two-pound lobster," the president would order if he liked who was there that evening.

Half an hour later, the elevator door would slide open and Truman, grinning from ear to ear, would step into the dining room. "What the hell!" he'd say to his friends. "Don't you guys ever work?"

I would have his lobster, a bottle of Old Fitzgerald, and a pitcher of water sitting on his table. Surrounded by his friends, Truman was the happiest man in the world. Harvey's was filled with laughter and songs. As I watched him clown, I sensed that Truman really missed the Hill.

In my excitement to drive to Houston, I made a foolish mistake. Every chauffeur who drove a congressman's car south had a "nigger letter," signed by the congressman, saying that so and so was supposed to be driving his car. I had no such letter—just a new car registered to LBJ and a pocket full of cash. I drove nonstop from Washington to Bristol, Tennessee, which is on the Virginia-Tennessee border. Then I stopped for gas.

"Fill it up, please," I told the white attendant. "Could you tell me where the restroom is?"

"We don't have a restroom for niggers," he said. "There's an outhouse in the back."

I didn't allow the insult to get to me. "Would you please check the air and water?"

"We don't check air and water for niggers," he said.

"This is a congressman's car!" I was beginning to lose my cool. "If anything happens, I'm going to report you."

Too angry to check the water and air myself, I paid for the gas and drove off. A few minutes after I left Bristol, I heard sirens. Through the rearview mirror, I saw half a dozen policemen on motorcycles. One sped ahead of the pack and pulled alongside me. The policeman drew a pistol and shouted, "Pull this car over, nigger, and stop, or I'll blow your brains out."

I skidded the car to a halt on the shoulder. Gun still drawn, the officer parked behind me and came over to my open window. "Get outta this car, nigger," he ordered. "The boys back at the gas station said that a smart nigger congressman just came through town."

"I ain't a congressman." I was scared and had decided to play his game. "But I am a nigger. I'm driving Congressman Johnson's car to Houston."

"Well, boy, you better show me some identification."

"I don't have any." I began to panic. "All I have is eighty-nine dollars that belongs to Congressman Johnson, and his registration card."

"Well, boy, I'm gonna have to take you back to town and check out your story."

With sirens blaring, the motorcycles escorted me to the Bristol police station, where an officer grilled me about the car and the money. I repeated over and over again what I had said when I was stopped. Then I added, "Listen, sir, I'm also meeting the president

48

of the United States at the Rice Hotel." I thought that might impress him.

"Ain't no nigger in the world meets the president anywhere," the officer snarled. Then he shouted to the policemen in the other room, "Do y'all hear this crazy nigger?"

After they had a good laugh, the officer pulled me up from my chair and gave me a push. I sailed across the room and cracked my head on the cement-block wall. Blood trickled down my face. Then the officer locked me in a cell without a window. No one called a doctor to stitch me up, and I still have the scar on my forehead where the cut did not heal properly.

Later that evening, two plain-clothes detectives came in and asked, "Boy, where did you get that money and car from?"

I repeated my story.

"What kind of work you do?"

"I work for the post office in Washington," I said. "Sometimes for Congressman Johnson."

They left. Three hours later two more detectives, one of them big and mean, came to question me. "Listen, boy," the mean one said, "we found a white man's body. You murdered him and took his car."

Now I was really scared. All I could think of was swinging from an oak tree. Lynching was still a popular sport in 1948. I was alone in Tennessee. I knew no one. I had no proper identification. I was driving a big black Mercury and I had eighty-nine dollars—a lot of money in those days. A white man lay dead somewhere. All I could do was repeat my story.

The county sheriff walked into my cell the first thing in the morning. He looked like he had come straight from Hollywood. Tall, red-faced, and sweaty, his curly black hair hung down over his forehead. He was chomping a cigar, and his gunbelt hung low under his big belly.

"I want to tell you something, boy!" he said without an introduction. "You're in a whole lot of trouble. That mob outside wants you real bad. They think you killed that white man we found dead."

That was the first I had heard of a mob, and the thought sent an icy chill up my spine. I could hear voices floating through the window in the cell next to me. I believed the sheriff, and I repeated my story for the fifth time.

"I can save you from that mob," the sheriff offered. "I can ease you out of here to the county jail. But you gotta tell me the truth."

"Sir," I said, "just call Washington, D.C., Cannon Office Building, Room 231. That's Congressman Johnson's office. Ask to speak to Walter Jenkins."

The sheriff walked out of my cell and, as I learned later, placed the call and spoke to Jenkins's secretary. She confirmed that a "colored boy," Robert Parker, was indeed driving Lyndon Johnson's black Mercury to Houston. Although I couldn't hear the phone conversation, I did hear the sheriff yelling, "Y'all locked up the wrong nigger!"

I sighed so loudly that I thought the whole world heard me. The sheriff was a different man when he returned to my cell. He was nervous, even a bit frightened. "You're a good nigger," he said. "I checked out your story."

The sheriff went outside as the white man in the cell next to me watched from his window. "Nigger, what did you tell that sheriff?" he asked me. "He's kicking asses like hell out there."

I waited for the sheriff to come back. I knew I had won, and all I wanted to do was put Tennessee behind me before they found another white body somewhere. One of the deputies had taken LBJ's car home with him for the night, and when he brought it back, the sheriff chewed him out, too.

"Listen, boy," the sheriff said as he unlocked my cell and led me to the car, "when you get down to Texas, you tell Congressman Johnson and President Harry Truman we were just trying to protect them. Niggers been stealing cars in New York and Philadelphia and coming down here to sell 'um. We saw you riding in this new car, and you looked like nothing but a suspect."

"Yes, sir." I would have agreed to anything just to get out of there.

A police escort took me out of town. The Tennessee state police led me to the Arkansas border, where the Arkansas state police guided me to Texas. The Rangers escorted me right to the Rice Hotel. The police even paid for my gas.

Once I got out of Bristol and was no longer afraid, my anger began to boil over. I had promised myself after the Philadelphia convention that I would build a wall of inner peace and not allow insults and hatred to penetrate it. But the Bristol police had broken

50

through. I couldn't help myself. That September day in 1948 was one of the lowest points of my life. I had left Washington proud and happy. I was wearing my World War II veteran's button. I was on the way to meet Congressman Johnson and President Truman. But I was treated like a dog, beaten, almost lynched. And they laughed at me. Looking back, that hurt more than the knock on the head and my fear of the noose.

When I arrived in Houston, I went straight to the Rice Hotel, where I waited for Johnson in the lobby. I was exhausted for I had driven nonstop from Bristol to be on time. When Johnson came for his keys, I began to tell him what had happened along the way. He cut me short. "I don't want to hear, boy," he said. "I already know all about it."

Johnson had too many troubles of his own to be concerned about mine. Former Governor Coke Stevenson, whom Johnson had beaten in the Democratic primary for the Senate, had accused LBJ of stuffing the ballot boxes. Federal Judge T. Whitfield Davidson issued a temporary injunction against placing Johnson's name on the November ballot and ordered an election investigation in the three counties where Johnson had won by the widest margin. LBJ appealed to Supreme Court Justice Hugo Black. A decision on the whole smelly mess was pending when Truman's train whistled into El Paso.

Given the uncertainty of Johnson's primary victory, President Truman was not eager to be seen with LBJ. He allowed Johnson to stand on the platform with him in San Antonio, and he said a few nice words about him in Waco. But for the most part, Truman kept his distance. I was disappointed, because I had been hoping to chauffeur the president around the state. On September 28, the day Truman left Texas for Oklahoma, Justice Black decided in favor of LBJ, subject to the review of the full Supreme Court the following week.

Johnson had told me to wait around until he had finished his business in Texas. After that, I was to drive his car back to Washington. I couldn't stay at the Rice Hotel because I was black, so Jenkins arranged for me to stay with a black family until it was time to go home.

Before I left for Washington, Jenkins handed me a letter signed by LBJ. "Don't get smart if you're stopped again," he warned. "Just keep your mouth shut and show them this."

I stuffed the letter into the glove compartment without looking at it and began the trip back to Washington. When I stopped for gas, I read it. "To whom it may concern," it said. "This nigger drives for me."

I was hurt and angry at Lyndon Johnson. To him, I was nothing more than a no-name nigger. On the lonely drive home, I debated whether to show the letter to the police if I was stopped. In the end, I decided I would use it only as a last resort. Better another humiliation than death.

Over the next twenty years, I frequently pulled out that old letter. The more I read it, the more I realized that the two-line "nigger letter" was a piece of political wisdom. If Johnson had written of me with respect or even used my name, no one would have believed the letter came from him. I would have been lynched as fast as you could say LBJ. I began directing my anger away from Johnson toward the system that made "nigger letters" necessary and toward those who kept the system alive.

Although Johnson's letter was destroyed by a flood in my basement in the 1960s, my anger never cooled. That letter became the one thing that managed to destroy my inner peace every time I thought of it. There was nothing I could do to make the hurt go away.

At six o'clock on election eve, November 2, 1948, I took a streetcar to the elegant Georgetown home of Dean Acheson to serve a party for forty to fifty congressmen and politicians who were gathered in gloom to wait for the election returns. Acheson was Truman's choice for secretary of state if he won. Of course, Democratic Party Chairman Howard McGrath was there, with Leslie Biffle and key congressmen who supported Truman. Averell Harriman was there, too. At the time, Harriman was U.S. special representative in Europe for the Economic Cooperation Administration.

Most congressmen and cabinet members voted in their home states and, if they could, returned to Washington to sweat it out at a "poll watching" party. Acheson's was the most important party during the 1948 election and, if Truman had been in town and inclined to sit it out with friends, he undoubtedly would have been there.

Truman or Dewey? No one knew, although it looked like Truman would lose. Acheson's guests were pouring down the drinks as the returns started to dribble in, napping in chairs, drinking coffee so they could drink more booze, eating sandwiches to keep the booze down. I had seen a lot of drinking, but nothing like that 1948 election eve in Georgetown.

My feelings about the election were confused. I admired and respected the president for his stand on civil rights, and I knew he meant what he said. But I liked Wisconsin Senator Joe McCarthy as a person, and McCarthy had been attacking Truman for months.

Of all the bigshots in Washington, McCarthy treated me in the most humane way, as an equal. I knew he wasn't putting me on for, as a matter of survival, I had become good at reading faces, voices, and motives. McCarthy was on my mail route, and when I opened the gate to his northwest Washington home, he frequently met me halfway. "You must be tired from carrying such a heavy bag," he'd say. "There's no need to walk all the way up the stairs." Sometimes he would invite me inside for a sandwich or a cold drink on a hot day. When I served his parties—I was his first choice—he always invited me to have a drink afterward, and many times he would join me at the bar for a nightcap. He tipped well, not like McClellan, who didn't tip at all, or Kefauver, who was so cheap no one wanted to work for him.

Whiskey had not yet pickled McCarthy's mind in 1948. When he called Truman a communist and traitor, I began to wonder, for I had no reason to mistrust him. But when he began saying the same things about Edward R. Murrow, whom I liked and who also treated me with dignity, I became confused. "I'd love to take that son-of-a-bitch Ed Murrow," McCarthy used to say, "tar and feather him, and leave him to freeze in one of our Wisconsin lakes." So on election eve 1948, I wasn't sure how I felt about Truman. Between pouring drinks, preparing food, and managing the other four or five waiters, I observed as best I could in a detached sort of way.

As polls closed across the nation with the results still in doubt, Acheson kept trying to reach President Truman in Independence, where he had cast his vote earlier in the day. But the president had disappeared, and no one would tell Acheson where he was. (Actually, he was hiding at the Elm Hotel in Excelsior Springs in the Ozarks.) Truman's disappearance became a running joke at the party. After all, what can you expect from a haberdasher?

Around five in the morning somebody yelled, "Make up a big batch of Bloody Marys!" Even though I was not glued to the TV set as most of Acheson's sober guests were, I knew it was over. The mood in the house had changed. There was shouting and back-slapping and toasting, Bloody Mary after Bloody Mary. I knew Truman had won, but I was so busy that I didn't even feel happy for him.

The phone rang, and Acheson took the call in the alcove of a large sitting room. Even the drunks were quiet. When he returned to his guests, Acheson announced with a sweeping regal gesture, "Ladies and gentlemen, that was the president."

The guests let out such a loud cheer that the glasses on my

serving tray rattled. "What did he say?" someone shouted. "Is he ready to make his victory statement?"

Acheson twirled his moustache, then said, "Mr. Truman—Mr. Truman— Well, Mr. Truman told me he doesn't have a victory statement. 'Dean,' he told me, 'I have nothing to say right now.' "

When the laughter died, Harriman shot back, "Show me the day ol' Harry can't find something to say. He's never been at a loss for words before."

The cabs and limousines finally began to drive off with Acheson's guests. Soon I and my helpers were left alone to wash the dirty glasses, wipe up the spilt drinks, and toss the half-eaten sandwiches into the garbage. I felt depressed and, although I had promised myself not to allow it to happen, a little sorry for myself. I had just worked for twelve straight hours for some of the most powerful men in Washington. An important moment in history was unfolding and, although I was present, I wasn't part of it. No one had thanked me. No one had asked me to have a sandwich, to stop for a drink. To them I was invisible. They paid more attention to the marble-topped mahogany furniture and crystal chandeliers than to me. They went home in cabs and limos. I cleaned up their mess and walked to the streetcar stop.

As tired as I was, all President Truman's talk about civil rights and dignity seemed like clouds, fluffy and pretty and far away. I got on the streetcar and took my seat in the colored section with the other black men and women in white Washington.

Adam Clayton Powell offered one of the few rays of hope to me and other blacks. I met him for the first time in Congressman Kenneth Keating's Washington home, where I was serving a party, sometime in 1948. I had seen Powell in the after-hours clubs, and like most blacks, I admired him immensely. From the pulpit in the Abyssinian Baptist Church in Harlem, he had been a civil rights advocate long before Montgomery and Selma, and he was brilliant. Even his most bitter enemies granted him that. He spoke with thunder and wit, and when he decided to attack someone on the House floor, his words were darts. Unlike William Dawson, a black congressman from Illinois who "kept his place," Powell bowed to no one. He waged a personal campaign against hypocrisy and found enough of it on the Hill to keep him busy for twenty-two years.

Powell had style. He slicked back his hair, chomped on a cigar, and dressed in flashy three-piece suits. To whites, he looked like a Harlem pimp, outrageously flamboyant. "Keep the faith, baby," he'd call to racists like Senator McClellan. They would squirm, while blacks like me secretly cheered. And Powell knew it. In a way, he stood proud for all of us who had to say "Yes, sir" all day long.

It was a pleasant summer evening, and most of the guests had already left Keating's patio party. Powell was sitting in a lawn chair sipping Scotch and milk.

"Robert, will you come over here, please?" Keating was always polite. Tall and straight, with a mane of white hair, pink cheeks, and beetling eyebrows, he looked like one of those marble or bronze statues of congressmen that line the halls of the Capitol. "Adam, this is Robert," Keating said. "Robert Parker. If you want a successful party, he's your man."

I shook Powell's hand and returned to clean up the bar for the evening. Before I finished, Keating and Powell came over for a nightcap. Both from New York, they were friends who had come to Congress just two years apart. Keating was one of those rare liberal Republicans who supported Truman on civil rights because he believed it was the just thing to do. Powell was in a talkative mood that night. He spoke in a voice that was powerful even when it was low, with sweeping gestures and dramatic pauses as if he were waiting for his congregation to say "Amen, brother." He recalled the day in 1945 when he arrived in Washington to take his seat in the U.S. House of Representatives.

He had pulled into the House parking lot, he said, in a shiny black Cadillac. He got out of the car, straightened his tie in the sideview mirror, and marched right up the marble steps into the rotunda. Adam Clayton Powell wasn't about to use the street level entrance like everyone else.

Powell went on to reminisce about a trip he had taken to Richmond one Sunday to preach in a Baptist church as a favor to the pastor. He was light-skinned for a black man, and he used it to his advantage. Many white congressmen, for example, believed that the lighter the Negro, the smarter he was, and Powell did nothing to dissuade them. On the way back to Washington, the pastor's car broke down, forcing Adam to hop a train to be on time for an important Monday-morning vote. When he got to the station, the train was already pulling out. He made a dash for the "colored" car. A conductor, who didn't recognize him as black, motioned him into a white one. Adam sat down and began to relax. Shortly after the train left the station, the conductor burst through the door shouting, "Anyone see a nigger? Someone said a nigger came in here."

Powell jumped out of his seat as if insulted. "A nigger?" he gasped. "In here? Where? Where is he?" The conductor looked around the car, then left.

After telling me the story, Powell flashed that toothy smile of his. For him, the train conductor was a symbol of the Hill: bigoted, hypocritical, and not very bright.

Powell continued. When he walked into his House office for the first time, he said, a memo from the Speaker greeted him. It was a list of "Do's and Don'ts for Negro Congressmen." Close to the top was, Don't eat in the House Dining Room. When Keating came to Congress in 1947, two years later, Powell still couldn't get seated in either the House or the Senate Dining Room. Outraged, Keating decided to attack the Jim Crow law on the Senate side, where the ripples would be greater. It was in the Senate Dining Room that the vice president ate when he lunched on the Hill. Keating asked a liberal senator to invite him to lunch. Keating, in turn, invited Adam and his wife, Hazel Scott, a jazz pianist and singer.

When Keating, Adam, and Hazel walked into the Senate Dining Room, the black headwaiter, Paul Johnson, almost passed out. Paul had been working the room since 1908, and he knew he would be held responsible for not enforcing the color barrier. "Congressman," he told Keating, "you know that no colored folks are allowed to eat here. You're going to get me in a lot of trouble."

Keating was the perfect gentleman. He told Paul not to worry because he and the senator would assume full responsibility for their guests. The lunch caused some screaming and kicking, but Keating had made his point. Once Powell got a little power, he crashed the color barrier in the House Dining Room on his own. He also became the first black to use the congressional shower and to get a haircut in the congressional barbershop. He fought racial prejudice in the Capitol Police and in other places on the Hill as well. Black policemen had always worked the parking lots in the heat and the cold while whites grabbed the cushy inside jobs. Powell changed that. He even got black policemen into the Senate side, which was more prestigious and, therefore, had been all white.

I was stunned by the Powell-Keating story, but not because Adam hadn't been able to get into the congressional dining rooms. We had all known he would be excluded, even though there was no sign. I was upset because Harvard-educated Keating hadn't even known that black congressmen couldn't eat with the men who passed civil rights legislation for others and he had been there several years. He hadn't been aware, as Adam would often tell me later, that there are two sides of the Hill, one white and one black. If Keating hadn't known that, how many other congressmen had their heads in the sand? It seemed to me that it was a congressman's job to know about the extent of discrimination on the Hill.

I listened spellbound to Powell's stories about the first years on the Hill. I got to know him well over the years, and he had a great influence on my life. He was the first black man who I ever heard call a white man by his first name. I'll never forget the shiver of shock and delight that I felt the first time I heard him do it. I was in my mid-twenties. I had lived on a farm, in a city, on an army base, and in the nation's capital. I had worked for the powerful, educated, and wealthy for five years, but I had never heard a black man call a white man by his first name.

"Keep the faith, Lyndon," Powell used to call out to LBJ in a crowded Senate corridor. It was music. "See you later, John!" he loved to tell McClellan and smile as the senator blushed. It was the first and only time racists like McClellan had had a black call them by their given names. Blacks in the South couldn't do it because the Klan would take care of them as "uppity niggers." Blacks in Washington couldn't do it because they'd lose their jobs. But Adam Clayton Powell could shout first names in public—an equal among equals. He committed the capital sins of refusing to be a token and refusing to allow anyone else to think of him as one.

It's impossible to understand Powell's courage from the vantage point of the 1980s. It is relatively easy to think black pride when everyone is shouting it from the rooftops. But to live black pride when the rest of the world is silent takes unusual strength.

I never realized how much I resented my father's not standing up to Mr. Yawn until I met Powell, who became everything on the Hill that I had wanted my father to be in Magnolia, Texas. Powell stood up to the white man; my father had cringed. Powell said no; my father had said yes. Powell fought the system; my father had accepted it. Powell chastised the world from his pulpit in the House; my father had shed bitter tears in private. Powell called white men John and Lyndon; my father had said, "Yes, suh!"

It's not that I blamed my father, for I came to understand one important difference between Adam and him. Adam *had* power; my father had none. Adam's courageous use of that power made me feel proud. My father's helpless "Yes, suh" made me feel ashamed.

Most important, Powell taught me to aim high. "I can do anything the white man can," he used to say. That was revolutionary talk in the 1940s. It would be another twenty years before a black man would stand up and say "I have a dream" and find millions who dared to share it. As I watched Powell flaunt his power and fight the system, I made up my mind that if I ever got a share of power, I, too, would use it for my people.

One evening in the mid-1950s, Adam proved a major point at Harvey's. The third floor elevator door slid open, and there he stood in a three-piece suit, a cigar clenched in his white teeth. On each arm was a beautiful white woman. He was the first black I ever saw on the third floor, and he was so important by that time that no one dared show him the door. He sat at a table near two southern senators.

"If you were down in my part of the country," one of them said loud enough for everyone to hear, "you'd get strung up."

"I can't understand why," Powell shot right back. "You white cats been doing what you please with our black women for as long as you wanted to."

The senators forced a laugh, but they never forgot the "insult." Neither did the waiters. We felt as if Powell had put those senators in their place just for us. The story became one of our favorites, and every time we recalled it, we laughed just as hard as we had the first time we heard it.

Many years after I met him at Keating's party, sometime during the mid-1960s, Powell, then chairman of the House Committee on Education and Labor, tangled with Senator McClellan. Powell was trying to pry out of committee his amendment that would deny federal aid to schools still discriminating against blacks in spite of the Supreme Court order to integrate. Arkansas stood to lose a

59

chunk of federal funds if the amendment passed, and McClellan was determined to kill it in committee. He began to lean on President Kennedy, who supported the measure. JFK in turn leaned on Vice President Johnson. "Talk to McClellan," he told LBJ. "And ask Adam to lighten up on the pressure."

Johnson told me to set up a luncheon in his Hill office, S–208. I ordered an LBJ special from the Senate Dining Room for Johnson and McClellan: a quarter-pound of chopped steak on a sesame-seed roll with sliced tomatoes and a king-size root beer.

Determined to broker a cease-fire, LBJ heard McClellan out, then told an aide, "Get Adam Clayton Powell over here!" I stood by, listening. The aide returned with a message from Adam: "Tell Mr. Vice President that I am in the middle of a committee meeting. With his permission, I'll come over in a few minutes."

Johnson exploded. "Wait just one goddamn minute," he shouted at the aide. "You tell that nigger I said to get his ass over here right now! Ain't no nigger in the world ever been that busy." LBJ looked over at McClellan in disgust. "Ain't that a goddamn shame," he said.

Anger rose to my cheeks as I waited for McClellan to spout his usual "The only good nigger is a dead one." It was McClellan's answer to every civil rights question. I had naïvely expected LBJ and McClellan to at least show respect for the office of United States Representative if not for the man. But standing there invisible in the vice presidential office, I understood that to LBJ, race was a political game. In front of McClellan, he played the Texas racist. Later, with Powell, he was apologetic and respectful, a liberal Democrat. When the Powell amendment finally passed, President Kennedy sent Johnson back to the Hill to congratulate Adam personally. Johnson shook his hand, slapped him on the back, and meant it.

Every time I stroll through the halls of the Capitol and see the marble and bronze statues of congressmen, I think of Powell. One afternoon in the mid-1960s, as I walked down one of those corridors with him after lunch in the Senate Dining Room, I asked, "Do you think you'll ever stand up in here?" I thought he most certainly would.

"No, Bob, never!" he said. "I fought the system too much."

He was right, of course. His last outrage was the congressional junket he took to Europe with a white secretary. He had just lost a libel case in New York and refused either to appear in court or to pay damages. Congress went coon-hunting. One of the worst was Joel Broyhill from northern Virginia, who wanted Adam's hide so badly that he made no attempt to conceal his glee. "We'll get him now," he'd say during the Powell ethics hearings. "We'll get him now." Congressional staffers, who are more powerful on the Hill than most people are willing to admit, wanted him just as badly, as they would later want Martin Luther King.

Congress censured Powell in 1967 for misuse of public funds and stripped away his twenty-two years of seniority. His defense had been vintage Powell, a variation of what he had said publicly many times: "As a member of Congress I have done nothing more than any member of Congress and, by the Grace of God, I intend to do not one bit less." The problem was, he flaunted it. The following year, Congress refused to seat him—all for doing what many were, and still are, doing privately.

When the Supreme Court ruled in 1969 that his constitutional rights had been violated, Powell took his seat once again. It brought tears to my eyes to watch him. He had always been so proud, the fourth man in his favorite joke. There were four men on the deck of a luxury liner, he liked to say. A Frenchman, a German, an Englishman, and an American black. They all stopped to light a cigar. The difference between the four was that the black man struck a wooden match on the seat of his pants and tossed it overboard. It landed in an oil slick. "Nigger scratch his backside," Powell would say, "and set the world on fire."

When he returned to Congress in 1969, there was no longer any fire in Adam Clayton Powell. He still came to his office each morning in a three-piece suit, hair slicked back, chomping a cigar, but he looked haggard and defeated. He spoke rarely, and when he did, his voice lacked the Powell confidence and conviction. He had challenged the other side of the Hill once too often. It had lynched him with as much hatred and satisfaction as I have ever seen. All because he wouldn't say "Yes, sir."

CHAPTER

In April 1951, Senator Hubert Humphrey gave me his box-seat ticket to the opening baseball game at Griffith Stadium. Vice President Alben Barkley was going to march onto the field for the flag-raising while the army band played the national anthem. President Truman would be tossing out the game ball. Naturally, I was eager to watch the Washington Senators beat the Yankees, along with a lot of congressmen.

The first game of the season was always a big event in Washington. The D.C. commissioner gave free tickets to congressmen and sent a bus filled with cold beer and liquor to the Hill to pick them up. The Senate kitchen packed box lunches of ham sandwiches and fruit, paid for by the D.C. commissioner. I usually traveled along to serve and clean up the bus before and after the game. The 1951 opener was an exception. Proud and pleased, I had a reserved box seat next to Congressman Keating.

It was fun to watch the congressmen on the bus. Laying aside legislation and power plays, they became red-blooded sports fans, chattering about how the Senators were going to whip the world champions while they wolfed down free sandwiches, washed them down with free beer, and made small bets.

The congressmen piled out of the bus calling "See you inside, Robert." I didn't want to miss seeing President Truman throw out the game ball. This was his first public appearance since he had relieved Douglas MacArthur of his Far Eastern command. At that very moment, the general was riding through Manhattan, waving to seven-and-a-half million fans.

In the stadium was a standing-room-only crowd of twenty-seven thousand. As I walked toward the section reserved for congressmen, a white usher blocked me. "You can't go in the VIP section," he said firmly. "Colored aren't allowed. You'll have to sit over there."

He pointed to the bleachers. I showed him my box-seat ticket. He was polite. "Sorry, but you still can't sit here."

I forced a smile and walked toward the bleachers. I wasn't totally surprised. Although Jackie Robinson had crossed the major league color line in 1947, Senators owner Clark Griffith had not yet integrated the team and wouldn't until 1954, three years later. But I was very disappointed. I had hoped that since I worked for the congressmen and had my own ticket, the usher would let me pass.

I was waiting on the bus when the game was over. The Nats had beaten the Yankees 5–3, and the congressmen were in a good mood. "Where were you, Robert?" Ken Keating asked. "I saved your seat."

"Well, Congressman," I said softly, "I tried to sit with you but the usher wouldn't let me in."

"Is that right?" Keating was truly surprised. "I didn't know. You can sit anywhere you want to in Yankee Stadium. That's too bad."

Other congressmen on the bus had the same reaction. I smiled, but inside I was hurt, especially by Keating. He had said the same thing to Adam Clayton Powell five years earlier, and he hadn't learned a thing about racial hatred since then. Few if any of the congressmen who weren't from the South realized that Washington was still two cities. They never bothered to look out their office windows, much less take a walk in the real world. After a few years on the Hill, they began to confuse Congress with life. If power hadn't blinded them, indifference did.

Neither Keating nor anyone else on the bus complained to the D.C. commissioner who had given them the tickets, beer, and ham sandwiches. No one read an angry speech into the Congressional Record or publicly protested the segregation that he privately seemed to condemn.

In due time, of course, it all changed. Ten years later, almost to the day, I went to the opening game with Senator Hubert Humphrey. I sat in the box with him and was treated with respect and a certain amount of envy. But ten years is a long time to wait for the right to sit in the shade during an afternoon ball game in the nation's capital.

Because I was Lyndon Johnson's man, I did get a place close to the inauguration stand where, in January 1953, I greeted the Eisenhower administration with mixed feelings. In one way I was pleased: Lyndon Johnson had just been elected minority leader, the youngest man ever to hold the post. All the years of doing favors for Richard Russell had paid off. The most powerful man in the Senate, Russell had declined to take the job and recommended LBJ instead. The acclamation vote was unanimous. On the other hand, I hated to see Harry Truman go. I've heard a number of people say that under his tough skin, Truman was a racist. If he was, he never showed it, and what he had accomplished in civil rights was significant.

As far as I was concerned, the overcast inaugural afternoon foreshadowed the years ahead. Even though Ike had not yet taken office, the mood in the city had already changed. Republicans moving into town were spending more money than the Democrats ever had, but they threw fewer parties and seemed to enjoy them less. Since most of the people I served were Democrats, work was drying up. And Eisenhower wasn't even in the White House yet.

I will never forget how weary President Truman looked as he passed in front of me to take his place in the stand. Each big issue had left a mark on his face: the death of FDR, Hiroshima, Potsdam, the birth of Israel, Korea, and Douglas MacArthur. But in spite of the crushing problems, Truman had taken the time and political risk to lay a solid civil rights foundation for Kennedy and Johnson to build on in later years.

With Johnson as minority leader in 1953, then majority leader the following year, I became cocky. The more he pulled me away from the post office, the more I took advantage of his protection. Though never nasty with my bosses, I bent every rule in the book. I'd have lunch in one home and a cold drink in another—against the rules. I'd set my bag on the sidewalk and toss a football with the kids or help them cross the street—against the rules. I'd accept gifts. Complaints began to pile up. There were reprimands and threats of suspension, but LBJ always fixed things up.

At one point in 1953 or 1954, I got friendly with Betty, a black live-in maid who served in a home on my postal route. She put me off for a while, then invited me up to her attic room at nine o'clock one evening after she had put the children to bed and while her employers were out to dinner. To get to her room, I had to walk through the master bedroom, then climb the creaky steps to the attic. It was just my luck that the mistress had gotten sick during dinner and came home shortly after Betty had let me in. I was trapped in the attic. There was no fire escape; it was a long drop to the garden below; and I couldn't walk into the woman's bedroom and say, "Hi! It's just me, Robert the mailman." I decided to spend the night and sneak to work after the lady of the house got out of bed the next morning. But she didn't. She was so sick, she stayed in bed for three days.

I was in a state of panic. The post office had no idea where I was. Neither did my wife (Modean and I were back together again, but our relationship was still strained); nor did LBJ's office. There was no phone in the attic, and I had no idea how long the woman would stay in bed. Deciding to take my chances, I sent Betty to break the news to her employer while I eavesdropped at the attic door. Betty was close to tears because she was certain she would lose her job.

"Ma'am?" I heard Betty say. "The postman is here."

"Fine," the woman said. "Does he have any mail?"

"I don't mean like that," Betty said. She was so frightened, she couldn't explain herself.

I opened the attic door and walked into the bedroom. "Oh, Robert! What in the world—" the woman said. Then she smiled.

"I've been here three days," I said, "and I'm going to get fired."

"Maybe I can help," she offered.

I think she felt guilty about Betty living in her attic without a social life. She reached for the phone and called the post office. But she said all the wrong things, and I got suspended anyway.

It took me a week to muster enough courage to ask for Johnson's help. When I finally got to see him, he wasn't the least bit angry. I think he envied me. "Did you lay her?" he asked. "I hope it was good." The next day I was back on the job, convinced I could get away with anything.

But at least I had learned an important lesson, and I was determined not to make the same mistake twice. For me, I concluded, women and work did not mix. There was no way I was going to lose my job over a woman.

Gambling, however, was another story. One important rule for mail carriers was to leave personal cars in the lot and take the streetcar to and from mail routes. The post office was afraid that if a carrier got into an accident, it would be liable. I didn't like the rule.

I got into the habit of driving to my Cleveland Park route because I wanted to make a quick getaway when I finished my deliveries. I used to drive out to Pimlico in Baltimore to play the horses instead of going straight back to the post office for another assignment. When questioned, I would always say that I was working for Senator Johnson.

My supervisor called me in one day after I had failed to return on time from my route. He asked me where I had been, and I fed him the usual excuse. Unknown to me, however, he had been watching my movements and checking with Johnson's office. I wasn't worried, because I knew no one could touch me. I was Lyndon Johnson's man. I had pulled a top civil service rating without an exam, hadn't I? I got a "preferred route," in which patrons showered me with twenty-year-old Scotch, silk ties and shirts, and Christmas gift certificates to the best Georgetown shops. Robert Parker was invincible.

A week later, I got a pink slip in the mail. The bill of particulars was impressive: unauthorized leave time, false statements to postal inspectors, actions unbecoming a member of the federal post office, acceptance of breakfasts, lunches, and gifts. I nearly passed out. How could I be fired? Where was Lyndon Johnson?

I fretted for four days, then went to see LBJ. When I explained what had happened and why, he exploded. Only once before had I seen him so angry with me: In the early 1950s, while driving his car downtown, I had been stopped for accidentally using the high beams, a traffic violation in the District. Before the officer who gave me a ticket pulled away, I shouted, "That's all right! Judge Scally will take care of it." Scally would fix anything for any congressman. I didn't know it at the time, but he was under investigation.

The officer told his superior what I had said, and the superior called the judge, who phoned LBJ. Johnson ordered me into his office. "Boy," he had shouted, "the two worst goddamn things in the world are a troublemaker and a nigger lover. Now I'm damned tired of gettin' your ass outta trouble. If I hear about you causin' anymore, I'm finished with you. Now you're gonna pay this damn ticket, and stay outta trouble. I mean it. You hear?"

This time, pink slip in hand, I stood staring at the floor and expecting the worst. Johnson pounded his desk, cursed me, and again gave me his "I'm damned tired of gettin' your ass outta trouble" speech. When he finished roasting me, he called the postmaster. I got my job back and never tried the Pimlico caper again.

I thought my world had crashed in on July 2, 1955, when I heard on the radio that LBJ had had a heart attack while visiting a friend in Middleburg, Virginia. He was rushed to the Naval Medical Center in Bethesda. Assuming that he would always be around, I had never asked myself what I would do if he died or retired. Even though I hated him much of the time, I felt truly sorry for him at that moment, but I was just as concerned about my own neck. Without his protection, I would lose my job and probably never find another patron. The party circuit was almost dry, which forced me to spend more and more evenings working at Harvey's.

Out of gratitude, concern, and self-interest, I tried to see LBJ. I drove out to the Naval Medical Center several times, but I couldn't get beyond the security guard at the front desk. I explained that I was a friend of Senator Johnson. Coming from a black man, it must have sounded ridiculous. "Sure, fella," the guard said each time I came. His refusal reminded me of the time the Tennessee police had arrested me. "I'm going to Houston to see Congressman Johnson and President Harry Truman," I had explained. "Sure, boy . . ."

Determined to crack the security system, I bought a get-well card and penned a short message inside, addressing it to Johnson's home, which was on my mail route. Then I got it registered at the post office, which required that Johnson sign the receipt for the letter. When the card ended up in my mailbag, I finished my deliveries, then headed straight for Bethesda. I had no trouble getting past the desk in my postman's uniform. I'm sure they didn't even recognize me. When I stepped off the elevator onto the VIP floor and walked toward Johnson's door, a guard stopped me. "What do you have there?" he asked.

"A registered letter for Senator Johnson. He has to sign for it."

"I'll take it in."

"I'm sorry," I said, "but the Senator must sign in my presence."

The guard cracked the door and beckoned an aide. A thin young man in a black suit and horn-rimmed glasses slipped into the hall to look me over. I refused to give him the letter, and I spoke loud enough for Johnson to hear. I was counting on the fact that his curiosity would get the better of him.

I heard the mighty Texas voice. "What in the hell is so important about that goddamn letter?" he shouted. "Bring the damn thing in here!"

The aide led me into Johnson's room. Far from being an invalid, the majority leader was holding court. I sighed in relief. His bed was covered with papers. Aides were handing him letters. He would read them and either toss them aside or dictate an answer. He didn't even look up to see who the mailman was. I stood there for a moment, looking for an opening. Finally, I said, "This is for you, Mr. Majority Leader. It's from me. Nothing really important."

Johnson recognized my voice. "Boy, what in the goddamned hell are you doing out here?" He was reproachful as if asking, "What kind of trouble are you in this time?"

Johnson tore open the envelope and read the card. "Boy, this is mighty nice of you," he said. "Mighty nice!"

I explained as quickly as I could that I had been unable to see him any other way. He smiled broadly and rumbled that he appreciated my coming. Then, so he wouldn't appear to be getting soft, he said as I left the room, "You better behave yourself, you hear!"

Lyndon Johnson never forgot that visit to his bedside. As brutal as he could be, he was always touched by simple acts of kindness. That was the side of Johnson I grew to know and appreciate over the years. I recall a luncheon I served for congressional leaders nearly a decade later. President Johnson hadn't forgotten me. It was one of the few times in the nearly twenty years I had worked for him that he called me by my first name. He told the congressmen how I had conned my way into his hospital room. "Robert went to a lot of trouble back then, just to see me," he said almost with pride.

CHAPTER

* 9 *

When he became majority leader, LBJ was entitled to a chauffeur and a Capitol Hill messenger. I let his aide, Walter Jenkins, know that I wanted one of those positions as soon as there was an opening. I had to wait till someone either quit or retired. It was clear to me that LBJ was going places, maybe even to the top. Not only did I want to ride on his wagon, but I enjoyed serving. Most people think that men and women serve because they can't find other work. That may be true in many cases, but not in mine.

Johnson hired me as his messenger in January 1956 when he returned to Congress after his heart attack. I was thirty-five years old, had two children (Edwin was born in 1950), and owned a home on Capitol Hill. It had taken me thirteen years, working two jobs, to get that far. I kept my civil service rating, and the Architect of the Capitol paid my salary. I never could figure out what running messages had to do with preserving buildings, but then, a lot of things on the Hill didn't make sense.

Until Johnson became vice president in 1960, my duties were fairly routine: pick up mail, deliver messages and documents, serve lunch and cocktails, drive Johnson around town, pick up his friends and contributors at the airport, and chauffeur them to their hotels and meetings at the White House or the State Department. I'd fetch LBJ's dry cleaning, take his dogs to the pound, and shine his cowboy boots. In a word, I was on call at all times to do anything Johnson requested. At night, I still served his dinner parties, worked at Harvey's, or chauffeured his friends, especially McClellan and Kefauver, neither of whom had full-time drivers. But if my duties were routine, what I saw and heard was not.

By 1956, Kefauver had turned into a real womanizer. Besides continuing to drop him off at the Rhode Island Avenue Plaza, I used to drive him to the La Salle and Commodore hotels, frequently with a woman. Very discreet in those days, I never lifted my eyes to see who they were or even what color hair they had. I'd sit in LBJ's car all night and wait. I have to admit that I found taking the senator to call girls amusing, for it was Kefauver who had headed the Senate investigation into interstate gambling and racketeering in 1950.

It wasn't just Kefauver. Johnson used to make similar arrangements for Texas oilmen and people important to his Armed Services Committee. At first, during the day a Johnson aide would simply instruct me to get a room at the Mayflower next door to Harvey's, or at the Commodore, just down the street from the Capitol, in my name and bring back the key. (The District of Columbia had abolished its Jim Crow laws in 1951, and by 1956 most public places were desegregated.) In the evening, I would drive LBJ's friend to the hotel, usually to a side entrance. Soon the procurement system became more efficient. An LBJ aide got me a credit card in my own name. It was my first. I would be told to get a room at such and such a hotel, pay for it with my credit card, and bring back the key. At the end of the month, I'd hand in the credit card statement, and LBJ's office would pay the bill. No cash was exchanged. I never had to line up the women, just be the fall guy.

Chores like that didn't bother me. Call girls were, and still are, part of the other side of the Hill. I recognized that Johnson was using them, as he was using me and just about everyone else, to build a power base. He was satisfying his contributors so they would give more next time. He was taking care of the constituents of other senators, who didn't want to get their hands dirty. In the end, they would owe him, just as I did.

Once LBJ became majority leader, he was entitled to a Capitol hideaway, as well as a messenger and a chauffeur. Room S–208, the "LBJ Room," where he held his lunches and informal cocktail parties, became the center of Johnson's kingdom on the Hill.

There are as many as fifty secret offices or "escape rooms" hidden behind unmarked doors along the Capitol's busy corridors or within its remote tunnels. Some are little more than cubicles; others are elegant apartments where congressmen can nap during late-night sessions or meet contributors. No one is sure how the hideaways got started, but rumor has it that in the 1920s a bootlegger named Cassidy managed to find an empty room, which he then used as a liquor store for congressmen. He began a tradition that is still very much alive today.

Hideaways are status symbols. As Speaker of the House, Sam Rayburn had H–128, where he and his cronies would sit after official business and sip bourbon. They called themselves "The Board of Education." It was in Sam Rayburn's hideaway that Vice President Harry Truman had learned of President Roosevelt's death. I served drinks there many times.

LBJ's hideaway was a large, beautifully carpeted room done up in French Provincial decor. Its narrow, castlelike windows were covered with gold drapes, and an elegant crystal chandelier hung from the high ceiling. The hideaway served as an office, bedroom (there was a Murphy bed in one wall), and a kitchen. A bar, refrigerator, and stove were hidden behind panels. Before he left the Hill for the White House, Johnson had acquired seven hideaways on two floors of the Capitol. He called them the Johnson Ranch East.

Louisiana Senator Allen Ellender also had a hideaway, S–304, and for years he ordered seafood sent up from Louisiana for an annual gumbo party, to which he invited the incumbent president and fifteen of his southern cronies. The chairman of the Committee on Agriculture and Forestry, Ellender was a powerful racist who was elected to the Senate in 1936 and had been reelected unopposed ever since. I usually tended bar at his gumbo fest and helped him stir the jambalaya. Party regulars were LBJ, Senators Long, Russell, Kefauver, Johnston, McClellan, Kerr, and James Eastland of Mississippi, one of the most bitter racists on the Hill. The party usually began in midafternoon and ended by ten or eleven in the evening with almost everyone drunk. Ellender had a new "nigger" joke each year. I remember one in particular that LBJ loved:

When Louisiana built a freeway through a small parish, it cut a town in half. The townspeople complained that they couldn't cross the freeway to visit their friends because the traffic was too heavy. So the state installed a traffic light. "One day, a nigger was driving through town and ran a red light," Ellender continued. "The sheriff caught him. 'Nigger, didn't you see that red light?' the sheriff asked. 'Yassah, boss,' the nigger said. 'But there be only two lights—a red one an' a green one. I knows the green is for you white folks to go, so I figured the red one be for us niggers.' The sheriff said, 'Boy,

71

you are the smartest nigger I seen in a long time. I'm gonna let you go, but you be careful, you hear!' "

Johnson laughed so hard he was literally crawling on his knees, then rolling over and over on the floor. That was one of the few times I wished I had a secret camera. I laughed just as hard as everyone else, but for a different reason. I admired the black man's survival instincts. He knew exactly how to con the white man. Act dumb and poke fun at himself. The sheriff was the fool, not the black man.

In the hideaways, serving lunches, dinners, and drinks, I saw a side of Johnson that I had never glimpsed before. In private, he was as crude as he could be charming in public. During a conference with a wealthy oilman, he'd kick his cowboy boots off and scratch his toes. I saw him blow his nose in the corner of the tablecloth during lunch, or pop up, strip off his shirt and tie, and lunch with his guests in his undershirt. I saw him and other congressmen like Kefauver lounge around the hideaways, drinking in their shorts, no matter who was there. I heard him say right in the middle of a discussion with a constituent, "Have you been laid lately? You need to go out and get some pussy. I'm gonna get you fixed up. Right now."

One time I was serving drinks in the LBJ Room after a busy day. Johnson had just returned the day before from Texas, where a rancher had given him a huge contribution. The rancher had called that morning while LBJ was in an important conference. Johnson took the call anyway. "He wanted me to put my prize bull in a trailer and send him to East Texas to screw his goddamned cow," Johnson told his friends that evening. "I hit the desk with my fist. 'Let me tell you one goddamned thing,' I told the sonofabitch, 'if you want my bull to screw your cow you can bring her up here!' " With that he laughed until the tears came to his eyes.

The press conference over a crisis in Berlin during the height of the Cold War was the most shocking example of LBJ's earthiness. President Eisenhower had told reporters that he ruled out using ground forces in any war with the Soviet Union, but he declined to rule out nuclear arms. Sniffing a good story, the Washington press corps wanted to hear what the Democrats thought. Johnson was holed up in his hideaway for lunch. As usual, Bobby Baker was there.

*　*　*

I remember a special lunch LBJ had with Baker. Johnson had returned to Washington as a newly elected senator in the fall of 1948. Although he knew House politics well, he didn't know the Senate side and he was in a hurry to learn. He had heard about a twenty-one-year-old Senate page who, so the rumor went, made it his business to know everything. Johnson invited Baker to lunch.

I understood Baker, for we had much in common. Like me, he had come to Washington from the South (South Carolina) on a patronage job. He soon realized that to go places on the Hill, he needed power. The only power open to him was the knowledge he could trade. Like me, he was in a unique position to hear and see things. Baker's strategy paid off, for Johnson recruited him as one does a high-class spy. As I poured cups of black coffee, I heard Johnson tell the young Baker, "I understand you're one of those real bright boys on Capitol Hill." Johnson didn't wait for an answer. "Well, listen, I need a man who can keep me in touch with everything that goes on. I wanna have my finger right on the pulse."

As I listened to Johnson, I watched Baker. He leaned across the table as if drawn to LBJ by some invisible magnet. Johnson was talking his language, and I was fascinated. A deal was in the making.

"I don't want a goddamned thing going on in this Capitol that I don't know about," Johnson emphasized. "I want to know everytime they piss and where they do it."

They shook hands. Johnson had just hired one of the smoothest sleuths I have ever seen. Baker became Johnson's eyes and ears. Before the year was out, Johnson knew more than J. Edgar Hoover about deals, power plays, and private lives—who was sleeping with whom and where, who was gay, who drank too much and who had marital problems, and who was in whose back pocket over what. He never kept files; he stored the grubby details in his head and pulled them out whenever he needed to bend a vote.

But back to that hideaway lunch. The reporters following the Berlin story camped outside Johnson's office, and LBJ was plainly irritated because he could hear their chatter and shouting. By the time lunch was over, he had lost what little patience he had.

"Mr. Majority Leader," an aide said, "you are going to have to say something about Berlin. Those reporters are not going away."

"Okay, let them in!" Johnson said. It was more of a challenge than a concession, and his voice filled the whole hideaway. "I'll give them a statement if they want to interview me while I take a crap!"

Johnson walked into the bathroom, unzipped his pants, and sat on the toilet. The aide let the reporters in. Standing as close to the open bathroom door as they could, they began firing questions.

I'll never forget that scene. The majority leader of the Senate of the United States seated in the bathroom, his pants down to his ankles, the door wide open, discussing the real threat of a nuclear war in barnyard language.

"Mr. Majority Leader," one reporter shouted, "we want your views on the Berlin crisis."

"It stinks," Johnson grunted. "Not my shit, either. Anyway, that's Ike's problem. If he had let George [Patton] go into Berlin at the end of the war, we wouldn't have a goddamn Berlin problem to worry about. Let Ike handle it!"

With that, he wiped himself, flushed the toilet, and zipped up his pants. As vulgar as the scene was, it was a key to understanding LBJ. The affairs of the nation and the machinery of politics were the fibers of his life. He never let go of them even during the most private times.

After blowing more steam at President Eisenhower, Johnson marched off to an official press conference from the stage of his office, where he spoke of Berlin and world peace in reasoned and unemotional terms.

I never could figure out why LBJ said and did those crude things. Some days, I thought he was trying to shock people just for the fun of it. Other times, I believed he did them because he actually *was* a crude man.

During those four years as LBJ's man, I also learned that Johnson was a strange womanizer. He frequently turned his hideaway into a love nest. He would invite a woman there at the end of the day to "take dictation." Most of the time, I prepared snacks and drinks. The woman would come in and, after I served him and her, Johnson would order, "Stand out by the door. If I need you, I'll call."

Three or four white women and at least three black ones used to come to the hideaway regularly during those years. Johnson used to pinch and slap bottoms so hard that some of the women could hardly walk to the elevator afterward. I remember one time LBJ told me to stand outside his door and let in a secretary who apparently was really coming to work. I was to stay there and let no one else in until he gave the word.

"That sonofabitch in there alone?" the secretary asked when she got off the elevator.

"Yes," I said.

"Will you go in with me? I don't feel like a fight tonight."

I said that I had my orders. She heaved a sigh and went inside the lion's den.

Even though Johnson was crude and cruel, I grew to admire him. It was an education just to watch him work. He was like a spider who spun a gigantic web. By the time he was finished, he had entangled half the Hill in it. He'd do favors for straight-laced men like Richard Russell, help womanizers like Kefauver, support bills for this senator, get jobs for the friends of that senator, make introductions for this one, send me to pick up Mr. So-and-So for Senator So-and-So. With the help of Bobby Baker, he knew where every body was buried on the Hill. He even lured J. Edgar Hoover into his hideaway. What information they exchanged or deals they made must have been important, for Hoover always dismissed me when it was time for serious talk.

What was important to me as a black man was that LBJ used his power not only to enhance his own political career but also to make important contributions to civil rights. The 1956 National Democratic Convention was key to all the civil rights legislation that would follow.

I looked forward to the 1956 Democratic Convention in Chicago. Lyndon Johnson was a Texas favorite son candidate for the presidency, and even though his bid for the White House was not serious, I was interested in seeing how he would deal with civil rights.

A lot had happened since the Freedom Train of 1947. In 1954, the Supreme Court had ruled that racial segregation in public schools was unconstitutional, and the following year it banned segregation in public recreational facilities. That same year, 1955, the Interstate Commerce Commission banned segregation in buses and waiting rooms involved in interstate travel; Rosa Parks was arrested in December after refusing to give her seat to a white man on a Montgomery bus, sparking the Montgomery bus boycott, led by the Reverend Martin Luther King, Jr. Blacks were beginning to organize politically. The pressure they applied was slight, but it was there.

Johnson was still wearing two political faces. To southerners, he played the racist; to liberal northerners like Hubert Humphrey, he was a practical civil rights advocate. No one in 1956, including me, knew where LBJ really stood. Most of the time I thought he didn't have a clear position. He was licking his finger, holding it up, and seeing which way the winds were blowing, as illustrated by the following story.

One day, Johnson jumped off the subway that runs between the Capitol and the Senate and House office buildings and raced down the corridor to the elevator. He was in a Texas-size hurry to get to the Senate floor for a critical vote. He punched the "Senators Only" button and swore as he waited. When the door slid open, the only person on the elevator was a black waiter carrying a silver tray with lunch for South Dakota Senator Karl Mundt. Johnson cursed as the elevator creaked to the next floor. It never made it. LBJ and the waiter were stuck between floors for nearly twenty minutes.

The black waiter's name was Lamb. He told me later that LBJ was very nice to him. "Put the tray down and rest your arms," Johnson had told him. They both sat on the floor and chatted while mechanics tinkered with the elevator. Johnson was up for reelection that year, and the next morning he called a press conference. To cover himself, he explained why he had missed the important vote. Then he said that he had issued orders preventing colored waiters from riding the "Senators Only" elevators. They were to deliver food by way of the stairs.

Texas papers ate it up. Unlike 1948, when he won the Democratic primary by a trickle, LBJ won by a landslide in 1954. "Lyndon, you shoulda had a nigger on the elevator with you in 1948," I later heard one of LBJ's friends comment during lunch. Johnson's face lighted up with an ear-to-ear grin. "Yeah," he said, "it's always good to have a nigger in the woodpile."

Just as in 1948, the civil rights plank was the major issue at the 1956 Democratic Convention. Simply put, the question was: Would the Democrats demand a national program to implement the Supreme Court's school desegregation decision, or would they remain silent? As in 1948, the minority proposed a "hard" plank, demanding not only the implementation of the school decision but also a ban on segregation in all public transportation, as well as federal legislation for fair employment, personal security, and full voting rights. The debate was hot. But unlike 1948, the majority, including presidential candidates Adlai Stevenson and Governor Averell Harriman, chose silence.

When the smoke cleared, blacks stood solidly behind Adlai Stevenson, even though his stand on civil rights was moderate. If they knew and believed in Lyndon Johnson, they didn't show it. Illinois Congressman William Dawson, the first black to chair a House standing committee, was the exception. Most black leaders had long since dismissed Dawson as a sellout to the white establishment if not an out-and-out Uncle Tom. When Chicago's South Side sent him to Washington in 1942, he was the only black in the House of Representatives. Blacks sent him back over and over again. But because he didn't give rabble-rousing civil rights speeches, black leaders soon dubbed him "William the Silent." They couldn't have been further from the truth. I watched Dawson for several years. Where Adam Clayton Powell dazzled and bullied, Dawson worked quietly. Both men were playing the same game, but with very different styles. Adam challenged and bent the rules; Dawson used them. His theme was consistent: political power represented the best hope for blacks.

I had discussed civil rights with Dawson several times on the Hill. He was the only black leader I knew who seemed to understand Johnson's power. "Potential for real national leadership," Dawson told me. "A force to be dealt with." I think Dawson saw in Johnson the same man I had glimpsed when there was no southern audience to please: a driven man, with a streak of kindness, who truly understood discrimination and powerlessness.

Dawson liked Adlai Stevenson but felt he wasn't strong enough to become president. I wasn't surprised when he sought out Johnson during the convention. Sensing that President Eisenhower would trounce Stevenson, Dawson began looking toward 1960, when the black vote would be a power to contend with. I served lunch in LBJ's private hospitality room; I don't recall which other congressmen were present, but I do remember the gist of the conversation. Dawson told Johnson he would support him for 1960 and try to convince other black leaders to do the same if Johnson would put his shoulder behind civil rights legislation. Johnson said he would.

I believed Johnson and was proud of him in a strange sort of way. Rarely did he commit himself to anything, but when he did, he meant it.

Dawson went on to say that blacks could eventually overcome their fear of a southerner in the White House, a fox in the chicken coop. An astute politician, Dawson told Johnson that he knew how difficult it would be for a Texan to endorse civil rights for blacks, and that the black community would come to appreciate LBJ's courage. And so a fragile and difficult alliance was born.

Johnson's chance to prove himself to blacks came soon after Eisenhower defeated Stevenson. Early in 1957, the House passed the first civil rights bill in eighty years. Even though the Eisenhower-backed measure had few teeth, it was symbolic. If the bill's supporters could steer it through the Senate, which had successfully blocked every civil rights measure originating in the House for eighty years, it would be a victory of gigantic proportions. The Senate version of the bill was locked in the Judiciary Committee, where

Senator Eastland of Mississippi was determined to kill it. Chairman Eastland was another of those southern racists who had called the 1954 Supreme Court school desegregation ruling a "monstrous decision." Also on the Judiciary Committee were racists like Olin Johnston and John McClellan.

In effect, the Eisenhower bill permitted the Department of Justice to intervene for the first time in history on behalf of persons deprived of their civil rights. In particular, it called for a federal Civil Rights Commission with subpoena powers, and a Civil Rights Division in the Justice Department. It also empowered federal prosecutors to obtain a court injunction against those who interfered or threatened to interfere with anyone's right to vote. Those refusing to obey the injunction could be imprisoned for civil contempt by a federal judge sitting without a jury, and held until they consented to comply. Blacks weren't pleased with the bill because, although it created useful civil rights machinery, there were no provisions saying that the machinery had to be used.

I recall how Humphrey, Paul Douglas of Illinois, and Phil Hart of Michigan came to Lyndon Johnson to ask for his support as majority leader in getting the bill out of Judiciary and onto the floor. I served them lunch in LBJ's hideaway. From that day on, I knew exactly where Johnson stood on civil rights. His analysis was as perceptive as it turned out to be accurate.

"For the first time, colored people have a powerful leader," Johnson lectured the three northern liberals, referring to Dr. Martin Luther King. I smiled to myself, because LBJ didn't say niggers. "A religious leader. A nonviolent man of the cloth. Do you know what that means? Have you ever seen a colored Baptist preacher from the South in action? Well, let me tell you something. That's *one* man who controls the colored community. And I'll tell you another thing. These people are not breakin' any laws. They're demonstratin' peacefully, and the eyes of the world are on them."

Johnson barely paused for breath, and I sensed that his pragmatism surprised Humphrey, Douglas, and Hart. What he said rang true to me, for my daddy was a preacher, and I had seen firsthand what power he had.

Johnson continued, "You know the boycott in Alabama was successful. Very successful. J. Edgar Hoover was saying just the other day how he was hoping niggers would flock behind militant leaders like Malcolm X, 'cause then they could lock 'um all up and throw away the key. Even old Hoover admits his hands are tied. The colored are not going to give up. They're determined. They've been oppressed long enough."

By the time the lunch was over, Lyndon Johnson's position was not only clear, it was vintage LBJ. He stood behind civil rights because the country had no choice. Justice and injustice, ethics and morality had little to do with it. Behind powerful leaders like Martin Luther King, blacks were beginning to demand equal rights, and if they were denied, there would be violence. To Johnson, it was as simple as that. Understanding both the anger and frustration of blacks and the fear and hatred of whites, Johnson wanted to avoid a "new civil war."

LBJ was at least six years ahead of other southern senators who would eventually share his pragmatic viewpoint. In 1968, after Martin Luther King's funeral, Senator Ellender joked about the potential for black violence during his annual gumbo party, which I served. Johnson, then president, had urged all employers to give blacks the day off so they could attend local memorial services for Dr. King.

"There was this old nigger woman," Ellender began. She worked for a white lady who had been bedridden for twenty years and who was as mean as a rattler in a shoebox. The mammy would come to work, mouth full of snuff, head bowed, and wondering what the old shrew would do to her next. On the day they buried King, the mammy came to work as usual, but instead of being grim and silent, she was humming and singing.

"Mornin', Miss Sally," she said as she walked into the white woman's bedroom.

"Why, Delila, what are you doing here?" Miss Sally said. "You know they're burying Dr. King today. I want you to go right back home. President Johnson said all good people should let their help off today."

"No, ma'am, Miss Sally," Delila said. "I'm gonna sit right here by you and watch it all on the television."

Delila washed Miss Sally as usual, cooked her breakfast as usual, put the pitcher of water on the table, and gave her the newspaper as usual. Then she got the spit can for her snuff juice and sat down by Miss Sally's bedside. Miss Sally kept insisting that Delila take the day off, but the mammy refused.

"Why not?" Miss Sally finally asked.

"Dr. King's been preaching that nonviolent shit all these years, Miss Sally, ma'am," Delila said. "Every time I get mad and want to do somethin' about it, I remember Dr. King sayin' to turn the other cheek. But Dr. King be dead now. I'm gonna sit right here with you until they bury him. And just as soon as they throw the dirt on Dr. King's face, bitch, I'm gonna whip your ass!"

But back in 1957, a few months after Johnson had the meeting with Humphrey, Douglas, and Hart, I served another lunch for him and the same three northern senators. Johnson was hesitating to push the civil rights bill through the Senate publicly for fear of alienating his southern colleagues, especially Richard Russell, the most powerful man in the Senate and the one to whom LBJ owed his job as majority leader.

"Mr. Majority Leader," Humphrey asked, "do you know what it would mean to you to get this civil rights bill passed? Why, there hasn't been one since Reconstruction, over eighty years ago."

"Goddamn it, Hubert," Johnson said, "I'd get strung up by my balls in Texas if I'd get behind this bill."

"We'll do the footwork, Lyndon," Douglas argued. "Just use your office to get it onto the floor."

I didn't hear Johnson commit himself to anything at this luncheon, but then, LBJ rarely did. Nevertheless, he got behind the bill in his own special way. He started bringing Hubert Humphrey to meetings with Richard Russell. He dragged Hubert to Harvey's and introduced him to the Southern power bloc. He invited Humphrey to intimate dinner parties at his home. It was almost as if he were telling his southern colleagues, "Look, Hubert's a nice guy, and he makes sense in his own northern liberal way. We ought to listen to him." Whenever Johnson met with his southern cronies, either in a group or privately, I would hear him say, "We can't continue to push these things down their nigger throats. They won't sit still any longer. We have to give them *something*!"

That became Johnson's message to the South. "I'm on your side, not theirs. Be practical. We have to give them something. But we don't have to put teeth in it."

Johnson was especially smooth at the southern prayer breakfast held every Wednesday morning in S–138, the Vandenberg Room. They were all there: John Stennis, Richard Russell, Olin Johnston, Strom Thurmond, Spessard "Hangman" Holland, James Eastland, Estes Kefauver. Stennis usually led the prayers. Except for the bonfire and the white hoods, the prayer breakfast was as close to a KKK meeting as I have ever seen. It reminded me of how I used to lie in the woods near our farm in Magnolia and watch the Klansmen call on God to help keep niggers in their place.

As soon as the doors to the Vandenberg Room were closed, *God* and *nigger* were the two words I heard the most. The senators treated each other like preachers and deacons, and LBJ was marvelous. By this time, I knew he was tricking them into not opposing the civil rights bill, so I could watch him with fascination. "Give the goddamned niggers something," he'd tell them. I could almost hear God chuckling.

It worked. On June 20, the Senate voted to place the House-passed civil rights bill directly on the calendar for a floor vote, thus bypassing hostile hearings in the Judiciary Committee. Johnson had worked closely with California Senator William Knowland, the minority leader, to pull off the surprise end run.

Johnson's constant massaging of the southerners paid off as well. Although they opposed the bill in principle, they knew they couldn't stop it. Fearing that it might be strengthened if they tried to delay it, they kept quiet—all except Senator Thurmond, that is. He conducted a one-man filibuster for twenty-four hours and eighteen minutes, beating the record that had been set by Wayne Morse four years earlier. Thurmond's colleagues were angry at him for what they called a "grandstand" performance that made the South look unreasonable and that gave liberals an opportunity to tighten the filibuster rule. The South wanted to save the filibuster strategy for future civil rights bills that would have teeth. If anyone could take the credit for preventing a full Senate filibuster, it was LBJ, who had convinced his southern colleagues that the tactic would do more harm than good.

No one took Thurmond's last stand seriously. The senators speculated about how he had managed to stay on the floor for a full day with only one trip to the bathroom. Either he had an amazing bladder, they joked, or he was wearing rubber pants.

Shortly after Thurmond gave up the floor, the Civil Rights Act of 1957 was passed 72 to 18, with LBJ, Kefauver, and Ralph Yarborough of Texas voting for it. Even though it was, as NAACP leader Roy Wilkins put it, "soup made from the shadow of a thin chicken that had starved to death," it was still an important victory for LBJ. He had gotten it through the Senate, hiding behind men like Humphrey, without losing his credibility with his southern colleagues. Unfortunately, he had done it so smoothly that black leaders were not aware of how much they owed him.

Hubert Humphrey, for one, appreciated what LBJ had accomplished. His sister, Francis Howard, whose parties I served regularly, threw a bash for Johnson. "Lyndon has more balls than anyone alive," Humphrey told me after the party.

Coming from a man who had risked his entire political career on one short speech in Philadelphia, that was quite a compliment. LBJ had promised Dawson that he would get behind civil rights, and he had. Now the question was, could Dawson deliver for Johnson?

CHAPTER

I had not been impressed with Senator John F. Kennedy. I had met him and his friend, Florida Senator George Smathers, whom we called "the Arrow Shirt kid," in Harvey's not long after Kennedy came to town. Unlike most other senators, Kennedy rarely ate there. At first, he used to drop in to order dinner, which I carried to his love nest next door at the Mayflower Hotel. After a while, he started phoning in his order, and I and the other waiters, depending on how many friends JFK was entertaining, would carry the food to room 812 and serve it. It was not unusual for guests staying at the Mayflower or at the La Salle down the street to order their food from Harvey's, which had a reputation in the 1940s and 1950s for an excellent kitchen. I remember serving movie stars like Marilyn Monroe at the La Salle, which was noted for its small bar, its mediocre cuisine, its elegant suites, and its high-class call girls. Estes Kefauver and Olin Johnson loved the place.

I never took Kennedy seriously. Before he made his bid for the presidency, he seemed to be in Washington only to have a good time. He made no attempt to tunnel his way into the Hill power structure of Richard Russell and Lyndon Johnson. President Truman never ate or played poker with him when Kennedy was a representative. Age had little to do with it; Russell Long and JFK were born one year apart, and Long had joined the group. After he became a senator in 1952, Kennedy still did not seem to be developing his own power base on the Hill. As far as I could tell, he didn't stand for anything or fight for anything other than staying in office. He laughed, he smiled, and he had a good time. We dubbed room 812 at the Mayflower "the Playpen."

Kennedy always seemed to be having parties there. Sometimes he would be alone with a woman; sometimes it would be a small affair with a few men and their dates. He or an aide would call me early in the evening and ask me to get the room ready. I would set up the bar, prepare the snacks, and see that there was plenty of ice. Then I would leave the key with a room clerk who knew about the arrangements. Later, I would supervise the waiters who brought the hot food over in elegant dishes.

Besides the intimate parties in room 812 for Kennedy, his women and his friends, there were also larger bashes for celebrities. I remember serving Betty Grable and Harry James in room 812. Frank Sinatra was Kennedy's guest whenever he was in town. JFK would order a load of lobsters from Massachusetts, and Harvey's would cook and serve them with all the trimmings. I did enjoy watching Kennedy, even though I didn't like him. His fun-loving approach to Washington was a welcome change from that of the Eisenhower people, most of whom kept their lives as well balanced as their checkbooks.

I was surprised when Kennedy almost won the vice-presidential spot on the Democratic ticket in Chicago in 1956. Adlai Stevenson had given the delegates the right to select his running mate after he was nominated on the first ballot. Lyndon Johnson had advised Stevenson to pick his own ticket, warning him that if he left the choice to the delegates, they'd settle on Tennessee Senator Kefauver, who was popular in the North but unacceptable to the South. Kefauver had come out strongly in favor of civil rights, not because he believed in them but because, like LBJ, he had had a glimpse of the future.

LBJ was right. Kennedy came in a strong second on the first ballot, just behind Kefauver. Most black delegates didn't even know Kennedy. Those who did—like Adam Clayton Powell, who supported Eisenhower because his record on civil rights was better than that of the Democrats—didn't think much of JFK as a potential leader or as a civil rights advocate. As far as they were concerned, Kennedy was just a rich Catholic kid from Massachusetts. His speech nominating Stevenson had not impressed blacks, either. Although it was electric and full of promises, it didn't even hint that Kennedy was aware that there was a civil rights problem.

Kennedy lost to Kefauver on the second ballot. It was fascinating to me that, almost to a person, delegates from the Deep South voted for Kennedy. They sensed that even if he wasn't strongly on their side, at least he wouldn't push for civil rights.

After the 1956 convention, I began to watch Kennedy more closely on the Hill. It didn't take long to see that he knew absolutely nothing about blacks. He was respectful, but his Harvard education and his social circles had isolated him. He reminded me of Congressman Keating in the 1940s; concerned about justice in an abstract way, he was unaware of the black world around him.

John Kennedy stood in the shadows in 1959–60 while Lyndon Johnson steered through the Senate the House's civil rights bill aimed at guaranteeing the voting rights of blacks. Once again, it was almost as if Kennedy didn't want to offend the southern senators, whose support he was courting. I smiled to myself as I watched him duck for cover, a surprising move, for he had won the Pulitzer Prize for his book *Profiles in Courage*. Kennedy was not at all like Hubert Humphrey, who had defied the southern bloc at the convention in 1948, an act for which the South had never forgiven him.

Kennedy also kept quiet when the southern scalpel went to work on the Senate version of the civil rights bill. Measures dealing with school integration and job equality were cut from it. Added to it were sixteen amendments that all but castrated it. The only controversial provision left intact allowed federal district judges to appoint referees to enroll qualified black voters in areas where local authorities systematically denied their right to the polls.

To get the bill onto President Eisenhower's desk, Johnson, who worked closely with Senate Minority Leader Everett Dirksen of Illinois, played his usual game. He told the southerners, "I'm on your side, but we have to give 'um something." To the liberals, he promised to use all his power and skill to get the bill by the southern bloc. He kept the Senate in nonstop sessions for more than a week. I remember how reluctant he was to allow the senators to attend the opening game of the 1960 baseball season, and how he called them back for a critical vote before the last pitch. In spite of a six-day southern filibuster, the civil rights bill passed 71 to 18, with every senator from the Deep South, except Texas, voting against it. There was no doubt in anyone's mind that without Johnson's leadership, there would have been no 1960 civil rights bill. LBJ himself had no illusions about what he had accomplished. He knew the weak bill was, as he told the press, merely a "step forward."

I felt that Johnson had once again delivered on his promise to Congressman Dawson to put his shoulder behind civil rights legislation. In the end, however, the 1960 civil rights bill was a no-win for LBJ and a no-lose for Kennedy. Senate liberals and blacks called it a southern triumph. Thurgood Marshall, who had argued and won *Brown* v. *Board of Education* before the Supreme Court in 1954, put it this way: "It would take two or three years for a good lawyer to get someone registered under this bill." Blacks blamed Johnson for cooperating with his southern cronies to water the bill down. Southerners, on the other hand, saw the bill as one more crack in the wall of white supremacy. Some even blamed Johnson for getting the bill passed. I sympathized with his dilemma.

Kennedy, on the other hand, could smile at everyone's frustration. To liberals and blacks, he could say, "I didn't support the bill because it was a national disgrace." To the South, he could say, "You see, I'm not that liberal. Although I voted for the bill, I didn't push for it."

After the bill was passed, I could see Kennedy begin to go after the black vote from a safe distance. It was mostly talk and private promises. I remember one afternoon in 1960, long before the National Democratic Convention in Los Angeles. Kennedy joined Johnson for lunch in LBJ's hideaway, S–208. I served them and left the room to stand guard at the door without being asked, because I knew that Johnson wanted to meet with his rival for the presidency alone. Down the hallway stood a cluster of blacks waiting to see JFK, among them Roy Wilkins, who had succeeded Walter White as executive director of the NAACP. James Farmer of CORE and Whitney Young of the Urban League were also there. To see blacks lining up to talk to a presidential candidate was a delightful shock. Although I had been working for Johnson for almost fifteen years, I had never seen such a beautiful sight. As I waited for Kennedy to come out of Johnson's hideaway, I couldn't help but reflect on how much progress had been made since I had stepped onto the Freedom Train in 1947. Blacks still had no real power of their own, but powerful whites were beginning to listen to them and even court them. I remembered what Congressman Dawson had told me time and again: "We'll never get anywhere until we have some political power." I sensed that if the Democrats took the White House in the fall, we'd get some.

Kennedy came out of Johnson's hideaway and peered down the

corridor. Then he leaned over to me and asked, "Robert, which one is Wilkins?"

I was shocked. To Kennedy, all blacks still looked alike, even though Roy Wilkins, with his balding head, medium-to-light skin, and distinctive bearing, was easy to pick out of a crowd. Hardly a week passed without him and Martin Luther King being on national television. I was upset. Kennedy, who had been hiding from civil rights, was being courted by blacks, while Hubert Humphrey, who had stood by blacks for twelve years, was being nosed out.

I discreetly described Wilkins. With a bounce and a winning smile, Kennedy strode right over to Wilkins as if he had known him all his life. And that's how it would be for the next six months.

The National Democratic Convention proved to be everything I thought it would be. I worked the hospitality rooms at the Los Angeles Biltmore Hotel, where the Democratic Senatorial Campaign Committee was headquartered. Of all the hospitality rooms, this one was the most important. It buzzed with rumors and smelled of cigars and deals. From the day the convention opened, it was clear to everyone but Lyndon Johnson that Kennedy had the nomination locked up. The big issues were the civil rights platform and who Kennedy would choose to run with him.

I had seen few black faces at the 1948 and 1952 conventions, unless they were serving, as I was. In 1956 in Chicago, there had been a group of blacks flexing some political muscle. In Los Angeles, however, I could feel black power pulsing as never before. I found it exciting. Martin Luther King led six thousand chanting and singing protesters to the Sports Arena for a civil rights rally, which I attended for a few hours. Democratic National Chairman Paul Butler addressed us. I think he was shocked to see so many blacks demanding civil rights. "We dedicate ourselves to the elimination of all discriminatory practices at the earliest possible moment without violence," he promised.

We were sick of weak promises that had been wrung from politicians during the heat of a campaign. "No!" we chanted in one voice. "No! Now! Not later!"

The Sports Arena shook. Stunned, Butler quickly added, "I mean now."

Not satisfied with either Butler or his weak response, Roy Wilkins invited Hubert Humphrey and all the presidential candidates—

Johnson, Kennedy, Stevenson, and Missouri Senator Stewart Symington—to clarify their stands on civil rights at a second rally sponsored by the NAACP in the Shrine Auditorium. What a change! Blacks were actually demanding that leaders spell out where they stood on desegregation, and the media were there to record their words.

Blacks weren't happy with any of the candidates. Johnson hadn't convinced them that he really believed in civil rights, Kennedy appeared to be a moderate, afraid to make waves, Stevenson was not a serious candidate, Symington had not impressed blacks throughout the primaries. Humphrey had been their overwhelming choice, but he had pulled out of the race.

At the last minute, Lyndon Johnson backed out of addressing the rally and sent his aide, Oscar Chapman, to speak in his place. I felt sorry for the man. As soon as Chapman mentioned Johnson's name, the audience of six thousand hyped-up blacks and a few hundred whites began booing and catcalling. Ever the gentleman, Roy Wilkins quieted the audience down so that Chapman could finish.

John Kennedy spoke for himself. As he strode to the podium with confidence, the audience greeted him with a sprinkling of boos and light applause. Unruffled, he emphasized the need for a presidential leader willing to use his moral and legal authority to guarantee the constitutional rights of all. He spoke favorably but cautiously about sit-ins, the new civil rights technique born at a Woolworth's lunch counter early in 1960. (Southerners wanted a presidential candidate who would condemn such actions or at least not encourage them.) Kennedy spoke of discrimination in the North as well as in the South, calling for an end to segregation in all public facilities, in voting, in education, and in housing. He ended with a challenge: "My friends, if you are sober-minded enough to believe, then—to the extent that these tasks require the support, guidance and leadership of the President of the United States—I am bold enough to try."

There were no boos when Kennedy sat down, but neither was there thunderous applause. Most blacks remained skeptical and rightly so. JFK had not yet done one single thing for civil rights that he could point to with pride.

Stevenson, who was not seeking the nomination but who

wouldn't turn it down if it were offered, did not appear either. Agnes Meyer, author and lecturer, read a telegram from Eleanor Roosevelt singing Stevenson's praises, and former New York Governor Herbert Lehman spoke on his behalf. Blacks weren't impressed. If Stevenson won't face us, why should we support him? they asked themselves.

Symington spoke briefly and in general terms about civil rights. He said he stood on his record, and he spoke as if he were reading a statement into the Congressional Record. He sat down to moderate applause.

Hubert Humphrey walked to the podium to cheers and thunder. But not only was he no longer a serious presidential candidate, he had already declined to become JFK's running mate. Humphrey proudly told the rally that he would rather be right on civil rights than be president or vice president. We believed him. To Humphrey, Kennedy was a civil rights fraud trying to jump on the bandwagon that he, Humphrey, had kept rolling for twelve years.

When he took the mike, Hubert did not dance around the sit-in question to please the South. After praising the NAACP, he said the sit-in strikers were "as patriotic as the men who had fired the first shot at Lexington and Concord." The applause was deafening. In one sentence, he had summarized what the budding civil rights movement was all about, and no one in the Shrine Auditorium, including me, doubted that he meant those words. We also knew that his honesty had cost him the presidency, for he was totally unacceptable to the South.

I had come to the rally more out of curiosity than anything else. But I would not be honest if I didn't say that Kennedy impressed me for the first time. I believed his promises. He had spun a little magic. His voice rang with conviction. His timing was flawless. His words were like a balm. I didn't want them to stop. It made no difference to me at that moment that he was late in endorsing civil rights or that he was saying what Hubert Humphrey had been preaching since 1948. As the strongest contender to beat Vice President Richard Nixon, Kennedy was making serious commitments. I had never seen Kennedy welsh on a promise. And I recalled what Strom Thurmond had said about Harry Truman in 1948: "That haberdasher means business." Those words might apply just as appropriately to Kennedy.

From my vantage point in the hospitality room, where the powerful drank and chatted, I watched Symington's feeble efforts for the nomination crumble. I watched Johnson pumping hands, fighting against the Kennedy machine. I saw Stevenson heave a giant gasp in a last effort to be taken seriously. Nothing or nobody could stop Kennedy.

Carmine DeSapio said it best. A Johnson supporter and a New York political leader, DeSapio had Kennedy leaning on him all during the convention. The New Yorker was allergic to smoke and was always asking me to open the door or window. Every time Pierre Salinger, Kennedy's press secretary, came to talk to him, puffing on a cigar that never seemed to go out, DeSapio would try to hide. Not long before the balloting began, I heard DeSapio say to one of the delegates, "Those Kennedy people don't just ask. They grab you by the nuts and twist."

Late in the evening on which Kennedy won the nomination on the first ballot, I was working the hospitality room, serving gallons of wine, coffee, and Boston Mist (cranberry juice and vodka) to the Kennedy crowd. The debate over JFK's running mate was taking place behind a locked door near my serving table. At first, everyone took it for granted that Kennedy would choose Symington. But as the hours dragged on, I heard another name whispered over and over again as I opened doors and served: Lyndon Johnson. Some of Kennedy's advisers urged him to offer Johnson the right of first refusal because LBJ had been runner-up. They knew Johnson would reject a courtesy offer. But no one thought Kennedy would actually tell Johnson that he was his *real* choice or that Johnson would actually accept.

I recalled a dinner party that I had served about six weeks before the convention back at Lyndon Johnson's house in Washington. Sam Rayburn was the guest of honor. The Speaker and a few friends were mixing after-dinner drinks and political strategy when the talk turned to the Democratic ticket. Rayburn had stong feelings about who should be on it. No one but LBJ really thought he could wrest the presidential nomination from Kennedy. Rayburn was blunt. "Lyndon," he said, "if you're not on this ticket as vice president, we'll lose Texas to Nixon for sure! You were our favorite son in '56. Texas loves you!"

Johnson was insulted. "I wouldn't be caught dead running on a ticket with that goddamned Roman Catholic!"

From everything I saw and heard in those wee hours of the morning in the Los Angeles Biltmore, I knew that Bobby Kennedy was the biggest obstacle to LBJ. I had met Bobby once or twice at parties. With his boyish looks and glass of milk, he seemed harmless. But Bobby hated Lyndon Johnson if for no other reason than that he thought LBJ was crude. The pro-Johnson people inside the Kennedy camp spent most of the evening and part of the morning trying to convince Bobby that his brother needed Johnson to help win in the South. Bobby kept saying that he'd rather lose than have that "cornponed bastard" on the ticket.

When John Kennedy finally settled on LBJ, he knew it would not be easy to sell the Texan to blacks. Kennedy's concern was real. As word spread that Johnson was a serious contender, there was a sense of anger among blacks, then betrayal. They began accusing Kennedy of a sellout. They wanted Hubert Humphrey, who had stood by blacks for twelve years, never faltering, always delivering, totally honest. But when Humphrey had said that he wouldn't accept the vice presidency, he meant it. Sensing a black revolt, Kennedy made a brilliant move to cut it off at the pass.

Around seven in the morning, after Johnson had accepted the offer, Kennedy opened his locked door and came over to the couch where Frank Reeves, a black Washington, D.C., delegate and a Kennedy adviser, was sitting. There were still small groups of people all around the hospitality room sipping coffee and popping caffeine pills. As I served JFK a cup of black coffee, I heard him say, "Well, Frank, it'll be Lyndon Johnson."

I was all ears as I kept myself busy.

"Senator Kennedy," Reeves said, "there's no way black people are going to accept Lyndon Johnson as vice president."

Kennedy brushed the objection aside. The decision had been made, and he wasn't asking for Reeves's advice. "Get together all the black delegates you can at eleven this morning," Kennedy ordered. "I want to talk to them."

While I made arrangements to secure the Biltmore Bowl, an auditorium that seated several hundred people, Reeves sent out calls to more than three hundred blacks in Los Angeles—delegates, alternates, and community leaders from cities all over the country who had come to town to make their presence felt.

I wasn't sure what to expect when I walked into the Biltmore Bowl just after eleven o'clock. Although the vast majority of the hundred people who came were blacks, there was a sprinkling of whites. The Bowl hummed with anticipation. Not only were blacks angry about the nomination of LBJ, they were resentful of the snobbish tactics of Frank Reeves. He had all but ignored Congressman Dawson during the convention and seemed to be standing aloof from national black leadership. In a word, it was a hostile audience, and I didn't envy John F. Kennedy in the least.

When Kennedy and Johnson walked into the Bowl arm in arm, there was faint applause and a scattering of boos. After Roy Wilkins reprimanded the audience for the boos, many sat in their seats, arms folded across their chests in protest. Wilkins then introduced Kennedy, and the applause was respectful.

Once again, Kennedy seemed unruffled. He had gained in credibility since he had addressed the blacks in the Shrine Auditorium. For one thing, he now *was* the Democratic candidate for the presidency, like it or not. For another, he had stood firmly behind the strongest civil rights plank in the history of the Democratic party.

Kennedy took the podium, smiled, and waved. Then he introduced Johnson and sat back down as if to say, "Lyndon, you're on your own. Now let me see you get out of this one!"

Johnson was in top form. He warmly greeted Congressman Dawson, who was sitting at the head table. Then he began his short speech. As I recall it, he said, "My fellow Americans. I know just how you feel. If I were in your place, I would feel the same way. As a southerner, a poor white from a very depressed region of Texas, I know what hardship, yes, what discrimination means. I know what your desires are. Perhaps we have not always acted in those interests, but this is a country of growth and challenge and chance. Working together, we can as men and women of good faith, achieve those goals. . . .

"I'm going to run on the platform that this convention adopted. I stand beside and behind the leader. With your help, I think you will find at the end of the first Democratic administration that you have made more progress in four years than you have made in the past one hundred years. If you stand behind us, I don't think you folks will be sorry."

Loud applause shattered the tension that we all felt. Kennedy fielded a tough question-and-answer period, defending his choice of Johnson. When the conference was over, blacks rushed to the table to shake hands with LBJ. Some doubters remained seated with arms crossed, but the logjam of skepticism had been broken. Roy Wilkins spoke for many when he said that Johnson was neither a racist nor a knight on a white charger fighting for the strongest civil rights bills possible. But with Johnson as vice president, Wilkins added, Democrats can expect to get at least part of their civil rights platform enacted because LBJ was "a doer." I couldn't have agreed more.

The Hill is an exciting place during a presidential campaign. The future of everyone, from secretaries to senators, hangs in the balance. Campaign chatter is incessant, from the elevators to the men's room. Kennedy's campaign, however, brought an added dimension to the Hill: hundreds of black faces from all over the nation. For the first time in history, a presidential candidate was actually appealing to blacks for their votes. They responded by coming to the Hill to see Kennedy personally. To his credit, he opened his eyes and ears to them. Soon he began to see their problems and to hear their fears. Then he began to speak to their hopes, and his words were straight as an arrow. The magic he had spun at the convention, he spun across the nation. Blacks from every state began lining up outside his office. It was like the California gold rush. I had to pick my way through the crowd each morning just to get down the corridor. The southern bigots, who swelled the Senate payroll, were upset. The only blacks they had seen on the Hill before Kennedy's nomination pushed brooms, polished brass, and washed dishes. They became vicious.

"The Hill's turning black!" I heard them say.

"I was late for work this morning because of all those niggers."

"I couldn't get down the corridor with those niggers blocking the way."

One symbolic act—whether it was purely political or motivated by kindness is not clear—won Kennedy the hearts of millions of blacks. When Martin Luther King was jailed in Atlanta in October for a peaceful sit-in just a few weeks before Election Day, Kennedy called Dr. King's wife, Coretta, to express his concern. He promised to do what he could to get her husband released. The next day, Bobby Kennedy began leaning on the judge. Dr. King was released a day or two after the Kennedys intervened. Although JFK's symbolic action did not make major headlines, the news traveled through the black community like a brushfire. Coretta Scott King expressed her gratitude on national television. Martin Luther King, Sr., who had planned to vote against Kennedy because he was Catholic, told the media that the phone call to his daughter-in-law had changed his mind. He was now a Kennedy supporter. Southern racists dubbed Kennedy a "Catholic nigger-lover," which only made the Irishman more popular among blacks.

I was so smitten with Kennedy fever that I became his unofficial ward boss among the blacks on the Hill, urging them to register and then vote the Kennedy-Johnson ticket. When the battle was over and the smoke had finally lifted, I watched John F. Kennedy take the oath of office and heard his touching inaugural speech with the strongest feeling of hope that I had ever experienced. It no longer made any difference to me that JFK did not have the civil rights track record of Hubert Humphrey, whom I respected so much. Lyndon Johnson had promised more civil rights legislation in the next four years than in the previous one hundred. His word was good enough for me. And I believed in John F. Kennedy. As a black man, I sensed that, somehow, theirs would be a winning combination.

CHAPTER

For me, the Kennedy-Johnson administration began with a smile. I served LBJ's big party on the Hill soon after inauguration. It was a good-bye celebration for Mr. Majority Leader and a welcome-home party for Mr. Vice President. Every lion on the Hill crawled out of his lair to be present for the television cameras. Johnson and I appeared together on some footage that most Texas TV stations ran. My daddy, who had moved to Houston, saw me. He called the White House.

"My name is Robert Parker," he told the switchboard. "I got a boy there. He's been workin' for that white man a long time. The one that just became vice president. I want to talk to my boy."

The switchboard operator checked the directory for a Robert Parker. Of course, I was still working on the Hill. "There is no Robert Parker listed at the White House," she told him.

"Well, you find him and tell him his daddy wants to talk to him."

My father kept pestering the White House. "What's your number?" the switchboard finally asked. "If we find your son, we'll give it to him."

The switchboard called the Secret Service. Suspecting that Robert Parker, Sr., was a dangerous crank, they sent two agents to check him out. Over eighty years old, somewhat weak physically but still mentally sharp, my daddy was sitting in a chair in his front yard when the feds pulled up. Still suspicious of white folks, he eyed them carefully.

"Is your name Robert Parker?" they asked.

"Yes," he said.

"Have you been calling the White House?"

"Yes," he said. "I saw my son on the TV. The White House

won't let me talk to him. He works there. He's been feedin' that ol' white man for a long time."

When he saw them smiling, my daddy thought they didn't believe him, so he fetched a group picture that I had sent him with LBJ, me, and some other Hill staff.

"We'll find him and have him call you," the agents promised before they left.

Three or four days later, two Secret Service men with grim faces asked to see me. I knew them both and couldn't figure out why they were so serious. "Do you have a father named Robert Parker?" they asked.

"Yes," I said. "What's this all about?"

"Does he live in Houston?" They gave the address.

"Yes," I said. By that time I was getting nervous.

"You better call him, because he's been phoning the White House looking for you. We sent a couple of agents to see him."

"What did he say?"

"That you've been feedin' that old white man for years."

We all stood there laughing. I knew exactly what my daddy wanted to tell me. He was worried that being on TV and working for such an important man as LBJ would go to my head. I could almost hear him shouting from Houston, "You stay in your place, boy!"

So began the Kennedy-Johnson administration for me. I was happy for Lyndon Johnson, even though my own future was insecure. It would be difficult for me to work directly for the vice president because the Secret Service would take over much of what I had been doing for him. LBJ's aide Walter Jenkins told me he'd look for an opening, but he doubted there would be one.

As loyal as a godfather, Lyndon Johnson did not forget me. Since he had been chairman of the Armed Services Committee, he told me he would try to find me a civilian job with the military in Washington. I told him I was not interested. He offered me a number-three butler position at the White House. Again I declined. I didn't want to be number three, and I didn't want to be a butler to anyone, not even to President John F. Kennedy. The White House sounded like a plantation to me. And, although I liked the service profession, I never wanted to be a servant.

Almost as a last resort, Johnson told me that Senator Humphrey had a patronage job available as doorman in the visitors' gallery of the Senate. A white man usually held that job. Although the position wasn't exactly what I wanted, I made an appointment to see Humphrey.

Hubert greeted me as if I were the most important guest of his day. He told me the doorman position was mine if I wanted it. I said I did. He was surprised. "Why do you want to get out of food service?" he asked.

"There's no opening," I said.

"There's the headwaiter job," he said.

Paul Johnson, headwaiter in the Senate Dining Room for fifty-eight years, had died in 1957, and the office of the Architect of the Capitol hadn't been able to find a good replacement. It had hired and fired at least six men between 1957 and late 1960. I hadn't heard that the manager of the Senate Dining Room, Robert Sontag, had just fired another one.

I told Humphrey I would be delighted to get the job. Managing a restaurant was the kind of position I had always wanted, and I enjoyed working on the Hill. Even though as headwaiter I would not manage the entire restaurant, the position seemed perfect.

"By golly, Robert," Humphrey said, obviously pleased that I wanted the job, "come on, let's go downstairs."

The senators had been unhappy about the quality of food in their restaurant. The Architect of the Capitol had hired a food service company to plan the menu, find cooks, and prepare breakfast and lunch. The food was bland and of the cheapest quality. And the menu was so full of compromises, it looked like a Senate bill. Harry Byrd of Virginia insisted on baked Virginia apples for the breakfast menu. Several old southern Democrats wanted stewed prunes each morning. Someone fought for chili and another for bean soup. Naturally, the southerners wanted fried chicken. The Rules Committee, which oversaw the Senate restaurants, was thinking about changing food companies. It was a major crisis on the Hill.

Taking me by the elbow, Humphrey marched me out of his office to see Sontag. "Did we hire a new headwaiter yet?" Humphrey asked him, making it clear that he was speaking in the name of the entire Senate. "I hope not, because we've finally got the man we want."

Sontag hired me on the spot. What could he say to Senator Hubert Humphrey?

I was pleased. My years of hard work and grooming friends had paid off. I would be serving in one of the most important and prestigious dining rooms in Washington, where vice presidents, senators, and their powerful and wealthy guests ate. Movie stars like Frank Sinatra, Bette Davis, and Betty Grable, Humphrey Bogart and George Raft, Edward G. Robinson, Charlton Heston, and Sidney Poitier. Writers like Ernest Hemingway. Millionaires like the Gettys, Mellons, Rockefellers, Vanderbilts, and Hunts. Media heavies like Walter Cronkite and Chet Huntley. I would be working among friends, for I had served all but the most junior senators in parties all over town for seventeen years.

I was forty years old, it was 1961, and my life had taken another important turn—thanks to Lyndon Johnson, in a way.

As headwaiter, my main job was to supervise the twenty-five waiters and waitresses who served breakfast and lunch in six different rooms that together seated two hundred people and made up the Senate restaurant.

The largest was the Senate Dining Room itself, with twenty-one tables seating eighty people. Only senators and their personal guests were welcome there. A small group of senators and their aides usually breakfasted there to plan the day's business. Senators' wives frequently lunched there with friends. And the senators' constituents and campaign contributors liked to eat there, under the Capitol dome. It gave them something to tell the folks back home.

Across the corridor from the Senate Dining Room was what the senators called "the Inner Sanctum." It was divided into two rooms separated by an arched doorway. In each room—one for Democrats and the other for Republicans—stretched a long table with twelve high leather-backed chairs. Huge crystal chandeliers, trimmed in brass, dominated these two rooms, where only senators were allowed to eat.

The Inner Sanctum was so private, it took Hill freshmen years even to learn it existed. Although any senator was free to use it, there was a pecking order. Young senators rarely tried to eat there; female senators created chaos. I remember how difficult it was for the Republicans, who were more flexible than the old southern Democrats, to accept Senator Margaret Chase Smith into their side of the Inner Sanctum. The Democrats were beside themselves when Oregon Senator Maurine Neuberger, who finished out the term of her dead husband, dared to join them for lunch.

Inner Sanctum tradition was so strong that even Senator Barry Goldwater got a written reprimand for breaking the "Senators Only" rule. Goldwater was so proud of his son, Barry, Jr., who had just been elected to the House, that he invited him into the Inner Sanctum for lunch. One of the old southerners called me aside and said, "Look, you go over and tell Senator Goldwater he's not allowed to bring his son in here. You know the rules."

"I can't do that, Senator," I said. The old buzzard was trying to get me to do the dirty work. "He's like John Wayne! He'll just tell me to go to hell."

"I'll get a letter over to Everett Jordan," the senator said. Jordan of North Carolina was the chairman of the Rules Committee.

"You do that, Senator," I said.

He did, and Goldwater later apologized to him, saying that he didn't know the Inner Sanctum was for senators only.

Besides the Senate Dining Room and the Inner Sanctum, there was also a dining room for accredited members of the press, another for the public, seating thirty-three, and one for the Senate staff, which held thirty-five. Cooks prepared breakfast in a small kitchen next to the Senate Dining Room; lunch came from the large kitchen in the basement and was carried upstairs by conveyor belt.

Part of my job was to greet senators and their guests in the reception room off the main corridor, where I had a desk. I would entertain guests while they waited for a senator or his aide, and seat them when they were ready to eat. Many of the old southern Democrats who had been dining there for years had their own tables— Gore, Eastland, Stennis, McClellan, Holland, Russell.

I was resented from the moment I walked through the door. Robert Sontag, the manager, and Dan Gary, who handled Senate restaurant procurement in the office of the Architect of the Capitol, were not happy. Since they had not recruited me for the job, they had no special hold over me, as they had had on previous headwaiters. Furthermore, it was obvious from the start that my connections on the Hill were better than theirs. Even though I was black, I could get to more senators, faster, than they could. They found that embarrassing. And because I was under civil service, they couldn't fire me as easily as they could my predecessors. They soon learned that they couldn't push me around as they had Paul Johnson.

If Sontag and Gary resented me, so did the black staff, but for different reasons. For one thing, I had not come up through the ranks, and the men on the staff were jealous. For another, the head-waiters before me had shown no leadership, so the staff was used to thinking of anyone in the position as an equal, not as a supervisor. For Negroes conditioned for generations to work for white bosses, it was a difficult adjustment.

By the end of my first week on the job, everyone recognized that I had high standards. I dressed and spoke well, I thought. I greeted the senators and their wives as if I knew them, which I did. They called me Robert. And I demanded that my staff snap to it. "Uppity," I could hear them mumble.

That they resented me did not bother me. I had the job I wanted, and I intended to make the Senate Dining Room into a first-class restaurant. Accustomed to the classy standards of the Congressional Country Club and Harvey's, I was shocked at what I found on the Hill, the showpiece of the nation.

The Senate Dining Room itself had taken on the character of the old-line southerners, who ruled it by their presence and who brooked no change. The place was little more than a rundown plantation. All the waiters, cooks, and waitresses were black. All the managers were white. Gary, Sontag, and Sontag's assistants, Joe Diamond and Louis Hurst, were as redneck as Mississippi's Bilbo. Among the four of them, they had maybe twenty years of education, and it showed every time they opened their mouths. They treated the black staff with contempt, more like slaves than people.

Like the butlers in *Gone with the Wind,* Senate waiters sported red jackets (supplied by the Architect of the Capitol) with black pants, white shirts, and black ties. Their uniforms were tattered, and no one seemed to care. Waitresses wore black dresses with frayed white aprons and white caps—little Aunt Jemimas. Everyone bowed and smiled with gleaming white teeth. The staff was encouraged—never really ordered—to use the service entrance and the service elevator when entering or leaving the Capitol, not the main entrances like other Senate staff persons. The only thing missing to make the picture complete was an old hanging tree.

I remember an incident that seemed to sum up Hill attitudes

toward blacks in the early 1960s. One day I met a white woman leading four black women, hired that day to work in the Senate restaurant, through the tunnel under the Capitol. "Where are you going?" I asked the white woman.

"To get their pictures taken," she said. They needed mug shots for their Capitol ID cards.

"You need someone to lead you like that?" I asked the new employees.

"No, sir!"

My anger boiled up. It was fine for new white employees to find the Capitol photographer without a personal guide, but not four black women who probably had more street smarts than all the Hill staff put together. Those women could find their way anywhere. Their survival depended on it. I laid into the white woman: "They don't need you to lead them around like a bunch of dummies! Don't you have anything better to do?"

"Mr. Hurst told me to bring them," the woman said.

I sent her back to Hurst and told the four new employees to make their own way to the Capitol photographer.

Southern senators like Eastland and Holland loved the plantation atmosphere. If they couldn't save Mississippi and Florida from the evils of integration, at least they could enforce segregation in the Senate Dining Room. It didn't matter that it was right under the chamber where the civil rights laws had been passed.

Freshly polished each morning by black "servants," the brass gleamed: spittoons, handrails, coat hangers, window crossbars, doorknobs, door plates. The mirrors and chandeliers sparkled. Some of the mirrors were so long that waitresses had to clean them from ladders. Labor was cheap—and so were the senators when it came to fixing up the restaurant.

Faded green drapes with holes and frayed fringe covered the windows. The silverware was worn stainless steel; the dishes were the ordinary greasy-spoon variety, chipped and cracked. The serving platters were tinted yellow with age and soap. Paint, probably lead-based, peeled from the walls and ceiling. Waitresses had to wipe the flecks off the tables each morning.

Cockroaches roamed freely in the silverware drawers and dish cabinets. I am not talking about an occasional roach, scurrying for cover, but thousands hiding in every corner and boldly walking over every surface. To find them, all I had to do was lift the cover off anything. And it was impossible to keep them out of the actual Senate Dining Room. They'd run across the red carpets during breakfast. Occasionally, one would make its way up a tablecloth. Sometimes a guest would find one lunching under a lettuce leaf in the salad.

The number of rats and mice was even more frightening. Most of Washington had been built on a swamp, and the Capitol was no exception. The basement, where the food was stored and the lunches were prepared, was dank all year around. I'd flip a light switch and see rats and mice run for cover. Naturally, they worked their way up to the kitchen and dining rooms on the first floor. I'd find mice stealing crumbs from under tables and playing tag on the faded green drapes. One afternoon, after I had seated some guests and as I turned to walk back to the reception room, I saw a mouse charging across the floor toward me. I hated those furry things so much, I broke into a cold sweat. With no place to hide, I jumped up on the nearest table. The mouse quickly disappeared through a hole in the floor.

Pauline Gore, wife of Albert Gore of Tennessee, was one of the Senate Dining Room regulars. I knew her and her husband well since I had served parties in their apartment, across the street from the Capitol and the Supreme Court. Soft-spoken and beautifully dressed, Mrs. Gore appreciated order and class. Even though she constantly complained about conditions in the Senate Dining Room, she came to lunch there almost every day when Congress was in session. She would sit with her guests at her favorite round table, number twenty. One afternoon around two o'clock, when the restaurant was unusually crowded, one of her guests leaned over and whispered, white-faced, "I thought I saw a mouse run up the drape."

Assuring her that it wasn't possible, Mrs. Gore called me over. "Robert," she said, "I'm embarrassed. My guest thinks she saw a mouse on the drape. Would you check please?"

I shook the curtain gently, praying that the mouse, which I knew had to be there, was more frightened than I. Nothing moved. I went back to Mrs. Gore and told her that her friend must have seen a shadow. Unconvinced, the poor woman couldn't eat another bite. After we cleared the restaurant that afternoon, I gave the drapes a good tug. Two or three mice peeked out of the pleats, then dashed for cover.

If the mice and roaches were an embarrassment (not to mention a health hazard), the wages of the Senate restaurant workers were a national disgrace. The waiters and waitresses, who worked four hours a day when the Senate was in session, each got fifty cents per meal served. Given the unappetizing conditions, there were rarely more than twenty people eating in the Senate Dining Room at one time when I first became headwaiter. That left sixty empty plates. Sometimes the room was nearly empty. On an average, waiters and waitresses were making eighty-seven cents an hour, or $17.40 a week, excluding tips, which weren't generous. Since they were part-time workers, there were no health benefits, paid vacations, sick leave, or retirement plans. My staff couldn't even get free meals, although they were allowed snacks from the kitchen. No one fought for them. No one cared. No one wanted to ask the Rules Committee for more money to run the restaurant.

My predecessor, Paul Johnson, had had it even worse. As head-waiter, he didn't serve customers, so he didn't get fifty cents a meal. The Architect of the Capitol paid him no salary, even though his job was full-time for all practical purposes. Each year, the senators took up a collection for him, and that's what he lived on. When he died after fifty-eight years of service, he was penniless. Fortunately, his health had been good right up to the end. Without benefits, he could not have afforded hospital care.

Under those conditions, morale was low. Every waiter and waitress who could find work moonlighted at night. The only reason they continued to serve the Senate Dining Room was because employment there helped them find jobs at the best restaurants. After all, if they worked the Senate Dining Room, they must be good.

Most of them came to the Capitol each morning after just a few hours of sleep, tired and listless. Because the pay was so poor, they found other ways to compensate themselves. At the end of the day, many waiters, waitresses, and cooks stuffed whatever food they could find—sugar, butter, cereal, bacon, canned beans—into their bags or under their coats. Robert Sontag looked the other way. I suspect Dan Gary did, too.

Even more shocking, it was easy for the waiters and waitresses to chisel the senators themselves out of a few dollars a month. If a senator could not join his guests for lunch, he would send them to me with a letter, signed by him, indicating that they were his guests. Most of the time, guests paid for their own meals, which were the best deal in town. A breakfast of bacon, eggs, toast, home fries, and coffee was $1.50 in 1961; a quarter-pounder with fries and lettuce and tomato went for $.85. Sometimes the senator would say in his letter that the meal was on him. In that case, I would sign the senator's name on the check, and Sontag's office would bill the senator monthly. Naturally, the senator himself rarely checked the statement.

Some of the waiters and waitresses took advantage. They signed the senator's name on the check and pocketed the cash the guests paid for their meals. Although it didn't amount to a lot of money, it didn't help the morale of those who wouldn't cheat. The system was so rotten that waiters and waitresses knew that if they got caught, they wouldn't be fired. Sontag would simply get them to admit they had "made a mistake" and ask them to reimburse the senator.

Waiters and waitresses weren't the only ones stealing. From the way conversation died when I entered a room and from the nods and whispers, I could tell that something else was going on. It didn't take me long to figure out what it was. After a few weeks on the job, I caught the driver for Bergmann's Laundry and someone in the Architect of the Capitol's office working a scam. The driver would deliver our towels, napkins, and tablecloths, then drop a second load at a nearby restaurant. I knew we were sending in about 200 pieces. But when I checked the receipt, I saw we were being billed for 450. I figured that the Senate was losing about five hundred dollars a week. How much money was going into whose pockets, I didn't know.

I did know that Sontag was a petty thief. He regularly added 15 to 20 percent to the tab for the parties and receptions that the Senate Dining Room served all over the Hill. Although he was supposed to divide the tip money among the waiters and waitresses who served the particular party, he never gave them the full amount. I figured he was cheating the staff out of at least a hundred dollars a week. The staff grumbled but never openly complained because he closed an eye to their pilfering. He could get most of them fired at any time.

I watched this mess for six months and did what I could to improve morale without actually stepping on any toes. Then I did an end run around Sontag, Diamond, Hurst, Gary, and their bosses in the office of the Architect of the Capitol. I went directly to Senator Robert Byrd of West Virginia, who chaired the three-man subcommittee on Senate restaurants. When I first took the headwaiter job, Byrd had asked me to come to him if I had any suggestions for turning the Senate Dining Room into a first-class restaurant.

I sure did.

"obert, how's it going?" Senator Byrd asked me after lunch one day.

"Okay, but the morale is very bad," I said. He seemed surprised. "I want to come over and tell you about it," I added.

"Friday afternoon at three-thirty after you close down," Byrd said.

I met the senator in his office and told him everything I knew: low pay, discrimination, filthy conditions, no job security—all the frustrations I had stored up for six months.

"It's a license to steal," I said finally. It was a loaded statement, and I hoped Byrd would pick up on it.

"*Are* they stealing?" he asked. Naturally, he meant the black staff.

"Madly. They have to," I said. "Everything they can put in a bag. Sugar, flour, butter." And it wasn't just blacks taking home a pound of ground meat or pocketing a few dollars, I said. It was white managers chiseling as well.

Senator Byrd was a calm, smooth politician who rarely showed his true feelings. When I told him about the linen scam, his jaw muscles began working as if he were chewing a piece of gristle. I said I thought Dan Gary was letting out bids for restaurant contracts on a noncompetitive basis, against Senate rules. If this kind of skimming is going on with napkins and bids, I told Byrd, there's probably more that I don't know about.

Senator Byrd told me not to worry, that he'd see to the restaurant problems. But I did worry and rightly so. Although Byrd was concerned about theft, he showed little interest in sanitation. If the D.C. health inspector had ever dropped by, he would have closed us down faster than a mouse could climb a drape. But he didn't have jurisdiction inside the Capitol. No one did, except Byrd's three-man subcommittee. Nor did Byrd seem concerned about the low wages, discrimination, or lack of benefits—in a word, the slavery. He was only worried about managers ripping off the Senate and how it would look if the Washington press corps dug up the story.

I knew that Sontag and Gary would soon learn that I had leap-frogged over them, going directly to the subcommittee on restaurants. And I had been around the Hill and its petty politics long enough to know that sooner or later Sontag and Gary would try to lynch me. My only protection was to get them first. I began to watch Sontag like a detective.

One day I saw Clarence Higgins, a black who worked in the storeroom and who was supervised by Hurst, talking to Sontag. An hour later, I watched Higgins load an unmarked Capitol van with food: boxes of beef, hams, slabs of bacon. I followed Higgins with the Polaroid camera I had bought to document restaurant conditions. Higgins pulled into a Capitol parking lot just around the corner from the restaurant service entrance. As he unloaded the food into Sontag's black Lincoln Continental, I snapped two pictures.

"Why you doing this?" I asked Higgins.

"The boss told me," he said.

Afraid that Higgins would become too suspicious, I didn't ask how often he loaded Sontag's car or if anyone else, like Hurst or Gary, was in on the heist. When Senator Byrd called me into his office again two weeks after my first conference, I was prepared. With Byrd were the other two members of his subcommittee on restaurants, Senators Carl Curtis of Nebraska, a Republican, and Joseph Clark, a Democrat from Pennsylvania. Once again, I ticked off the list of problems. When I finished, I tossed the two photographs of Higgins stuffing Sontag's Lincoln with food onto Byrd's desk the way Lyndon Johnson would have done it—with a triumphant flourish and a gleam in my eye.

Although the thieving was a scandal, stopping it was not the most important thing I was after. Besides nipping scams and catching mice, I wanted decent wages and working conditions for my staff. Inspired by Adam Clayton Powell, I was determined to force the Senate to treat them fairly. I was facing some of the same problems Powell had. None of the three senators on the subcommittee had a clue about how poorly the restaurant staff was paid. Stunned when I told them, they recognized that I had tossed them another stick of political dynamite just waiting for a match.

"What do you recommend?" Senator Byrd asked.

For openers, I told him, the staff should get new uniforms and full-time jobs. That meant keeping the Senate Dining Room open all year from seven-thirty to four-thirty and putting the staff on a full-time pay scale. Next, restaurant staff should be given the same privileges as other Senate staff members, such as parking stickers, membership in the credit union, and membership in the Senate Staff Club.

As far as the waiters and waitresses are concerned, I said, I want to weed out those who won't follow orders or shape up. The subcommittee will have to back me when I fire someone because most of the staff have senators as patrons. The first thing they'll do when I give them a pink slip is to lean on their patron to get their jobs back. (If anyone knew that game, I did.)

If you want tasty lunches, I continued, you'll have to get rid of the food management company and take over the kitchen yourself. That way, you can have control over what is served and how.

Finally, I told them, the restaurant needs to be remodeled. Unless the carpets are replaced and the holes in the floors and walls are plugged, there is no way to control the roaches and mice. To call in an exterminator twice a month won't do. Everything needs to go: drapes, rugs, dishes, and silverware. It's the only way to clean the place up.

Senator Byrd promised to back me on replacing the dining room staff (that wouldn't cost anything), and he said he'd look into my other recommendations. I left his office feeling good about myself and the future of the restaurant. After all, I had just talked to the men who had the power to change things. Like Powell, I was fighting for my people. What I forgot were two lessons I had learned from Lyndon Johnson. One was that on the Hill, nothing gets done all at once. The other was that most congressmen are willing to settle for the appearance of progress instead of progress itself.

Senator Byrd ordered the Architect of the Capitol to fire Robert Sontag. His assistant, Joe Diamond, took his place. Louis Hurst moved into Diamond's old job. But even with Sontag gone, little changed.

Both were committed to working with Dan Gary to continue to run the Senate Dining Room like a plantation. Needless to say, the firing of Sontag put the staff on alert and did not endear me to the restaurant management.

I began to whip my staff into shape. I held meetings every morning and designed new uniforms to change the plantation image: blue and white uniforms for the waitresses and gold jackets with black pants for the waiters. Since they didn't cost much and improved appearances, I had little trouble getting subcommittee approval. I stressed from the start that I wanted everyone to come to work looking classy. If you walk into the Capitol looking like trash collectors, I said, they expect you to ride the trash elevators. I told the women to dress as if they were going to an office in the State Department, and the men to appear in jackets and ties, their shoes shined. Once you do that, I said, you can feel good about using the main entrances to the Capitol like other Senate staff. You can then proudly walk up the marble steps into the rotunda, just like Adam Clayton Powell did.

My speech worked. The staff started to take pride in their work.

Next, I got rid of the three brass spittoons in the reception room and Senate Dining Room. To get them removed, I needed the support of senators' wives like Mrs. Gore. I know it may sound silly to make an issue of brass spittoons, but they had become symbols of the power of the Southerners who resisted change in the Senate Dining Room almost as strongly as they fought civil rights on the Senate floor. The cuspidors offended everyone except three or four tobacco chewers like Senators Herman Talmadge of Georgia and Willis Robertson of Virginia. To junk the spittoons was to prove that change was possible.

When I finally hauled the spittoons away, the chambermaids who polished them every morning along with the rest of the brass in the dining rooms were upset to the point of tears. They thought I was trying to take their jobs away. I assured them that there was still plenty of brass to shine and that, to the contrary, I wanted it to sparkle like it never sparkled before. But seeing their fears made me sad: black women crying because they could no longer clean the spit of southern senators who despised them; victims of a system that gave them a clear choice—tobacco juice or hunger. Sometimes I felt that those racists wanted to keep the cuspidors just so they could brag back home, "Why, up in Washington, we *still* have nigger women shining our spittoons."

Since I had no control over the kitchen in the early 1960s, I couldn't stop my staff from taking home a few pounds of butter, but I could put an end to their pocketing the cash of paying guests and then charging the meal to the senator who had invited them. With the approval of Senators Jordan and Byrd, I appropriated the right to sign all checks. But I explained to both senators that if Senate Dining Room workers continued to be paid poorly, the pilfering would go on. Jordan and Byrd made promises.

Even if I had wanted to, there was no way I could fire the entire staff. I decided to replace bad waiters and waitresses gradually. It wasn't easy, and I didn't enjoy it. After several warnings, I let a couple of waiters go for coming in drunk. Naturally, they ran to their patrons to get their jobs back, but Byrd and Jordan stood by me.

A waiter named Girard was especially hostile. One day, he refused to serve Senator Claiborne Pell of Rhode Island. Pell motioned to me. "Robert," he said, "I've been sitting here for quite some time. No one has been by to take care of me."

I apologized and promised to send a waiter right over. No one liked to serve Pell, for although he was respectful, he was a poor tipper.

"Take care of Senator Pell right away," I ordered Girard.

"No," he said.

"He's on your station," I said.

"I don't care."

"You're fired," I said.

"You can't fire me," Girard said. Then he slugged me in the mouth and stomped out. I knew he would run to his sponsor, Senator Russell Long, so I got to Senator Byrd first. Byrd backed me up. Girard apologized later, but I didn't give him his job back.

The hardest thing to do was to weed out the old-timers who had been working in the Senate Dining Room for as long as fifty years. I felt sorry for them because I knew they wanted to continue working. Over seventy years old, they continued to shuffle from table to table. Given the youth and vigor of the Kennedy administration, which infected all of Washington, even the Hill, they just didn't fit. No matter how hard I tried, I couldn't teach them to serve

111

with enthusiasm, and I doubted that they would be able to keep up once I increased the number of meals served each day. I knew that if I didn't fire them, they'd drop dead on the job rather than quit. They simply did not fit into my plans for a first-class restaurant. I let several go and replaced them with energetic waitresses who needed part-time jobs to help support their families.

What I didn't know at the time was how badly the old black men had needed those poorly paying jobs. No sooner would I fire one than the phone would start to ring. The message was always the same: "You fired my daddy. Don't you have any feelings? He's worked there for forty-eight years. He has no other income. He can't get Social Security. Who in the hell do you think you are?" There was even talk of shooting me.

I hadn't realized until I fired those old men that, because the Senate paid so poorly, they had never even made enough to qualify for Social Security, and that the Senate had no retirement benefits at all for waiters and waitresses, as it did for Senate staffers. When I learned this, I felt so bad I couldn't sleep at night, not because I thought someone would actually try to assassinate me (that was idle, angry talk), but because I felt helpless and trapped. I eventually accepted the fact that, although I couldn't do anything for the old-timers, I could for those who took their places. I was more determined than ever to fight for them. I had to. I felt it was my duty.

I went to see Senator Byrd once again, as I would many, many times over the next ten years. Although he had promised to look into staff salaries, expanding restaurant hours, and creating full-time jobs for the staff, he hadn't done anything. He was shocked to hear that Senate restaurant workers didn't qualify for Social Security because they weren't covered by minimum wage laws. I pointed out to him how foolish the Senate would look to the rest of the country if it didn't extend minimum wage coverage to its own restaurant staff. He agreed but did nothing.

There was a lot of talk on the Hill in the early 1960s about raising the minimum wage and extending coverage. On the Labor and Public Welfare Committee, which proposed minimum wage legislation, sat Senators Wayne Morse of Oregon, Harrison "Pete" Williams of New Jersey, and Jacob Javits of New York. Since I had served their parties, I knew I could easily approach them. I had learned from Lyndon Johnson that if you can't get through an obstacle on the Hill, you can usually find a way to get around it. If the Rules Committee wouldn't help my staff, maybe Labor and Public Welfare would.

Morse, Williams, and Javits took time to see me. I didn't have to argue my point. They saw the irony. Labor and Public Welfare was legislating minimum wages for the rest of country while black Senate workers down the hall were getting a pittance. *The Washington Post* would have fun with that story.

Under pressure from these senators, the Architect of the Capitol began paying Senate restaurant workers more than the newly proposed minimum wage of $1.25 an hour. It was a sweet victory that pleased Senators Jordan and Byrd, since it made them look concerned and generous. But the concession did not endear me to Diamond, Hurst, Gary, and the other bureaucrats in the Architect's office. Once again, I had embarrassed them by going directly to the senators instead of to them. And I had made them look cheap and uncaring.

artin Luther King had a great impact on my life. I met him for the first time early in 1963, several months before his March on Washington. He came to the Hill with his colleagues Ralph Abernathy, Jesse Jackson, Hosea Williams, and Andrew Young in the hope of seeing Senator Jacob Javits, among others. Dr. King spent three days getting the runaround from Javits's staff, who thought it would be best for the senator if he weren't seen with the controversial civil rights leader. Javits himself didn't even know Dr. King was in town.

Tired of camping out in front of Javits's office, Dr. King and his colleagues walked over to the House side to meet black congressmen, among others. When I saw him coming down the hall outside the Senate Dining Room, I introduced myself. I admired his courage and his nonviolent approach to civil rights, and I was proud of him.

"If you ever want lunch on the Hill," I told him, "let me know. I'll arrange it for you. And if there's anything else I can do, just ask."

"I sure would like to see Senator Javits," Dr. King complained. He described his problem.

"Be here tomorrow at noon," I told him. "You may have to wait a little, but I'll introduce you to the senator."

Andy Young began chuckling. They had tried every trick they knew to reach Senator Javits except asking the headwaiter for an introduction.

"I don't believe it!" Young said. "Can you do that?"

"Wait and see," I told him.

I had known Javits for years, and I had always found him friendly and open—the type of person who liked to know things firsthand and size people up for himself. I couldn't imagine him refusing to see Dr. King, but I could well imagine his staff trying to block a meeting for appearances' sake. King was not popular on the Hill in 1963, and he hadn't even warmed up yet.

I knew it would be easy to reach Javits the following day, for he rarely lunched off the Hill. He would either come to the Senate Dining Room, have a sandwich delivered to his office, or entertain guests in his hideaway, S–122. If he lunched in the dining room, I would seat him. If he ate in his office or hideaway, I would deliver his food personally or go with the waitress who did.

Dr. King was right on time the next day. I asked him to have a seat in the reception room near my desk, out of the way. He didn't have long to wait. In walked Senator Javits with two guests. I seated them and, when the senator had almost finished his lunch, I walked over to his table.

"Senator," I said, "there's someone who wants to meet you."

I waited for Javits to push away from the table; then I told him, "It's Dr. Martin Luther King. He saw you walk into the dining room."

Javits and King shook hands. Then the senator led the civil rights leader to his hideaway just down the hall from the Senate Dining Room. I went with them to see if they needed anything. I served Dr. King a cup of coffee. Javits asked him if he wanted lunch. Dr. King said no, and I left them. It was the beginning of a five-year relationship that proved to be useful to both leaders.

"A very fine man. He's doing a great job," Javits told me later.

I was pleased I had been able to bring them together, for rarely did I hear a senator speak well of Martin Luther King.

Dr. King thanked me for the introduction.

"From now on," I told him, "when you want to see someone on the senate side, come to me. Everyone around here has to eat somewhere."

Dr. King said he was having a hard time getting to Senator George McGovern of South Dakota and Senator Ross Bass of Tennessee. Their staffs were blocking him as Javits's had.

I approached McGovern the very next day. He seemed eager to see Dr. King. "Set up a meeting," McGovern told me.

Knowing that Dr. King wouldn't be in Washington long and that the Hill moves slowly, I told McGovern that I could easily arrange a private lunch for the two of them. It wasn't necessary to go through his office. McGovern agreed. A few days later, I brought him and King together for lunch in S–120, a private dining room under my care.

Senator Bass seemed willing to meet Dr. King as well. "Tell you what you do," he said. "You go to my staff and ask them to set something up."

I didn't know Bass well in 1963. He was always pleasant, and he had the reputation of being an honest, no-nonsense legislator. But I didn't know if there was a streak of racism under his southern polish. I decided to take his advice. Repeating what Bass had told me, I asked his staff for a meeting. I waited. I reminded his staff. When nothing happened, I didn't push. I didn't feel it was good for me or for Dr. King to step on Bass's aides. In some ways, they were more powerful than the senator himself and, like snakes, they would strike back if riled.

A few months after I set up meetings for Dr. King with Javits and McGovern, the Hill was buzzing with talk abut King's plan to march on Washington. I heard nothing on the Hill but criticism and fears of violence, looting, riots, even attacks on the Capitol itself. That the Senate invited law enforcement officers from other cities to tell the nation's capital how to protect itself against the likes of Dr. King and his "mob" didn't do much to calm those fears.

I expected as much from racists like Eastland and Thurmond who sounded like identical broken records. The commies are behind this. . . . They'll tear up Washington. . . . The District Committee should stop the march. . . . Why give him a permit? But I didn't expect such hostile feelings from Hill liberals and Washington blacks. Senate staff lawyers kept pounding, day after day, "Robert, don't march, and don't let your staff take part." Some of the city's blacks turned out to be as skeptical as the Senate, even though few will admit it today. "He'll cause more trouble than good," I heard all over town after work. "He should stay in Atlanta!"

To be perfectly honest, all that talk convinced me that Dr. King's March on Washington was a dangerous mistake. I decided not to attend and told my staff that it would be better if they didn't either. Given what I had heard and what I knew about the Hill, my decision was logical. If Dr. King angered the senators, they would take it out on us. We stood to lose much of what we had already gained, and it would become even more difficult to squeeze benefits out of the subcommittee on restaurants or the Architect of the Capitol. I just applied Parker's Law: People on the bottom are the first to get stepped on.

My brother Richard, who was retired from the Navy, drove all the way from Jacksonville, Florida, to march with Dr. King. I joined Richard and his wife for dinner in the Mayflower Hotel next door to Harvey's.

"Goin' to march tomorrow?" Richard asked me after we caught up on family news.

"No," I said.

Richard dropped his spoon. "You mean to tell me that we drove all the way from Florida for this great march and you live here and won't go?"

"That's right," I said defensively. "What do you think you'll accomplish anyway? There's enough problems here without you creating more. We have a good president, and things are finally beginning to happen!"

Richard got hot. "What things?"

I couldn't answer because, although it looked like President Kennedy was doing a lot, his administration was mostly varnish. True, people were excited. New blood pulsed through the veins of the capital. The city was vibrant with excitement and hope. But the Kennedy administration hadn't passed one single piece of legislation helpful to minorities since he moved into the White House two and a half years earlier.

"Bob, you're just like the rest of these bourgeois black folks in Washington," Richard said. He made no effort to hide his disgust.

Angry and hurt, I went home only to toss and turn all night. Richard's words bothered me like a wood sliver under the skin. He had made an expensive trip to Washington just to be part of what he thought would be history. What did Richard see in the march that I didn't? Could I be so wrong? Was everyone I heard on the Hill and on the streets wrong, too?

The next morning, August 28, I went to the Senate Dining Room as usual. I repeated to the staff that I didn't think it would be in their best interest to attend the march, even out of curiosity. They all agreed to avoid it.

By half past one, my own curiosity got the best of me. I left my post in the dining room and walked up to the press room on the second floor near the press gallery. It was one of the few places I could find a TV set.

Insulated by the walls of the Capitol, I watched the television screen with my mouth hanging open. Packed on the mall, a short walk from where I was standing, were a quarter of a million people. I recalled what I had often heard Lyndon Johnson tell his southern cronies, who were looking for a way to stop Dr. King: "The most powerful man in the colored community is a nigger preacher. Y'all can search all the laws you want, but there ain't no law ever been written against peaceful people demonstratin'."

A quarter of a million people can't be wrong, I thought. The crowd drew me like honey. I was curious. I was confused. I was afraid I'd be missing something big and important.

As I stepped out of the shadow of the Capitol into the August sunlight, I almost stopped breathing. It was the biggest crowd I had ever seen. It stretched down the mall forever. And one "nigger preacher" had drawn them there.

I began walking toward the Lincoln Memorial. I heard singing, a sound that came from deep inside. Pent-up pain and fury in harmony. "If I had a hammer, I'd hammer in the morning, I'd hammer in the evening all over this land. I'd hammer out freedom . . ."

The singing drew me. My feet moved faster.

"I'd hammer out justice. I'd hammer out the love between my brothers and sisters all over this land."

My throat got tight. The monument seemed miles away.

Then I heard Mahalia Jackson. A lone woman with a passion and power to rock men's souls. "We shall overcome. We shall overcome someday!"

I believed her. "Yes, we shall!" I cried. I gave the crowd the victory sign. I began running. I sang. I joined the marchers, not as a curious watcher but as a man who wished he had a hammer. Tears rolled down my cheeks. I looked around me. I stood in a sea of black and white, rich, poor, young, old, lame, red, yellow. People from all walks of life.

I heard Dr. King's voice, strong and resonant: "Five score years ago . . ."

I stood at attention like a young soldier at Fort Leonard Wood.

" 'We hold these truths to be self-evident; that all men are created equal.' "

My hair felt as if it were standing straight up. There were goosepimples on my skin.

"So let freedom ring from the prodigious hilltops of New Hampshire. Let freedom ring from the mighty mountains of New York. Let freedom ring from the heightening Alleghenies of Pennsylvania! . . . From every mountainside, let freedom ring."

My sweat turned cold in the ninety-degree heat.

" . . . we will be able to speed up that day when all of God's children, black men and white men, Jews and Gentiles, Protestants and Catholics, will be able to join hands and sing in the words of the old Negro spiritual, 'Free at last! Free at last! Thank God Almighty, we are free at last!' "

For the first time in my life, I *did* feel free.

I couldn't wait to get to the Senate Dining Room the next morning. I felt so proud to be black. I was dying to hear what the senators had to say.

"I don't know how they did it," one senator commented. "There were two hundred and fifty thousand people out there, and the police didn't make one single arrest. I've never seen anything like it. Why, it was the most peaceful demonstration since Gandhi!" His observation was typical of what I heard most of the day.

The old southern crowd, however, remained unconvinced. "Too well organized," I heard Senator Eastland say to nods of approval from his colleagues. "It had to be financed by the communists."

But I was convinced. Dr. King's March on Washington touched me deeply. I recognized that my brother Richard had been right. The bright light of the Senate had blinded me to the real world. At forty-two, I was becoming a bourgeois black. And I felt embarrassed that I had not encouraged my staff to attend the march. Not realizing it, I had cheated them out of walking into history.

I resolved to make it up to them. I would work for them harder than I ever had before. I would not give in—or give up—until they had what every other Senate staffer on the Hill had.

I didn't realize just how long that would take and how many toes I would have to step on to do it.

It was time to integrate the Senate restaurant staff. If a quarter of a million blacks and whites could march in peace for equal rights, then both races could work together in peace in my dining room, even if they couldn't do so anywhere else on the Hill. I needed to prove that point.

Before the Architect of the Capitol had been embarrassed into paying Senate restaurant workers more than the minimum wage, I hadn't been able to find whites willing to wait on senators, who were known throughout Washington as the worst tippers in the world. But now that my waiters and waitresses were earning well above the minimum wage, I had several applications on my desk from white women.

Soon after the March on Washington, I began discussing integration during my morning meetings. Staff opposition was stronger than I thought it would be. "Don't do that!" they complained. "Before long we'll have all white waitresses. None of us will have jobs anymore. Besides, the management is against integrating."

"Don't you realize," I argued, "that if it ever looked like we were becoming lily-white, every member of the NAACP would picket the Capitol? You don't have to worry. I'm not going to replace you with whites. I'll hire one white waitress as soon as there's an opening."

They accepted my decision with reluctance and skepticism. Tina Panetti was the first white I hired. She's still working in the Senate Dining Room. The staff was chilly to her in the beginning, but she fit in well. When they saw that I didn't fire anyone to make room for her, they were relieved. Soon I added a few more whites. There were no racial problems. I felt I had done something important.

If it was easy to integrate my staff, it was a nightmare to integrate the Senate staff dining room, which I called "the KKK Room." I had long since learned that—in percentage terms as well as in sheer numbers—there were many more racist secretaries, legislative aides, committee workers, investigators, and attorneys than there were racist senators. They were the biggest obstacles to civil rights legislation, because they had the ears of the senators, who lived in the isolated and unreal world of power. I was determined to integrate their dining room, even if it cost me my job. I thought of Keating and Powell and how they had broken the color barrier in the Senate Dining Room in the 1940s. I made up my mind that Robert Parker was going to break the race barrier in the KKK Room in the 1960s.

President Kennedy had attracted bright, new faces to the Hill,

120

many of them liberal, some of them black. The change was startling. When I arrived in Washington in the early 1940s, there wasn't a black secretary or a black aide to be seen. Now, riding high on the Kennedy wake were more than a mere smattering of black men and women. They knew they weren't liked or welcomed. Most weren't even told that there was a staff dining room. Those who knew wisely stayed away, lunching either at their desks or in the crowded, noisy public cafeteria, where the iceberg lettuce was usually wilted.

One day, Dora Jean Lewis, an aide to Senator John Sherman Cooper of Kentucky, asked me if there was anywhere to eat on the Hill besides the public cafeteria. She was a stunningly beautiful woman, vivacious, smart, and pleasant. I had often said to myself that if I ever had the opportunity to select one person to break the "color" bar in the KKK Room, it would be Dora Jean. I told her about the staff dining room tucked behind the Senate Dining Room. But I didn't have the heart to warn her that, as the first black ever to eat in that room, she'd be testing an unwritten Jim Crow law.

"Come see me, and I'll seat you," I said.

As in the Inner Sanctum, there was a pecking order in the KKK Room. Although any staff member could theoretically eat there (there were less than forty places for the hundreds who worked on the Hill), several matriarchs controlled the room. They were top staff in the offices of the Architect of the Capitol and the Sergeant at Arms. Critical for the smooth running of the Senate, these two offices had been dominated by southerners for almost a hundred years. Ordinary staff found the KKK Room so cold and catty, they never came back. Poor Dora Jean!

There were three empty places on the afternoon Dora Jean came for lunch. According to the regulations of the Rules Committee, anyone could sit at any table, first come first serve. No one was allowed to reserve places or to refuse to have his or her table filled. I seated Dora Jean next to a racist who worked in the office of the Sergeant at Arms. She had been coming to the KKK Room for years and was the unofficial "Grand Dragon."

No sooner had I seated Dora Jean than the matriarch came over to me. "Get her out of here or make her move!" she ordered.

"I can't," I told her. "She works for Senator Cooper. You know the rules."

"Well, Robert, I don't care," she fumed. "I want her moved, or I'll report you to Senator Jordan."

Refusing to tell Dora Jean to move or leave, I got an urgent message to Jordan, who was on the floor of the Senate. He caught up with me later in the day in the Senate Dining Room.

"We have a problem in the family dining room," I told him. Jordan called the KKK Room the "family" room because senators and their families used to eat there before it became a staff restaurant.

"What kind, Robert?"

"As you know, Senator, we're now getting black staff in some—"

"No problem," he cut in. "You handle it as you see fit."

I never heard a word from the Grand Dragon after that. The KKK Room was open from that day on to every Senate staffer. But its integration didn't endear me to the racists who managed the Hill restaurants. When the Grand Dragon couldn't budge Senator Jordan, she and others began leaning on Joe Diamond, Louis Hurst, and Dan Gary to get rid of me. "Who's running this place?" they'd ask Diamond. "You or Parker?"

Diamond wouldn't fire me because Senator Humphrey had personally asked for me in the name of the entire Senate. Besides, I was still considered Lyndon Johnson's man.

But Diamond, Hurst, and Gary didn't forget the humiliation.

CHAPTER

From the first day I became headwaiter in the Senate Dining Room, I worked closely with Marie German, a special assistant first to Robert Sontag, then to Joe Diamond. German's job was to arrange for Senate parties, special dinners, and receptions. An expert at her job, which she held for more than twenty years, German taught me everything she knew. She was popular with the senators and their wives. "Hello, Miss G.," Senator Jordan used to say to her every day. "How's it going?"

"I got a good boy here," she'd answer, nodding toward me. I'd squirm at the subtle racism. "He's my right arm."

And I was. German's drinking problem was so bad that by early afternoon she could barely walk. I had to assign a waitress to escort her to the ladies' room. My staff used to joke about her during our morning meetings. "Who gotta take the white woman to the bathroom today?" someone would invariably snicker.

German got sick in 1963, two years after I had become headwaiter. During the several months she was out, I handled her job and mine both quite easily. She came back to work for a while, then took sick again and died. By that time, the senators and bureaucrats responsible for the restaurants were so used to me doing her job, which had traditionally been held by a white person, that I kept both. Senators Jordan and Byrd were pleased. Why hire another special assistant if Robert Parker could do both jobs on the salary of one? That's how I became the first maître d' in the history of the Senate. Though the office of the Architect of the Capitol did not have an official name or description for my new job, the press called me maître d'.

When the Rules Committee finally followed my suggestion to fire the food management company and allow the restaurant to hire its own kitchen staff and prepare its own food, my little kingdom grew. I now supervised the waiters, waitresses, chefs, and kitchen help—over two hundred people. I had responsibility for breakfast, lunch, private parties, receptions, and dinners. And I had final say over the menu and the general cleanliness of the kitchens and dining rooms. Joe Diamond, Dan Gary, and Louis Hurst resented me even more, but there was little they could do. I had everyone from Hubert Humphrey to Everett Jordan on my side, especially their wives.

One of the first things I did as maître d' was to improve the general menu. Since it didn't cost much, no one opposed me. I replaced frozen hamburger with fresh ground beef. I added four-ounce sirloin steaks, Maryland crabcakes, fresh fish every day, Chesapeake Bay rockfish once a week, and Senate club and Reuben sandwiches. I kept the traditional chili and bean soup and included a soup du jour. We had a black baker as old as water who made the best cornbread in the South. We called him Papa Hill. I asked Papa to make apple pie and southern biscuits every day. The fresh food and the new menu went a long way to make my staff and the senators' wives feel proud of the Senate Dining Room. More and more people started coming to lunch. Within a few years, we were serving two thousand meals a day, including private parties and receptions.

Next, I improved service in the Inner Sanctum, where senators in a hurry liked to eat. Two waiters were assigned to serve them as soon as they unfolded their napkins. Washington Senator Henry "Scoop" Jackson, who always seemed rushed, asked me one day, "Robert, can't you put something in here that's quick and special?"

Jackson loved rare prime rib on a seeded roll. It wasn't on the menu, but I always special-ordered it for him. Before the week was out, I had set up a buffet lunch in the Inner Sanctum with two waiters standing by to serve: there was soup du jour and the Senate's famous bean soup, fresh fruit, one entrée of meat or fish, and what I called the "Scoop Special"—rare prime rib.

Once my staff realized that I was fighting for better working conditions for them, they started coming to me with their personal problems, asking me to intervene for them since I knew the senators so well. Two incidents stand out in my mind.

Delia was the Senate Dining Room inspector who saw to it that every piece of silverware was clean, every napkin folded just so, and every crumb of bread swept from the carpet. Given our mice and roaches, her job was important. She kept her standards high. Soon after I had promoted her from waitress to inspector, a young black man with the same last name as Delia's shot Mississippi Senator John Stennis outside his home in an apparent robbery attempt. Word spread over the Hill that the alleged assassin was related to someone who worked in the Senate Dining Room. Hill racists made it sound as if there were a conspiracy afoot. Delia didn't even know the man.

Delia came to see me in my office. "Mr. Parker," she said, trembling and in tears, "I've been an honest, hardworking woman all my life. I've finally pulled myself up to a point where I can save a little money. Now this! What in God's name am I gonna do? Senator Stennis is one of the most powerful people here."

I tried to calm her, even though I knew she was right. If she and the robber had been white, no one would have thought twice of the matter. But because she and the robber were black, people concluded that they were related. It was a vicious kangaroo court, and it reminded me of how I almost got lynched in Bristol because no one believed a black man could be on his way to meet Congressman Johnson and President Truman. The only difference between my Tennessee escapade and Delia's Hill experience was twenty years of "progress."

"I don't think they will hurt you," I told her. Then I talked to everyone on her behalf—Joe Diamond, Senator Jordan, and members of the subcommittee on restaurants. The gossip quieted, and Delia kept her job.

On another occasion, a waitress told me that her uncle was almost destitute. He was a hard worker who wanted a job but couldn't find one. The reason, she said, was that he had served time for killing a man in self-defense. I told her I'd talk to him. After listening to his story, I concluded that the police and the courts had framed him, and I hired him. He proved to be one of my best busboys. The Secret Service found out much later that he was an ex-con, but because his record in the Senate Dining Room was so good, they let him keep his job—with one exception. Whenever the president paid Congress a visit, he got the day off.

After Marie German died, my job became so demanding that I quit moonlighting at Harvey's. But I still continued to do parties at night and on weekends as special favors to old friends. I'll never forget the wedding shower a few years later for Lynda Johnson and Charles Robb, who is now governor of Virginia. The White House called me one day to say that both the president and Mrs. Johnson had specifically asked for me. The party was to be held in Averell Harriman's home in Georgetown.

I was pleased to do it. With only thirty young men and women, friends of Lynda and Chuck, as guests, it wasn't an elaborate affair: mounds of hors d'oeuvres prepared in the Senate Dining Room kitchen and plenty of drinks. The party was for fun, and the atmosphere was relaxed. Guests brought empty gift-wrapped boxes or inexpensive funny presents. When I left the party to return to the Hill, a *Washington Post* reporter, whom I knew, was waiting in the alley behind Harriman's home, where I had parked my black, unmarked Capitol van. She asked me who was at the party, how many, what they ate, what kind of gifts—the usual society page stuff. I saw no harm in chatting with her. I liked reporters and knew quite a few who covered the Hill and ate in the press dining room, which was under my supervision. I thought the *Post* reporter and I were just having a friendly conversation. Like a piranha, she picked me clean. Her story appeared the next morning.

LBJ's office called me at breakfast time in the Senate Dining Room. "You should know better," an aide scolded. "Anything about the First Family has to be cleared through the White House."

I learned my lesson and never made that mistake again.

Part of my job as maître d' was to take care of hideaway lunches. A senator or an aide would call the Senate Dining Room and request lunch for two or three to be sent to a particular hideaway at a certain time. They would tell me what they wanted. I would place the order in the kitchen and assign a waitress to deliver the food. Within a year, I was the only person on the Hill with a passkey to every Senate hideaway. It all began with my checking each hideaway before lunch to make sure there were wine and cocktail glasses, ice, and fresh flowers. Before long, I was stocking each hideaway with snacks, beer, and liquor. I bought what I thought each senator wanted or needed and sent him the bill. Fresh Georgia peaches for Richard Russell's hideaway, Virginia apples for Harry Byrd's. Frank Church of Idaho and Gale McGee of Wyoming liked fresh-cut flowers each day, which I got delivered free from the U.S. Botanic Gardens across the street from the Capitol. Javits wanted fresh bagels; others craved junk food. Roman Hruska of Nebraska

With Vice President Mondale, who invited my family and me to the White House, 1976.

Serving astronauts John Young, left, and Gus Grissom, right, the brownies they requested from President Lyndon Johnson while in orbit, June 1965.

With Governor Ronald Reagan and Senator John Tower of
Texas, December 1967.

With Rev. Billy Graham and Mildred Smith, one of my staff
waitresses, on President Nixon's Inauguration Day, January
1969.

Vividell Holmes and I are serving Senator Ted Kennedy a whole salmon for a private luncheon in his hideaway, July 1969.

Vice President Hubert Humphrey with my Aunt Rebecca Durkee and me, 1967.

President Lyndon Johnson with the Senate Dining Room waiters and me in the Capitol, 1965.

With President Lyndon Johnson at the signing of the Voting Rights Act of 1965. Left to right—me, Senate Majority Leader Mike Mansfield, LBJ, Sergeant at Arms Joseph Duke, Vice President Hubert Humphrey, Senator John Sparkman of Alabama.

Marlon Brando always stopped in the Senate Dining Room to see me. He was a friend of Senator Eugene McCarthy of Wisconsin.

With my mother, 1922.

With my father, Robert Parker, Sr., on the beach in
Galveston, Texas, 1972.

(All photographs are from the author's private collection.)

asked for butterscotch candy; Herman Talmadge, peanuts; Spessard Holland, pretzels.

Once the senators realized that I was providing that kind of service, they came running to me with their private keys. I became even more powerful.

As maître d', I not only supplied the hideaways, but I got an even closer look at what was really happening behind their locked doors than I had as a messenger for Lyndon Johnson. My inside information, however, placed me in a delicate position. Every day for almost ten years, one or another senator's wife would ask, "Robert, where is my husband's hideaway?"

I would smile politely and say, "I don't know."

"Robert, where is my husband having lunch today?"

I would smile and say, "I don't know."

"Robert, who does my husband have lunch with?"

Without a smile, I would say, "I don't know."

One day, one of the wives got so peeved at my ignorance, she blurted out, "Robert, what the hell *do* you know?"

"Just my name!" I laughed, and so did she. But it was a sad laugh, for we both knew her husband was using his hideaway for more than lunch. So were a lot of other senators. They'd bring women there for a quickie at noontime or spend a more leisurely evening with them over cocktails.

Two prominent senators had affairs with Senate Dining Room waitresses. One day one met me in the hallway near the Senate Dining Room. "Say, Robert, you got a nice little doll in there I'd like to meet," he said, mentioning her name.

"I'll see what she has to say," I told him.

"I'll give you a call later," he said.

The senator phoned just before I closed the restaurant for the day to ask what the waitress had said. "She's here right now," I told him. "Do you want to talk to her?"

The senator said yes, so I called the waitress to the telephone. I believe that they had a close relationship that lasted for years.

The other senator wasn't so lucky. He came to the restaurant late one afternoon for coffee. Since the place was almost empty and he liked to chat with me, I joined him. He loved to tell dirty jokes, especially about prostitutes and call girls. That afternoon, he told me his latest story and had a good laugh. Then he got serious. "Robert, you got a nice little fox here I'd like to see."

"Which one?"

"There she goes out the door now," he said.

I caught up with the "fox" the next morning. "Senator So-and-So has eyes for you," I said. I figured if she wanted to see him, she knew how to reach him.

A few days later, I asked her if she had met the senator. "Yes, I saw that cheap bastard in his office," she said.

"What do you mean, cheap?" I asked.

"He didn't pay me," she complained. "He said he didn't have any change."

When I saw the senator alone in the hall later, I kidded him. "That fox went to see you, and you didn't even make it up to her," I said.

"She ought to be happy to play in the big leagues," the senator said. He meant it. He never did pay her, and she never saw him again.

Senators would frequently lend their hideaways to congressmen who wanted to entertain women but who didn't rate a private retreat; or their staff would make arrangements for politicians and important contributors from back home to use them.

The wife of a senator from the Far West was particularly insistent. She knew her husband was philandering, but didn't know where and with whom. She was deadly serious and she kept asking me to show her her husband's hideaway. I wouldn't.

One morning, the woman's husband ordered lunch for two in his hideaway. He specifically asked for long-stemmed roses and candlelight. When I walked into the hideaway shortly before lunch to inspect the room, I found his secretary leaning over a finely carved French Provincial table, wrapping a small gift she had bought for the senator. I said hello and began checking the room. I noted that two fresh red roses sat in a tapered vase, then walked over to the refrigerator to make sure there was enough ice. I heard a soft knock. Thinking it was a waitress with lunch, I opened the door ready to scold her for being early. The senator's wife brushed past me with fire in her eyes. Like a good detective, she had checked my appointment book and followed me.

"Robert, what the hell is going on here?" she yelled at me as if her husband's adultery were my fault. Before I could answer, she rushed over to the secretary. "What's that!" she cried, pointing at the gift.

With her hair perfectly coifed and smelling of fresh perfume, the secretary tried to bury the package in her purse. She wasn't fast enough. The senator's wife grabbed the handbag. The secretary wouldn't let go. "This is my personal property," she screamed.

Soon they were both calling each other bitches and worse. Then they began tossing dishes. It was a good thing their aim was poor. I quickly shut the door. When they began rolling on the carpet, pulling each other's hair and clawing at their blouses, I tried to separate them. I couldn't. They were scratching and biting. Never having seen anything like it, I was deeply embarrassed. When they tired, I snatched the secretary's purse, stuffed her gift inside, and pulled her up off the floor. I shoved her out of the hideaway—gift, purse, messed-up hair, torn blouse, and all. Then I locked the door.

The senator's wife picked herself up from the floor and went into the bathroom to tidy up. An hour later, I seated her in the Senate Dining Room, where she smiled and chatted with friends as if nothing important had happened. Soon after I had seated the senator's wife, his secretary called. "Robert, please cancel the luncheon in the senator's hideaway," she said sweetly. "He won't be able to make it today."

It went beyond senators just cavorting afternoons away with their secretaries. One morning, a senator from the Deep South ordered lunch for four in a hideaway on the first floor of the Capitol. He asked for rare New York sirloin steaks. I was in the room when the senator and his three male guests arrived. I seated them, served cocktails and then the steaks, standing by until the senator told me everything was fine and that he required nothing else. I left like a shadow, closing the door quietly behind me.

A few hours later, I escorted two waitresses back to the hideaway to clean up the lunch dishes. After unlocking the door for them, I continued down the hall to make my rounds. A moment later, one of the waitresses came chasing after me.

"Mr. Parker! Mr. Parker!" she half-shouted and half-whispered. "We can't go in there!"

"Why not?" I was irritated.

"There's naked men in there. They're on the couch making love. They yelled at us, 'Keep that door shut, you black bitches!' "

I was more angry at the way the senator treated my staff than I was shocked at his sexual antics. Homosexuality on the Hill was not exactly rare. I knew four gay senators who used their hideaways in the same way some of their heterosexual colleagues did. Many an evening I walked into a hideaway to check on ice, liquor, and snacks, only to find the senator and his male friend sitting in shorts or walking around in bathrobes. The senators and their lovers were not embarrassed, for they knew I was discreet. They even joked with me about their lovemaking. "My, what a big handsome black man!" the gay guest of an important senator from the West said one afternoon.

"Robert doesn't play around," the senator said.

As I left the hideaway, I winked at the senator and laughed all the way back to the Senate Dining Room.

Gay or straight, there was no excuse for calling Senate Dining Room waitresses "black bitches." But I didn't want to show my true feelings in front of my staff. "That's right," I told the waitress, "you keep that door—and your mouth—shut!"

I wasn't being harsh. They were young, and I was teaching them how to survive on the Hill. If they breathed the story in the wrong place, they would be fired and I wouldn't be able to help them. I knew they would gossip and that the "black bitch" story would soon be all over the kitchen. But it would die with my staff giggling and chuckling to themselves, if I had anything to say about it.

CHAPTER

I was in the Senate Dining Room when I heard that President John F. Kennedy had been shot in Dallas. Like everyone else in the Capitol, I couldn't believe it. At first I thought it was a mistake. The Hill feeds off rumors like mosquitoes feed off blood. Then I thought he had just been wounded. Since I didn't have a radio or a television set in my office, I rushed to the press room. I found people running down the corridor, some shouting, others crying. Senators deserted the Senate floor as if the plague had struck. The elevator was packed. The Capitol was in chaos. I couldn't get near the press room, there were so many senators trying to catch a few phrases from the newscast.

Worried that there might be a conspiracy to kill off the leadership of the United States, the Capitol Police took charge quickly. They cut off telephone service to and from the Capitol. Setting up ropes across corridors, they rounded up all tourists and herded them out of the building. By early evening, the Capitol had been turned into a funeral home. The Senate chamber was as still as a coffin. Guards stood quietly at their stations, with no one to guard but the marble and bronze statues. Janitors and maintenance men with brooms, mops, and wax began shining the Rotunda floor on which the bier of John F. Kennedy would rest.

I decided to spend the night in the Capitol, as close to the memory of John F. Kennedy as I could get, just in case I was needed to serve sandwiches. After brewing a huge urn of coffee for the guards, workers, and the few senators still in the Capitol—it was an unusually cold November night—I huddled next to the small Philco radio I had found in the waiters' locker room. Wrapped in grief, I said a personal good-bye to John Kennedy and waited for dawn to greet our new president.

It didn't take long for the enemies of Lyndon Johnson to crawl out of the Capitol woodwork. "Old LBJ must have had something to do with it," I heard them say the very next day. The suspicion echoed in every corridor from Senate staff attorneys, legislative aides, waitresses, and tourists. Their grief for John F. Kennedy made their cynicism and dislike of Lyndon Johnson even more intense.

Blacks, who as a group had always mistrusted LBJ, were no exception. A few days after President Kennedy was buried, Clarence Mitchell, director of the NAACP's Washington office, got into a heated discussion about President Johnson with Whitney Young, director of the Urban League. They were standing in the corridor outside the Senate Dining Room. Mitchell called me over. Like most people in the Kennedy camp, Young was upset. It was bad enough to lose a dynamic leader like John Kennedy, but to get Lyndon Johnson in exchange was to rub salt in the wounds of grief. Young was telling Mitchell that everywhere he went he heard someone say LBJ was behind the assassination of Kennedy. Young was concerned about the gossip.

"Johnson's not that kind of man," Mitchell said. Then he turned to me. "Tell him, Robert! You've known Johnson ever since you were a kid."

As depressed as I was over the death of the president, the accusations of murder leveled at Lyndon Johnson made me even sadder. Although he could be the meanest man in Washington, I knew he was no killer. I defended him. I felt that people like the ones Whitney Young heard gossiping didn't understand LBJ and were not being fair to him. That Lyndon Johnson was bored as vice president was clear to anyone who cared enough to watch him. I had seen him often on the Hill between January 1961, when he took his oath of office, and November 1963, when President Kennedy was assassinated. I had served dozens of his private lunches, as well as hideaway parties, which he attended for old times' sake. President Kennedy had turned him into his messenger boy on the Hill. And Johnson had let it be known that he didn't like being a toothless old lion.

A few weeks before Lyndon Johnson moved into the White House, I was in the Inner Sanctum when Senator Jordan walked to join a half-dozen of his southern friends. "Did y'all hear about ol' Lyndon?" he asked even before he sat down. "He's got himself in trouble already."

132

Jordan began fleshing out a story I had read that morning in *The Washington Post*. I'm sure he got his information from Johnson's aides, who were itching to take over the White House.

"Ol' Lyndon got on the phone and called Mrs. Kennedy the other day," Jordan drawled as if he were savoring each word. "He told her, 'Sweetheart, listen, you don't have to move out until you're good and ready. We're not rushing you.' "

Jordan and his friends laughed because they knew "ol' Lyndon" couldn't wait to swivel in the the Oval Office chair.

Jordan continued, "Jackie slammed down the phone and huffed to an aide, 'How dare that oversize, cowpunching son-of-a-bitch call me sweetheart! I want you to speak to him about it.' The aide went over to ol' Lyndon's office."

Jordan paused for the punchline.

"Well, ol' Lyndon pounded the desk with that big fist of his, got out of his chair, stretched tall, and said, 'I'm sick and tired of this horseshit! Where I come from, we always call our ladies "sweetheart" and they call us southern gentlemen "honey." ' "

Jordan could hardly stop laughing.

"Well, ol' Lyndon better not try being a southern gentleman with Jackie again!" he said.

I never believed for a minute that Johnson had been trying to drive Mrs. Kennedy out of the White House. Say what they would about the man, he had streak of genuine compassion in him. But as in all political stories that make the rounds on the Hill, there was a lesson buried in Jordan's. And the lesson was true for the first few months of the Johnson administration: no matter what President Johnson said or did, he'd be misunderstood. To the Kennedy crowd, Lyndon Johnson was still "a cornponed bastard." Kennedy fans were convinced that no one, especially Lyndon Johnson, could ever match the leadership of their slain president. And blacks mistrusted or hated him.

It didn't take long for a power struggle between the Kennedy and Johnson factions on the Hill to flare up. I felt it even in the Senate Dining Room. Most of the time, the fighting was petty, but it showed how deeply feelings ran.

I had two private dining rooms near the Senate restaurant (S–120 and S–138) and one reception room (S–207), which senators and staff would reserve for private lunches, parties, or dinners. Each seated thirty to forty people. The rooms were in such demand that there was usually a waiting list when the Senate was in session. The Kennedy and Johnson factions began waging a pitched battle over who had more of a right to use them first. The Kennedy people had been already scheduled for parties when Johnson hurriedly took the oath of office on Air Force One. The Johnson people began leaning on me to cancel their reservations.

Since the Senate Dining Room did not take reservations, a party of Kennedy people and a party of Johnson people would end up waiting together in the outer reception room for a table to open. The Johnson crowd felt they should be seated first, even though the Kennedy crowd had been waiting longer. And so it went.

Sometimes the petty became ridiculous. Oil billionaire H. L. Hunt used to eat in the Senate Dining Room every day he was in town, which could be for weeks on end. A penny-pinching eccentric, he used to roam the halls of Congress, papering it with petitions to reform the electoral process and to keep the Russians from taking over the country. He was harmless, and everyone knew that he was the unofficial guest of Lyndon Johnson. I had the authority to seat anyone I wanted in the Senate Dining Room, whether they had a letter from a sponsoring senator or not. I used my judgment. If the restaurant wasn't crowded and a dignitary or special friend of a senator wanted to eat there, I would seat him or her. The last thing any senator wanted was a scene in the reception room or an embarrassed, powerful guest. I had been seating Hunt for years, even though he didn't have a letter. No one objected because, although the billionaire wasn't popular, he ate in the shadow of LBJ.

Soon after Kennedy was assassinated, however, I felt pressure from Connecticut Senator Thomas Dodd to kick the old man out. Kennedy men like Dodd suspected Hunt of playing a role in the assassination: Hunt was rich; he was from Dallas; and he had been saying for years that Kennedy had turned soft on Fidel Castro.

Dodd cornered me one day at lunchtime when Hunt was eating in the Senate Dining Room. "Robert," he asked, "whose guest is he?"

"No one's," I said. "He used to come all the time when President Johnson was here."

"Don't let the man in again," advised Dodd. "Unless someone sponsors him, you'll get yourself in a lot of trouble."

I knew Dodd was right. A Kennedy supporter was bound to either create a scene or complain to Senator Jordan. Even if I didn't ask Hunt to leave that day, I knew I'd have to tell him the next day or the day after. Besides, I trusted Dodd's judgment, and I looked on him as a friend. He had taken me to Cape Canaveral in May 1962 to watch John Glenn blast off into space as the first man to orbit the earth. I sat in the VIP section with Dodd and other members of the Aeronautical and Space Sciences Committee—Chairman Clinton Anderson of New Mexico, Stuart Symington, Margaret Chase Smith, and Bourke Hickenlooper of Iowa. No bleachers for Robert Parker that time.

I went over to Hunt's table. "I can't let you eat here anymore without a letter from a senator," I said.

"Who told you that?" Hunt asked. I could see he was angry.

"Mr. Hunt, I just have orders. There are new rules. Senator Everett Jordan is the chairman of the Rules Committee. You'll have to see him."

Hunt left without a fuss and never came back again.

I did a similar favor for Dodd four years later in 1967, when syndicated columnist Drew Pearson began riding Dodd for misuse of campaign funds. Pearson came to the Senate Dining Room one day with three distinguished journalists as his guests. It was the first time he had tried to eat in the restaurant; he usually lunched in the press room when he was on the Hill. That particular afternoon, Pearson wanted to impress his guests, two of whom were foreign journalists. There were several free tables in the restaurant, so I let Pearson in.

The columnist came back four or five days later with another important guest. I was about to let him in, when Senator Dodd spotted him. Dodd called me aside without Pearson seeing him. "I don't want that man in the Senate Dining Room," Dodd told me.

I couldn't blame the senator. Pearson had skewered him and was slowly roasting him each morning in his column—not that Dodd was innocent of the allegations.

Drew Pearson may have been the most feared reporter in Washington in 1967, but he meant nothing to me. "I'm sorry," I told him, "but I can't seat you. You'll have to eat in the press room."

Pearson turned away quickly. I could see that he was more than annoyed. Dodd was delighted. A few days later, Pearson sought me out. "Let me tell you, young man," he said, "I've never been so embarrassed in my whole life. I brought a guest, and you refused to let me in the door!"

Hubert Humphrey, the Senate whip, became President Johnson's peacemaker on the Hill. Between the end of November, when Kennedy was assassinated, and the beginning of January, when President Johnson delivered his State of the Union address, the Hill was a mess. Normally, Congress has most of November, all of December, and part of January to change the guard when a new president is elected. It needs that time for the inevitable power struggle to be resolved. In Lyndon Johnson's case, however, there was no transition time. Legislative wheels almost ground to a halt as pro-Kennedy and pro-Johnson aides fought over committee rooms, while their bosses argued over committee assignments.

As usual, Humphrey was optimistic. He had seen Johnson perform a miracle in 1956 when he had raised from the dead the first civil rights legislation in eighty years. He was confident that if anyone could create unity from the chaos on the Hill, it was Lyndon Johnson. Exactly how, Humphrey wasn't sure. But his confidence in LBJ was as strong as his optimism.

I remember one lunch conversation in the Senate Dining Room a few weeks after President Johnson had taken the oath of office. It was an important discussion because it summarized the intense feelings on the Hill during those confusing first months. Lunching with Humphrey were Jennings Randolph of West Virginia, who also believed in the LBJ magic, and Senator George Smathers of Florida, an old Kennedy friend, who didn't.

As a suave man-about-town, Smathers couldn't swallow Johnson's earthy style. As a southerner, he considered Johnson a power-hungry and bossy turncoat. "Do you know ol' Lyndon's first order after he took the oath of office?" Smathers asked Humphrey and Randolph. Johnson, of course, had been sworn in on Air Force One while it was still on the ground at Love Field in Dallas. "Get this goddamn thing in the air, and let's get back to Washington!"

Smathers's laugh was bitter. As far as he was concerned, President Johnson's first command symbolized what life under LBJ's rule would be like.

Humphrey laughed, too, but for a different reason. He could hear LBJ, as I could, saying just those words. To Humphrey they meant, "Let's go to work. We have a long row to hoe."

Humphrey was especially upset that afternoon because the office of the Sergeant at Arms, which was supposed to keep order in the Senate, was caught in a Kennedy-Johnson power struggle of its own. "We have to keep order," Humphrey said. "We have to control the Senate staff. 'Who's going to get this room! Who's going to get that!' If we don't keep our heads, the whole Senate will collapse, and the Republicans will have a field day."

Randolph nodded in agreement, but Smathers was cynical. "Ol' Lyndon needs a bigger saddle for his ass before he can ride herd on this corral," he said.

If Smathers had perfectly described the Hill's skepticism for the leadership potential of President Johnson, it was Republican Senator Margaret Chase Smith who touchingly expressed the nation's deep feelings for Kennedy and the monumental task awaiting Lyndon Johnson. I had great respect for Smith's humaneness, for we had had many converstions about the plight of the poor in general and of restaurant workers in particular. She had been a great help to me in winning decent wages for my staff.

Early one morning a few days after Kennedy's assassination, while Senate pages were still placing copies of The Congressional Record on each desk in the Senate chamber and before most senators had had their first cup of coffee, one of the Capitol Policemen came over to me. "You want to see something?" He pointed to the small, trim figure of Senator Smith, dressed in a conservative business suit. "Watch! She does this every morning."

Senator Smith stole into the Senate chamber, a cavern of empty desks and galleries. Picking her way over to Senator John F. Kennedy's old seat, she reached into her handbag and laid a single red rose on the desktop.

Could Lyndon Johnson ever win the respect and cooperation of a Congress and a nation who felt so deeply about their slain leader?

Like Senator Humphrey, I was not one to underestimate LBJ. Not only was he a superb politician, but he was a man with deep feelings. Recognizing how the country and its leaders felt about John F. Kennedy, he found a way to use those feelings to unite the nation. It was a pleasure to watch him go back to work after a miserable three-year vacation as vice president.

CHAPTER

★ 17 ★

Not long after he moved into the Oval Office, President Johnson floated a trial balloon over the Capitol. As a memorial to John F. Kennedy, the rumor went, he was going to push through Congress the civil rights bill that the young president had left in knots in the House Judiciary Committee. Written in the Justice Department, a half-mile down Pennsylvania Avenue from the Capitol, the Kennedy bill had landed on the Hill in June 1963 just after the Birmingham race riots and just before Dr. King's March on Washington.

In sum, the Kennedy civil rights bill outlawed for the first time discrimination in such public accommodations as hotels, motels, restaurants, gas stations, theaters, as well as in publicly owned facilities such as parks, stadiums, swimming pools, and in publicly funded programs; it banned discrimination in employment and union membership; it prohibited voting registrars from using different standards for whites and blacks and from disqualifying anyone for trivial errors; it spared from a literacy test anyone with a sixth-grade education; and it gave the attorney general new powers to speed school desegregation and to enforce the voting rights of blacks.

Introduced by Brooklyn Congressman Emmanuel Celler, the measure immediately ran into trouble. Southerners vowed to kill it in committee or to filibuster it into the grave. Civil rights idealists, who thought it was too weak, began adding more teeth; moderates and conservatives, who thought it was too strong, began watering it down. It took Attorney General Robert Kennedy until October, a month before his brother was assassinated, to work out a compromise with House Republican Leader Charles Halleck of Indiana. Even so, HR–7152 made the 1956 Civil Rights Act look like a marshmallow.

President Johnson's promise to erect the civil rights bill as a memorial to John F. Kennedy was vintage LBJ. In one stroke, he told the Kennedy people that he was sensitive to their slain hero's memory; he signaled to Congress and the nation that he intended to continue the legacy of John F. Kennedy; he bought time from black leaders; and he put the South on notice. It shouldn't get mad at him if, for the sake of unity, he outwardly backed a bill distasteful to them. After all, what choice did he have?

The problem for President Johnson was not the House. With a compromise already in place, it was only a matter of a few months before the bill would be reported out of the Judiciary Committee and put to a floor vote. Like other House civil rights bills that reached the floor, it was sure to pass.

As usual, the Senate was the problem. The filibuster that the southerners were promising would lock a ball and chain onto every other piece of legislation President Johnson was calling for. The stall would drive him crazy. The southerners were counting on it.

To rally Senate Democrats behind the bill, Johnson could count on Majority Leader Mike Mansfield from Montana and Senate Whip Hubert Humphrey. To defeat the southern bloc, however, Johnson needed a pocketful of Republican votes, and he went to work on getting them. In particular, he courted Senator Everett Dirksen, the minority leader, who had helped him get the 1956 Civil Rights Act passed.

As LBJ applied his own special brand of pressure, the tone of Hill talk began to change. Instead of "Johnson can never unite us," it was "What's he up to now?" The talk got louder as January 8 approached, the day on which President Johnson would deliver his first State of the Union address.

Rarely did a State of the Union address cause a stir of anticipation on the Hill. Truman's addresses were long and boring. Eisenhower's were short and boring. Kennedy's sparked some enthusiasm, even though the Hill knew what he was going to say. He was so dynamic, it looked forward to *how* he would say it.

With Lyndon Johnson, it was different. The task of uniting the nation behind him was a Texas-size challenge. No one knew what he was going to say—except that he would announce a new war on poverty—or how. Most legislators and aides on the Hill were curious about how he'd handle the civil rights question, but for many different reasons.

Kennedy people were wondering, "Will he really get behind the civil rights bill as a memorial to John F. Kennedy? Or is he tossing us a rubber bone?"

Southerners were anxious. "Ol' Lyndon knows how to double-talk," I would hear them say in the Senate Dining Room. "Give a little here, take back a little there." For them, the problem was whose side "ol' Lyndon" was really on and precisely what he was going to "give" on civil rights.

Blacks were distrustful and unwilling to give the fox much ground around the chicken coop. "Let's hear what he has to say" was as far as they would go. As usual, Illinois Congressman William Dawson was the exception, as he had been during the 1956 Democratic Convention in Chicago. I chatted with him in the hall one afternoon several weeks after Kennedy's death. "I told you to watch LBJ," Dawson reminded me. "It's unfortunate he got here the way he did, but he's going to do fine. His heart is in the right place." I agreed with Dawson then as I had in 1956.

President Johnson delivered his first State of the Union at twelve-thirty on the afternoon of January 8, 1964, six weeks after Kennedy was assassinated. Recognizing that the speech was an important symbol, Johnson had worked hard on it right through breakfast that morning. I couldn't sit in the staff gallery to watch him deliver it because I had to work in the Senate Dining Room, but I heard it live over the radio. Forty minutes long, it was a confident, tough speech that told Congress it "must" thirty-three times. The press reported later that President Johnson smiled every time he said the word. As a senator, he had often bragged, "For Congress, there is no such thing as 'must.' "

Besides stressing unity, promising budget and tax cuts, and announcing his war on poverty, President Johnson put Congress and the nation on notice over civil rights. "Let this session of Congress be known as the session which did more for civil rights than the last hundred sessions combined," he challenged. Then he hit the promised filibuster head on: "Here in this Congress you can demonstrate effective legislative leadership by discharging the public business with clarity and dispatch, voting each important proposal up or voting it down, but at least bringing it to a fair and final vote.

"Let us carry forward the plans and programs of John Fitzgerald Kennedy, not because of our sorrow or sympathy, but because they are right."

The strength of President Johnson's words on civil rights shocked everyone who had been waiting to hear them: the Kennedy people, southerners, and blacks. "Let me make one principle of this administration abundantly clear," he warned. "All of these increased opportunities [he had described them earlier] in employment and education, in housing and in every field must be open to Americans of every color. As far as the writ of Federal law will run, we must abolish not some, but all, racial discrimination. For this is not merely an economic issue, or a social, political or international issue." The president paused, then said slowly, "It is a moral issue, and it must be met by the passage this session of the bill now pending in the House."

President Johnson continued to hammer softly in a slow rhythm: "All members of the public should have equal access to facilities open to the public.

"All members of the public should be equally eligible for Federal benefits that are financed by the public.

"All members of the public should have an equal chance to vote for public officials and to send their children to good public schools, and to contribute their talents to the public good."

There had been a rumor floating in the halls of the Capitol that President Johnson might permit the public accommodations section of the civil rights bill to be either stricken or watered down to please the South. Johnson put that rumor to rest. "Today, Americans of all races stand side by side in Berlin and in Vietnam. They died side by side in Korea." He paused. It was the most dramatic part of his speech. "Surely, they can work and eat and travel side by side in their own country."

The applause was loud and long. President Johnson had drawn the battle line as straight as a plumb line. Those who didn't know Lyndon Johnson thought his threats and promises were just election-year speechmaking. But those who understood him, like Senator Richard Russell, weren't so sure.

The Judiciary Committee finally sent the Kennedy civil rights bill to the full House three weeks after the State of the Union address. On its way there, the bill had visited six committees, which sat for eighty-one days and heard 269 witnesses, whose testimony covered 5,791 printed pages in eight volumes weighing 13¹/₄ pounds. The House debated the bill for eleven days, then passed it. On March 9, it reached the Senate floor. Debate soon turned into the filibuster the southern bloc had promised. To end it, Johnson needed a two-thirds majority. The votes weren't there, and the filibuster dragged on for seventy-five days, the longest and bitterest in the history of the Senate.

It was both fun and agony to watch the Hill during the filibuster. Every morning except Wednesdays, the senators from the southern bloc—Virginia, North Carolina, South Carolina, Florida, Georgia, Alabama, Arkansas, Mississippi, Louisiana—caucused in the Senate Dining Room at a long table with eighteen high-backed leather chairs.

Senator Russell managed the filibuster. I found him an interesting sort of racist. He was polite to me in a gentlemanly southern way and called me "chief," as Lyndon Johnson did most of the time, never "nigger." In his bones, he was not a bitter, rigid racist like "Hangman" Holland, McClellan, Ellender, and Eastland. Rather, he was a practical racist, like Kefauver and LBJ. I was convinced that if Russell had had national ambitions, he, too, would have supported integration for the same reason that Kefauver and Johnson did—they had no choice. But because his constituency was limited to Georgians and the southern bloc senators, Russell's stand on civil rights was narrow: kill or castrate the Kennedy civil rights bill.

Senator Russell was usually the first to arrive for breakfast in the Dining Room. He'd order his usual fresh peaches (flown in from Georgia), graham crackers, and black coffee with honey. It was the breakfast that had helped him through countless floor fights, filibusters, roll calls, and committee meetings in his thirty-two years on the Hill. At sixty-seven, he looked as fit as a Georgia fiddle.

The rest of the old lions lumbered in. Like Russell, they were men of habit. James Eastland of Mississippi and John McClellan of Arkansas, who ate breakfast at home or in their offices, ordered coffee. The others never varied their menus: Allen Ellender of Louisiana and Willis Robertson of Virginia, stewed prunes; Harry Byrd, fried Virginia apples; Sam Ervin, sausage (flown in from North Carolina) and toasted cornbread with a fried egg; John Stennis of Mississippi, a hard-boiled egg and black toast; Herman Talmadge, ham (flown in from Georgia), eggs, and steaming black coffee.

On Wednesdays, the southerners held their regular prayer breakfast in the Vandenberg Room, where, with Senator Stennis as moderator, they asked God's help in defeating the civil rights bill.

President Johnson had them all fooled. Time and again, I would hear them say, "Ol' Lyndon is just like ol' FDR." They spoke of Franklin Delano Roosevelt, whom LBJ greatly admired, with affection and joked about the way he would promise one thing to one group, another to a second group, and then do a third without blushing. They thought that Johnson was backing civil rights only to satisfy the Kennedy crowd and to keep blacks quiet, and that he would help the South make the bill as weak as possible.

It wasn't President Johnson who irked the southerners during the filibuster. It was Martin Luther King, who was kicking up civil rights dust all over the south. I chuckled to myself when I heard Senator Lister Hill of Alabama complain to Senator Russell one morning. "Dick," he said, "we ran that nigger out of Alabama, and sent him over to you in Georgia hoping you'd keep him quiet. Now he's back stirrin' up the niggers. What happened, Dick?"

I watched Russell stir his coffee and shake his head. "I don't know Lister. I just *don't* know."

In contrast to the southern bloc, the Senate leaders who were behind the civil rights bill met privately a few times a week in S–138. I reserved the room and set it up for them. As Senate whip, hence responsible for getting the votes, Humphrey was in charge. With him were Democrats Joe Clark of Pennsylvania, Phil Hart and Pat McNamara of Michigan, Warren Magnuson of Washington, Ted Kennedy of Massachusetts, Paul Douglas of Illinois, and John Pastore of Rhode Island. A select group of Republicans joined them: Tom Kuchel of California, the minority whip; Ken Keating and Jake Javits of New York; and Clifford Case of New Jersey.

Their talk was always the same. How many votes do we still need for a two-thirds majority to kill the filibuster? Who's wavering? Which way? How can we get him?

It was clear to them that if they could stop the filibuster, they could easily collect a simple majority to pass the civil rights bill.

Humphrey was especially good at keeping Bobby Kennedy, who had agreed to stay on as attorney general, quiet and cooperative. As he had many others, Johnson had the younger Kennedy hog-tied.

On the one hand, Bobby detested LBJ; on the other, he wanted to see the civil rights bill passed in memory of his brother.

In the early months of 1964, Humphrey frequently invited Bobby to his hideaway, S–309. He kept reminding the attorney general that the civil rights measure had originally been proposed by his brother and therefore it was John F. Kennedy's bill, not Lyndon Johnson's. It worked. Bobby Kennedy swallowed his bitterness—at least for a while.

During the seventy-five-day filibuster, I did my modest share to help the bill along. As maître d', I held a coveted parking place in the Capitol lot near the east steps. Civil rights leaders like Roy Wilkins, Whitney Young, and Clarence Mitchell were lobbying and caucusing all over town. To save them time, I shuttled them to the White House for meetings with Johnson's aides or to Justice Department meetings with Kennedy's staff. And as I had done earlier for Dr. King, I arranged private meetings for them in S–120 or S–138 with senators who didn't want to be seen talking to black activists.

I had a system. I would reserve one of the private dining rooms for a senator who was committed to the civil rights bill without actually telling him. When the coast was clear, I'd hide the black leaders in it with a pot of coffee. Locking the door behind me, I would stalk the senator they wanted to meet, usually catching him in the cloakroom after he left the Senate floor. I would tell him Wilkins, Mitchell, Young, or whoever, wanted to meet him privately. I would describe how I had set up the secret caucus. If he was willing to meet, I unlocked the door and let him in. If Joe Diamond asked how civilians were getting into private rooms, I told him that a senator asked me to arrange a meeting there for him.

Once, I got caught. Joseph Rauh, a noted Washington attorney and general counsel to the Leadership Conference on Civil Rights, frequently lobbied the Hill with Clarence Mitchell. Rauh was a close friend of Senator Humphrey. If the Senate Dining Room wasn't crowded, I'd let them have a quiet table. One day, Rauh, Mitchell, Yvonne Price, and Aaron Henry (both civil rights activists) needed a place to meet. Since the Senate Dining Room was nearly empty, I gave them a table.

To my surprise, the restaurant began to fill. All the tables were soon taken. In walked Senator McClellan. Standing in the doorway, he scanned the restaurant, table by table. By the time I reached him, he was livid.

"What the hell is goin' on here!" he blasted me. To him, Rauh was one of the commies responsible for the civil rights bill. "I'd have a table if you didn't have that damn Jew-lawyer sitting there. Who invited him?"

"He's a guest of Senator Humphrey," I said.

Fortunately, a table opened up almost immediately. But Mc-Clellan didn't drop the matter. As exhausted as he was from filibustering, he found enough energy to complain to Joe Diamond and to write to Senator Jordan.

I was lucky. No one really challenged my explanation.

During the frustrating months of the filibuster, while other important legislation collected dust on the Senate calendar, President Johnson wasn't sitting still. He came to the Hill regularly to meet with Senator Dirksen, who controlled the Republican votes needed for cloture. They met either in Dirksen's hideaway (S–228) or in the presidential hideaway, EF–100. I would serve them coffee or, if it was an evening meeting and President Johnson wanted to play cards, I'd tend bar.

I thought I knew Lyndon Johnson, but during those sessions with Dirksen I saw another side of the man. He was as soft and as sweet as a kitten. "Ev, my friend," he'd purr, "I need your help. This will be a tough one. I'm counting on you." In public, he'd stroke Dirksen, calling him "my friend, the great Senator from that great state of Illinois."

But old Ev was as cagey as old Lyndon. He never committed himself early in the filibuster. He merely said he would see what he could do. Naturally, Dirksen wanted something in return for his cooperation, and President Johnson patiently waited to hear what it was. Fortunately for the sake of the 1964 Civil Rights Act, the price was not high. I remember the deal-making well.

Dirksen asked for several amendments to the House-passed bill. Together, the changes gave states and local communities more time and scope to deal with complaints about discrimination in hiring and in public accommodations. The amendments, Dirksen argued, would make the bill more acceptable to several Republicans who were wavering. They might vote for cloture when the time came. Johnson agreed to support the amendments.

Dirksen also wanted Johnson to give him credit publicly for helping steer the bill through the Senate. Since it was Kennedy's bill, Johnson agreed.

It was understood from the tone of the conversation that President Johnson would owe Dirksen at least one favor. I remember the day Dirksen called in a chit.

"Mr. President," I heard Dirksen say several years after Johnson had signed the civil rights bill into law, "you have a colored boy that's just a bit too big for his britches. He's been giving my people hell. I want you to pull him back."

"Who is he?" Johnson asked.

"Cliff Alexander."

Clifford Alexander was then Johnson's chairman of the Equal Employment Opportunity Commission. President Kennedy had recruited Alexander to work for the National Security Council. President Jimmy Carter would appoint him secretary of the army.

"He's one of Kennedy's blacks," President Johnson said. "I'll take care of that."

It wasn't only Dirksen whom Johnson leaned on during the 1964 filibuster. Three or four times a week, he would call Senator Russell during breakfast. I would get the call from the White House and ask Russell to come to the phone. "Yes, Mr. President," I heard Russell say one day, "but I don't think that's possible."

When Russell returned to his table, I followed as discreetly as I could. "That was the President," I heard him report to his cronies. "He really wants to bring this filibuster to a close. He's very upset."

A few days later, Johnson called Russell again. I heard the senator say, "Mr. President, if you get that bill to the floor, you're going to lose by two votes."

I followed Russell back to his table. Imitating Johnson's Texas twang well, he told his colleagues what the president had said: "Dick, I don't give a goddamn how many votes I lose. Just end the fuckin' filibuster and bring it to a vote so I can get Dirksen's foot out of my ass and these niggers off my back."

At that point, Johnson had Russell convinced that the only reason he wanted to end the filibuster was to appease Dirksen, who as minority leader wanted to move on to other business, and to satisfy blacks, who were blaming him for the delay tactic. All the time, LBJ was lining up votes.

When he felt he had a two-thirds majority, Johnson told Mansfield and Humphrey it was time for a vote. The Senate had attempted cloture on a filibuster twenty-eight times since the rule was adopted in 1917, but it had succeeded only six times, and never against a civil rights bill.

On the morning of June 10, 1964, I sat in the second row of the gallery with Rauh, Mitchell, and Price. My heart was pounding. I didn't know who to believe—Russell, who was certain Johnson didn't have the votes, or Humphrey, who was sure he did. It was like *High Noon*.

18

With the approval of President Johnson, Mansfield and Dirksen had made a deal with a small group of jittery Republicans. If Senate leaders would permit action on three of their amendments before the cloture vote, they would support cloture, even if their amendments failed to pass. It was another small price for big Republican votes.

On Monday, June 8, Senator Mike Mansfield filed a motion to cut off all debate on the civil rights bill. According to Senate rules, the cloture vote had to be taken two days later and one hour after the President of the Senate pounded his gavel.

On Tuesday, June 9, the Senate heard the three Republican amendments to the civil rights bill. Senator Norris Cotton from New Hampshire proposed that companies with less than a hundred employees be exempted from complying with the ban on discrimination in employment. Defeated, 63 to 34.

Senator Bourke Hickenlooper of Iowa proposed to strike the bill's provision for training institutes and in-service training programs to help teachers deal with problems of desegregation. Defeated, 56 to 40.

Senator Thurston Morton of Kentucky asked for jury trials in all cases of criminal contempt arising from the bill's antidiscrimination bans. Passed, 51 to 48.

Testing the water for southern Democrats, Senator Sam Ervin proposed to strike the entire title banning discrimination by employers and unions. Defeated, 63 to 33.

After voting on the amendments, it looked as if the southerners had a firm thirty votes against cloture. They needed thirty-four to keep the filibuster alive.

Senator Humphrey counted noses all day Tuesday. At four in the afternoon, his aide David Gardner called me as I was closing the Senate Dining Room for the the day. Humphrey was still on the Senate floor. "The boss wants to meet with some senators down-stairs," Gardner said. "Do you have a room?"

"You can have one-twenty," I said.

"How about some iced tea and ice water? And the boss would love to have a cold beer."

I ran out and bought a six-pack of Miller High Life, Hum-phrey's favorite. When Humphrey and Gardner arrived at five-thirty, the room was ready. A small group of Republicans, headed by Ev-erett Dirsken, joined them. Realizing it was an important caucus, I hung around as long as I could.

Humphrey told Dirksen that he was concerned about four Democrats: Ralph Yarborough of Texas, William Fulbright of Ar-kansas, Albert Gore of Tennessee, and Howard Edmonson of Okla-homa. Humphrey said he thought he had Yarborough because the Texan was such a good friend of LBJ, and Edmonson because he had already lost the reelection primary and had nothing to lose by voting for cloture. But he was less sure of Gore and Fulbright.

"I'm certain they've all made up their minds," Humphrey said, indicating he didn't know which way. "I'm going to tell the president I don't have the votes tonight."

Dirksen pulled out his yellow pad. He, Humphrey, and Mans-field, who had joined them later, went over the list of sure votes. They were short. Besides Humphrey's four "maybes," Dirksen had two wavering Republicans—Carl Curtis of Nebraska and John Wil-liams of Delaware, who could vote either way. And Democrat Clair Engle of California, a sure Johnson vote, was still recovering from a brain operation. Partially paralyzed and unable to speak, he hadn't been seen on the Hill since April. Humphrey called the White House and broke the bad news to LBJ.

President Johnson went to work.

At precisely ten o'clock the next morning, Senator Lee Metcalf of Montana called the Senate to order. The legislators unanimously agreed to equally divide the hour remaining before the cloture vote between Senator Mansfield and Senator Russell.

Mansfield took the floor first. I was waiting for that moment. The day before, I had served lunch for seventeen people in the ma-jority leader's hideaway, S–208—homemade vegetable soup, four-ounce sirloin steaks, and salad. I had heard Mansfield say "I have a letter from a woman in Montana that I'm going to read on the floor tomorrow. It would bring the nation to tears if they could hear it." I was anxious to hear that letter, and I had told both Clarence Mitchell and Yvonne Price about it. They were with me now.

"The Senate now stands at the crossroads of history, and the time for decision is at hand," Senator Mansfield said. He then unfolded the letter from a twenty-nine-year-old mother of four. It was so eloquent and passionate, so right for the moment, that it sent a shiver right through me. It still does as I reread parts of it. Mansfield delivered it in a booming, professorial voice, peppered with dramatic pauses.

"How can we, as responsible Americans, continue talking, arguing, bickering over civil rights as though the privileges, responsibilities, and birthrights of a great percentage of our people were favors or rewards to be handed out by a benevolent few?

"I am white. By a simple accident in birth, I was allowed to grow up believing in the laws of God and our country. As a child, I learned to recite the Preamble to the Constitution. I learned the Bill of Rights, and memorized the Lincoln Gettysburg Address. I accepted these things as truth. I grew up with the right to feel that I, as an individual, was as good as anyone else, that I had the opportunity to climb as high as my ability, my intelligence, and my ambition would take me. While I did not learn to consider myself as a superior being, I could look upon myself with a lack of inferiority. I did not learn to regard my color with a great sense of pride, but never with guilt or shame.

"I was conceived by a pair of good, respectable, hard-working white parents. I was allowed to grow and mature, to have faith in myself and my future, and when I married and gave birth to my lovely children, to have faith in them and their future.

"I know that my children may go to the school nearest our home. I know that when I give my children a coin to buy an ice cream cone, that coin is good in any store in town. When we are traveling, we can stop at any hotel or motel of our choice. When we go out to eat, we may do so in any cafe or club we wish and can afford. I can sit in any vacant seat in a bus, I can use a public restroom, and if I am thirsty, I may quench my thirst at any public drinking fountain. These things I consider my rights. I take them for granted and know that no one may deny me these rights.

"This morning, the thought occurred to me, that by the same accident of birth, I could have been conceived by a pair of equally good, respectable, hard-working Negro parents. The process is the same, but what immense differences there would have been in my life and upbringing.

"How heartbreaking it must be for a child to have to learn that his future is sharply limited even if his intelligence and his ability is not. How confusing it must be for a child to learn that he may not buy an ice cream cone or a Coke in the same shop as a lighter skinned child, even though his dime has the same value as the other. How could my parents have logically explained to me that a dime from a white hand is worth ten cents, but that the same coin in a brown or black hand is unacceptable? . . .

"At night, when I kiss my children good night, I offer a small prayer of thanks to God for making them so perfect, so healthy, so lovely, and I find myself tempted to thank Him for letting them be born white. Then I am not so proud, neither of myself nor of our society which forces such a temptation upon us.

"And that is why I don't feel that this is a southern problem, it is a northern problem, a western problem, an eastern problem. It is an American problem for all Americans. It is my problem.

"I am only one person, one woman. I wish there was something I could do in this issue. I want to help. The only way I know how to start is to educate my children that justice and freedom and ambition are not merely privileges, but their birthrights. I must try to impress upon them that these rights must be given, not held tightly unto themselves, for what cannot be given, we do not really have for ourselves.

"These are the thoughts of but one of your citizens. I realize that no earth-shaking changes will develop from having written this letter, but it is a beginning. If more can be done by people like me, please tell me what I can do. Thank you for your time."

By the time Mansfield had finished the letter, I was in tears. So were Mitchell and Price next to me. In a few hundred words which it took the senator exactly twelve minutes to read, that ordinary Montana woman had made a fool out of the filibuster and those who supported it. She stunned the gallery. Mansfield sat down without another word.

Senator Russell took the floor next. The Montana mother was

a hard act to follow. In the face of her honesty and emotion, Russell's prepared speech sounded like fifteen minutes of well-turned hypocrisy.

"Mr. President," Russell intoned, "at this hour we must decide whether we will proceed, in summary fashion, to gag the Senate, or whether we will proceed, in orderly fashion, to debate comprehensive amendments and to vote upon them, in a conscientious, studied effort to enable the Senate to develop a definitive measure which will not be an unbridled grant of power to appointive officers of the Government. . . .

"Ours is not a perfect system; the American system of law and order and economy has many defects. But, Mr. President, with all its errors and all its weaknesses, it is the finest system yet devised by man. It has brought more of the good things of life, more happiness, and a greater degree of freedom to more people than have ever before been enjoyed by any other people, under any other governmental system. . . .

"Mr. President, what does equality mean?

"It does not mean that a child can stand on the street corner and cry for a car in which he sees another child of his own age riding. That is not equality. Equality does not mean that one person shall be admitted to a club merely because he desires to be, and because to be refused admission would cause him embarrassment or anguish. Our system never contemplated any such 'equality' as that. If it had, we would not have achieved our present greatness; instead we would be wandering in the chaos and the poverty, and the distress that accompany a tyrannical government, whether it be Fascist or whether it be Communist. . . .

"Mr. President, have we now seen the dawn of the day when—in the name of passing a law to help one group of our people—we shall insist upon the destruction of some of the most important rights of all Americans? Would that be equality for all the American people?"

Senator Russell then took issue with President Johnson and many religious leaders like Dr. King, who were calling civil rights a "moral" issue. "This is the second time in my lifetime that an effort has been made by the clergy to make a moral question of a political issue," Russell said. "The other was prohibition. We know something of the results of that."

153

Russell made his final appeal: "Mr. President, those of us who have opposed this bill have done so from a profound conviction that the bill not only is contrary to the *spirit* of the Constitution of the United States, but also violates the *letter* of the Constitution. . . .

"I appeal to Senators to rise above the pressures to which they have been subjected and to reject this legislation that will result in vast changes, not only in our social order, but in our very form of government."

After Senator Russell sat down, Senator Mansfield gave a few minutes of his time to Senator Humphrey. The old civil rights warrior was brief and to the point.

"In the Senate," he said, "the Constitution of the United States is on trial. The question is whether we will have two types of citizenship in this nation, or first-class citizenship for all. The question is whether where will be two kinds of justice, or equal justice under the law for every American. The question is whether this Nation will be divided, or as we are taught in our youth in the pledge of allegiance, one Nation, under God, indivisible, and with liberty and justice for all."

Stressing the importance of the historic vote just minutes away, Humphrey concluded, "I say to my colleagues of the Senate that perhaps in your lives you will be able to tell your children's children that you were here for America to make the year 1964 our freedom year."

Senator Dirksen was the next to take the floor. His was a calm, reasoned appeal.

"There are many reasons why cloture should be invoked and a good civil rights measure enacted," he said. "First. It is said that on the night he died, Victor Hugo wrote in his diary, substantially this sentiment: 'Stronger than all the armies is an idea whose time has come.' The time has come for equality of opportunity in sharing, in government, in education, and in employment. It will not be stayed or denied. It is here. . . .

"Second. Years ago, a professor who thought he had developed an incontrovertible scientific premise submitted it to his faculty associates. Quickly they picked it apart. In agony he cried out, 'Is nothing eternal?' To this, one of his associates replied, 'Nothing is eternal except change.'

"America grows. America changes. And on the civil rights issue we must rise with the occasion. That calls for cloture and for the enactment of a civil rights bill.

"Third. There is another reason—our covenant with the people. For many years, each political party has given major consideration to a civil rights plank in its platform. Go back and re-examine our pledges to the country as we sought the suffrage of the people and for a grant of authority to manage and direct their affairs. Were these pledges so much campaign stuff or did we mean it? Were these promises on civil rights but idle words for vote-getting purposes, or were they a covenant meant to be kept? If all this was mere pretense, let us confess the sin of hypocrisy now and vow not to delude the people again. . . .

"Fourth. There is another reason why we dare not temporize with the issue which is before us. It is essentially moral in character. It must be resolved. It will not go away. Its time has come. . . .

"Today let us not be found wanting in whatever it takes by way of moral and spiritual substance to face up to the issue and to vote cloture."

The hour was up.

Senator Metcalf instructed the Sergeant at Arms to call the roll to make sure, for the record, that a quorum was present. Every senator but Clair Engle was in the chamber.

Senator Metcalf then ordered all Senate staff off the floor. Although they are technically not allowed on the floor unless they are helping a senator discharge his official duty, the rule is rarely enforced. June 10, 1964, was very special. They cleared the floor.

"A quorum being present," Metcalf announced, "the Chair submits to the Senate, without debate, the question: Is it the sense of the Senate that the debate shall be brought to a close?

"The yeas and nays are required by the rule; and the Secretary will call the roll."

It seemed like such a harmless, simple question. The galleries were packed. I have never before or since heard the Senate Chamber so still. The voting took ten minutes.

"Mr. Aiken."

"Aye," said George Aiken, a Republican from Vermont.

"Mr. Allott."

"Aye," said the Colorado Republican.

A ripple ran through the Senate just after Senator Eastland cast

155

his nay. There was a pause in the rhythm of the ayes and nays. Heads turned toward the Senate door, which I couldn't see from the balcony. Moments later, an orderly wheeled a stretcher down the aisle as close to the secretary as he could push it. On the stretcher lay Senator Engle. It was the calling of Lazarus from the tomb. Engle was smiling.

"Mr. Edmonson," the secretary continued.

"Aye."

'Mr. Ellender."

"Nay!"

"Mr. Engle."

There was no answer. The secretary waited. All eyes were on the old man. Except for the smile, he looked dead. I saw him move his lips. Words refused to form. I saw him slowly raise his left hand and point to his right eye while nodding his head yes. The nod was so slight, the secretary would have missed it had he not been looking for a sign.

"Aye!" said the secretary. The gurney left the chamber as silently as it had arrived. Engle would die just seven weeks later.

With each vote, it became clearer that Russell had lost. Everyone was keeping his own count.

"Mr. Williams," the clerk said.

"Aye!"

There was a sigh. It was over. The Senate had killed the first civil rights filibuster in history. "That's it," I heard someone say from below. Senator Mansfield relaxed in his chair. Senator Russell frowned, then began scribbling on a yellow pad. I felt like leaping over the balcony onto the Senate floor and bear-hugging Senators Mansfield, Humphrey, and Dirksen.

When the voting was completed, the final tally was 71 to 29, four votes more than Mansfield, Humphrey, and Dirksen needed to win. President Johnson had had a very busy night.

At breakfast the next morning, the southerners acted like football players in a locker room after losing the big one. "All we needed was one of them nigger choirs in there," Senator Eastland whined, "an' we'd a had everyone cryin'."

As a group, they accused LBJ of a doublecross, pretending that all he wanted was an end to the filibuster so he could get Dirksen's "foot out of his ass," while all the time he was actually trying to get the civil rights bill passed.

Strom Thurmond was especially bitter. "You see that ol' Clair Engle comin' in there on a stretcher?" I heard him say. The Capitol ambulance, parked near the presidential hideaway and driven by a black man, had whisked Engle to the Hill for the vote. "Lyndon sent those niggers up there to get him in that ambulance. Lyndon'll do anything in the world for a vote."

Senator Russell didn't seem to share Thurmond's bitterness. I sensed that whatever he felt in his gut, in his mind he admired his old friend and student. As president, Lyndon Johnson had done what the nation had expected of him, and he had done it with great skill. And he, Richard Russell, had done what Georgia and the South had expected of him, and he did it with almost equal skill.

When the Senate passed the 1964 Civil Rights Bill, as amended by Senator Dirksen, on June 19 by a vote of 73 to 27, civil rights activists were numb. They had never doubted that a bill of some sort would eventually pass. But they had never dreamed that the 1964 Civil Rights Act would be *stronger* than the bill President John F. Kennedy had sent to the House a year earlier.

More than a thousand people had gathered in the floodlit plaza under the east steps of the Capitol to cheer Mansfield and Dirksen. Almost as if President Johnson were whispering in his ear, Mansfield gave the full credit to Dirksen. "This is his finest hour," Mansfield told the crowd. I stood on the Capitol steps just behind him. "The Senate and the whole country are in debt to the Senator from Illinois."

Television cameras captured the words of Mansfield and the smile of Everett Dirksen. The crowd cheered. President Johnson signed the bill into law on July 2, only seven months after he had taken office. He had kept his promise to Congressman Dawson in 1956 to do what he could for civil rights, and he had kept his promise to do it in memory of John F. Kennedy.

When Mansfield had draped the civil rights garland around Everett Dirksen's shaggy neck, he hadn't fooled Richard Russell. "Lyndon Johnson had more to do with this than any one man," he told the media.

CHAPTER

* 19 *

In the spring of 1964, the Hill was buzzing. Whom would President Johnson pick as his running mate against Senator Barry Goldwater?

It was a game, and the chess player in the Oval Office kept everyone guessing. It seemed as if every day a new name floated down Pennsylvania Avenue to the Capitol: Cabinet members like Labor Secretary Willard Wirtz and Defense Secretary Robert McNamara. Senators Eugene McCarthy and Hubert Humphrey of Minnesota, Abraham Ribicoff and Thomas Dodd of Connecticut, Edmund Muskie of Maine, Stuart Symington of Missouri. A grab bag of others like Governor Pat Brown of California, Mayor Robert Wagner of New York, old pro Adlai Stevenson, and Kennedy holdover Sargent Shriver. But the most popular was Attorney General Robert F. Kennedy.

I remember a lunch I served for Hubert Humphrey and Bobby Kennedy in Humphrey's hideaway late in the spring. Hubert and Bobby were more than colleagues. I sensed that they liked each other as much as they disliked J. Edgar Hoover. Bobby used to complain how the FBI chief would barge into his office unannounced, apparently trying to catch the attorney general at something, as he did with everyone else in town. Bobby told Humphrey that he had had a buzzer attached to Hoover's phone so Hoover could let him know he was coming over for a visit. Hoover had ripped the buzzer out.

Like other Democrats in 1964, Humphrey was concerned about uniting the party and the nation, still shrouded in grief, behind Lyndon Johnson. Humphrey settled back with a glass of beer for some serious talk.

"Bobby, you know that you're the people's choice for vice president," he said.

Bobby set his ginger ale onto the table, leaned forward in his chair, and looked Humphrey in the eye. "Yes," he said, "but I'm not that asshole's choice!"

"Well, I don't give a damn who he picks," Humphrey said. "The Republicans are going to catch hell. That sonofabitch is so popular now, he's going to put both of those cowboy boots right up Goldwater's ass."

They both laughed. Humphrey didn't use foul language much, but when he did, the words were well chosen.

"Speaking of Goldwater," Bobby said, "did you notice that item in the paper? Someone asked Barry who he thought would be Lyndon's running mate, and he said, 'Well, there are a lot of Bobbys to choose from. There's Bobby Kennedy, Bobby Baker, and then there's that what's-his-name—Bobby Sol Estes—or is it Billy?' " Billy Sol Estes was a Texas white-collar crook.

Between the laughs and from the drift of the conversation, I sensed that Bobby Kennedy looked upon the vice presidency the same way LBJ did when John Kennedy was looking for a running mate. Bobby would accept the vice presidency for the sake of unity, if Lyndon Johnson really *wanted* him. But Bobby wasn't at all sure Johnson did want him.

"He might pick *you*, Hubie," Bobby suggested.

"No!" Humphrey said. "I talk too fast in front of him. He doesn't want anyone to out-talk him!"

I wasn't surprised when President Johnson scratched Bobby Kennedy from his list at the end of July, a month before the convention. As usual, his timing was perfect and his method flawless. There was a popular storm building up behind "Bobby for Vice President," but LBJ didn't want to be pressured into making a choice. He knew that the inexperienced attorney general was not the best man for the job, but he also knew how popular Kennedy was in the polls. Unwilling to single out the attorney general as unacceptable, Johnson announced that no one in his cabinet was being considered as a running mate. By eliminating all cabinet members, including Kennedy, he narrowed the field and made the guessing even more fun.

To blacks, Johnson's choice of running mate was not a game; we felt that it would be a sign of LBJ's commitment to racial justice. Would he pick someone with a strong civil rights record, even if that meant further angering his southern colleagues? Or would he pick a moderate to please the South?

The decision was not just a symbolic one, either. Johnson had had a severe heart attack in the 1950s. His running mate could be the next president.

When the Democratic convention opened at the end of August, it was more like a gala than a political caucus. There were no burning questions. Civil rights, which had played such an important role in the Democratic conventions I had attended since 1948, were barely mentioned. Why rock the boat? Polls indicated that President Johnson was thirty-six points ahead of Goldwater, and that 86 percent of blacks planned to vote for him. We had nowhere else to go. Goldwater had supported the filibuster and had voted against the civil rights bill, calling it unconstitutional.

Where the convention was held and how it was organized said even more to the nation than the soft Democratic platform. Democrats chose Atlantic City to host the meeting. With its Boardwalk, beaches, call girls, and seven-acre Convention Hall, best known for Bert Parks and Miss America, it was the playground of the East Coast.

As the convention motto, LBJ chose "Let Us Continue . . ." The words were strung high on the wall behind the podium, along with pictures of Franklin Roosevelt, Harry Truman, and John Kennedy. Dwarfing everything else were two forty-foot-high portraits of Lyndon Johnson.

As the convention theme song, LBJ chose "Hello, Lyndon," to be sung by Carol "Hello, Dolly" Channing. LBJ planned to deliver his acceptance speech on the evening of his fifty-sixth birthday, to be commemorated with the biggest fireworks display Atlantic City had ever seen. And as a memorial tribute to John F. Kennedy, whose shadow fell on Atlantic City, LBJ would allow the delegates to view the twenty-minute film *A Thousand Days,* to be introduced by Bobby Kennedy himself.

It was to be a Texas-style convention, big and brash. President Johnson and his staff composed it like a square dance. There were only five sour notes in the four-day hoedown.

The first came from the president's old colleagues. As if to punish him for the 1964 Civil Rights Act and to warn him not to stray from the pack, key southern senators stayed home: Richard Russell and Herman Talmadge of Georgia, Allen Ellender and Russell Long of Louisiana, John Stennis and James Eastland of Mississippi, and John Sparkman and Lister Hill of Alabama. I heard Johnson's men complaining about the insult in the hospitality room, which I supervised. To them, the boycott was a cloud over LBJ's rainbow of unity.

If the southern senators had turned their backs on LBJ, Atlantic City bared its bosom. Instead of streets jammed with civil rights marchers, as in Los Angeles four years earlier, they were filled with party-goers. One of them was Averell Harriman, who sounded the second sour note.

A distinguished Kennedy fan, Harriman didn't like LBJ's down-home approach to the presidency. Almost as an affront to Johnson, he threw a party at the Deauville Hotel for the delegates and alternates. What angered Johnson's staff was that the sole purpose of the party was to present Jackie Kennedy, the dethroned "queen of Camelot." I didn't work Harriman's party, but I calculated that if all of the almost six thousand delegates and alternates tried to meet Jackie, she would have to smile to seventeen hundred people per hour. Each smile could last no longer than twenty seconds. The whole thing was as silly and petty as the Kennedy and Johnson people fighting over who should be seated first in the Senate Dining Room. Harriman's pettiness was just more glamorous and expensive.

Johnson's advance men in Atlantic City caught the message of the Kennedy supporters. They would come into the hospitality room for a drink with long faces. I never heard them trash the Kennedys, but I could feel their envy and hatred.

Perle Mesta, the famous "hostess with the mostest," wouldn't allow Harriman to get away with socially slapping Lyndon Johnson in the face at his own convention. She disliked the Kennedys as much as Harriman loved them. A millionaire from Oklahoma, she had a dash of LBJ's down-home style herself, and she really liked Lyndon Johnson as a person. He had been going to her parties since he first came to Washington as a skinny congressman in 1938. When John and Jackie Kennedy moved into the White House, Mesta let Lyndon and Lady Bird live in her mansion in Spring Valley, Maryland. The Kennedys snubbed her. To punish them, she refused to throw a single Washington party during Kennedy's thousand-day rule.

Mesta came out of mothballs for the convention. She rented a twelve-room oceanfront villa near Atlantic City and threw four stand-up buffets there, inviting two hundred guests to each. Removing all the furniture from the main floor, she converted it into an Italian garden with artificial shrubs and rented marble statues.

Mesta also threw a supper dance at the Claridge Hotel for seven hundred of her "most intimate friends." To her credit, a good many of them were black. I supervised the bash with thirty-five waiters that I hand-picked from the Senate Dining Room and the best hotels in Washington. To keep out the party crashers, Mesta hired a special security force, and to shuttle her guests to the Claridge and her villa, she rented minibuses blazoned with "Perle's Party Line."

Though smaller than Harriman's party, Mesta outdid him in wall-to-wall celebrities and oil millionaires. Everywhere I looked I saw cowboy boots, diamonds, and ten-gallon hats with feathers. It seemed as if all of Texas and most of the South had turned out to help Lyndon celebrate. Lionel Hampton played his xylophone, and Pearl Bailey, a good friend of Mesta's, belted out a few songs.

If the setting in Atlantic City was staged, so was the convention itself. Lyndon Johnson watched from the White House, and when he sensed the delegates were getting bored, he livened things up. I had a floor pass as well as security clearance for every room in the convention complex, including the presidential suite across the street from Convention Hall. It was obviously Johnson's show, and I wouldn't have missed it for anything in the world.

On Monday evening, August 24, Senator John Pastore of Rhode Island delivered a blistering keynote address painting Barry Goldwater as a trigger-happy extremist ready to unleash the bomb as soon as the Russian bear sneezed. Pastore pulled out all the emotional stops. When he finished, the hall went wild. Eddie Fisher sang "America the Beautiful." An announcement rang over the loudspeaker: "The President is on the phone with Senator Pastore." The telephone was placed on the speaker's platform in such a way that we could all watch the senator receive a pat on the back from the White House. The hall went wild again as LBJ knew it would. Still, no hint about his running mate.

On Tuesday, a rather dead convention day, President Johnson kept teasing the Washington press corps with vague hints about who his running mate might be. Although Senator Eugene McCarthy had withdrawn his name the day before, asking President Johnson to pick Humphrey instead, LBJ didn't tell reporters. The hospitality room in Atlantic City was going crazy from curiosity. Hubert Humphrey, Eugene McCarthy, and Stuart Symington were the front-runners. The smart money was on Humphrey.

There were two sour notes on Tuesday. An integrated unofficial Mississippi delegation challenged the legality of the all-white official delegation. Blacks supported the challengers. Johnson's staff fretted all day that such a trivial problem as an all-white delegation from the Deep South might tear the convention apart. They kept asking me, "After all Lyndon Johnson has done for blacks, why do they want to challenge his convention?"

It never dawned on Johnson's people that the all-white Mississippi delegation was trampling on the 1964 Civil Rights Act, which blacks had hoped meant something. They were asking the convention, "If you believe in the new law, why do you still accept this kind of discrimination?"

The convention found the perfect political solution to the Mississippi problem. It voted to allow two blacks from the unofficial delegation to be seated with the official whites. Rather than integrate, the Mississippi delegation stomped out, just as Strom Thurmond and his Dixiecrats had done in Philadelphia in 1948. I could almost hear Senator Eastland applauding all the way from Mississippi.

Also on Tuesday, Bobby Kennedy announced that he had made New York his home state and that he was running for the Senate in November. When he arrived in Atlantic City, he was mobbed on the Boardwalk and in Convention Hall. Every time I saw him, at least fifty of the people trying to get his autograph were black. That angered Johnson's staff. They considered the timing of the announcement to be insensitive, and they were upset that Bobby had such a hold on blacks. "He hasn't done a damn thing for civil rights," they complained to me. "Look at what Lyndon Johnson accomplished! Why are they flocking to Bobby?"

It was a good question, and I didn't have an answer. I could only speculate that whatever LBJ said about civil rights sounded insincere to the blacks, and whatever the Kennedys said or did rang true.

On Wednesday, Lyndon Johnson invited Senators Humphrey

and Pastore to the White House. Word rippled across Atlantic City like an ocean breeze. Who was it going to be? Pastore or Humphrey? Did that mean McCarthy and Symington were definitely out?

Johnson told the press at seven o'clock Wednesday evening that he would personally announce his choice to the delegates that night. No president had ever done that before. With Humphrey in tow, Johnson boarded Air Force One at Andrews Air Force Base for Atlantic City. Johnson waited in the presidential suite until the right moment. I was on the convention floor close to the podium. Excitement had reached fever pitch, as Johnson knew it would.

After Texas Governor John Connally nominated Lyndon Baines Johnson, and California Governor Pat Brown conominated him, the delegates rioted for twenty minutes. Californians banged garbage-can lids together. The huge Convention Hall pipe organ pealed "Happy Days Are Here Again," and "The Eyes of Texas." Balloons headed for the ceiling on cue. Lady Bird, Lynda, and Luci tossed confetti from their box onto the mob below. Foghorns bellowed, and bells rang. One poster said it all: "We Absolutely Adore Lyndon."

Johnson waited.

I was as excited and as proud as every other Texan. But more than that, I had actually worked for the man everyone was cheering. As my daddy had put it, I "fed that ol' white man for a long time." I knew him. And it was good to see the boss reach the top. At that moment, I loved Lyndon Johnson.

When the seven nominating speeches were over and the delegates had proclaimed Lyndon Baines Johnson their choice for the presidency by acclamation, into the hall strode LBJ. Lady Bird, Lynda, and Luci stood on the podium with him. As if to prove he was in complete charge, he pounded the gavel himself to bring the mob to order.

Describing what he wanted to see in his vice president without dropping any name, Johnson stretched out his remarks for as long as he could, wearing that sly grin I had seen so often. At just the right moment, when the delegates began to stir impatiently, he finally said, "I hope that you will choose as the next vice president of the United States my close—my long-time—my trusted colleague—Senator Hubert Humphrey of Minnesota."

We let out a mighty roar.

The rest of the show that night was LBJ's, too. Under his pressure, Senator Eugene McCarthy nominated Humphrey as a symbol of unity. Senator George Smathers, a strong Kennedy supporter and a southerner, seconded the nomination. And Senator Olin Johnston, a bitter racist, moved to approve Humphrey's nomination by acclamation. Johnson was taking no chances on a convention stampede for Bobby Kennedy.

Blacks were surprised and delighted with Johnson's choice. Humphrey's stand on civil rights was legendary. For the first time, I sensed that black leaders were beginning to trust Lyndon Johnson a little. Personally, I was more than pleased. Together, Johnson and Humphrey would make the strongest practical civil rights team I could think of.

On Thursday evening, I heard the fifth and last sour note. I was on the floor, close to the front, to watch *A Thousand Days*. The delegates were disappointed because Jackie Kennedy wasn't there. When Bobby stood up to introduce the film, however, they broke into a spontaneous fifteen-minute frenzy of applause, hooting, and marching. The morning newspapers called it the longest and most spontaneous demonstration in political history.

I could see tears rolling down Bobby's cheeks. He tried to pound the convention back to order, but it wouldn't obey. I thought the delegates would never let him talk. When Convention Hall finally quieted to a hum, Bobby quoted from Shakespeare's *Romeo and Juliet*. He picked the right words to memorialize his brother. They were the last ones Lyndon Johnson wanted to hear:

> When he shall die,
> Take him and cut him out in little stars,
> And he will make the face of heaven so fine
> That all the world will be in love with night,
> And pay no worship to the garish sun.

To me it sounded as if Bobby Kennedy were calling LBJ the garish sun and telling him that no matter what he said or did, he would never outshine JFK's star. Bobby Kennedy was calling LBJ a "cornponed bastard" in public on his birthday.

It seemed as if everyone was crying. I was choked up, too, as much for Lyndon Johnson as for John Kennedy. I thought it was very big of LBJ to allow the Kennedy people to show the movie and to invite Bobby Kennedy to introduce it. I couldn't think of any other political leader who would have been so generous to the Kennedys at his own convention. And I was convinced that LBJ had acted out of the best of motives. He wanted to unite the country, and he felt deep sympathy for the family.

Bobby had trampled on his generosity.

"I accept your nomination," President Johnson said later that evening. "I accept the duty of leading this party to victory. I thank you for placing at my side the man you so wisely selected to be the next vice president."

The delegates roared in delight.

"Let us now turn to our task," Johnson concluded. "Let us be on our way."

I thought of the Biltmore Hotel in Los Angeles in 1960 and Lyndon Johnson standing in front of a mostly black, hostile audience. I heard him promise that if they supported the Kennedy-Johnson ticket, they would see more civil rights progress in four years than they had in the previous hundred. I also thought of Hubert Humphrey in Philadelphia in 1948. I recalled how he had placed his political future on the line for a strong civil rights platform. Together, would these two men continue to win civil rights victories?

We cheered longer for LBJ than we had for Bobby. But then, Johnson was president, not a candidate for the Senate; and his demonstration was planned, not entirely from the heart. I'm sure LBJ saw the difference. And I'm also sure that even sounds of twenty thousand people singing "Happy Birthday, Lyndon" outside his hotel suite window that night—and the explosion of a six-hundred-square-foot pyrotechnic portrait of Lyndon into red, white, and blue sparks could not drown out that pointed quote from Shakespeare and the wild cheers for Bobby Kennedy.

20

President Johnson buried Senator Goldwater under the biggest landslide in political history. To emphasize that he was no longer president by accident but his own man, the following January Johnson broke with tradition and announced that he would deliver his State of the Union message at nine in the evening, during prime time. The only other president to give a State of the Union at night was Johnson's mentor, Franklin Roosevelt. To signal Congress that he was impatient to start building his Great Society, Johnson scheduled his address for Monday, January 4, the very day Congress opened.

Given that he wanted every American to see and hear him, Johnson's decision was a good one. Every other president but Roosevelt had delivered the address at high noon to a half-empty House Chamber. Congressional staff were not encouraged to attend. Most congressional wives stayed home. Their children were usually in school, and the nation was at work. Unable to watch or listen live, most people heard excerpts on the evening news or scanned boring stories in the morning papers.

Johnson sent word to the Hill that he wanted every congressman and senator to attend with their wives. He made it clear that the Senate staff was not only invited to sit in the gallery but was expected to. In a word, Johnson wanted to play to a full house. To make it easier for representatives and their spouses to attend, the White House asked the Senate Dining Room to serve a special State of the Union dinner—the first ever.

I arranged to have three sittings for dinner on January 4, beginning at five-thirty, and I selected three entrées: chicken cordon bleu, prime rib, and veal Oscar. I accepted reservations, and the places were quickly filled.

The evening reminded me of Academy Award night without

fans, for the police had closed the parking lot to visitors on the east side of the Capitol nearest the Senate Dining Room. It seemed as if everyone pulled up to the east steps in a rented limousine with a chauffeur in a black suit and hat. The Texans, in particular, dressed for the occasion. The men wore their finest cowboy hats with tuxedos, string ties, and cowboy boots of every style and color—white, gray, blue, alligator skin. The only things missing were spurs and the smell of stables. The women were draped in Texas-size, full-length furs.

Part of my job that evening was to prepare the presidential hideaway, EF–100, where Johnson would wait until he was ready to enter the House chamber. I served coffee, sherry, and cookies for President Johnson and his entourage of thirty-five, including Lady Bird, Lynda, Luci, his close aides, and his makeup man. Senate Majority Leader Mike Mansfield and House Speaker Carl Albert were there to greet him in the name of Congress. Johnson seemed subdued and calm.

Just before the president left EF–100 to deliver his address, I went to the staff gallery. The House was packed and so was the family gallery. Reporters were stuffed into the press gallery. Dignitaries sat in the VIP gallery looking important. I suspect that every black staffer on the Hill was in the balcony with me. I felt proud. This was the first State of the Union I could attend, for the others had been at my peak serving period in the restaurant. I was also excited. I knew that Lyndon Johnson was about to take his first step into the civil rights snakepit as an elected president.

Most of Johnson's fifty-minute address, which he delivered very slowly even for Lyndon Johnson, dealt with his Great Society program. Typical of LBJ, there was one big surprise. He invited Soviet leaders to visit the United States and to appear on TV with U.S. leaders. He also announced a small surprise: he would visit Europe and Latin America in 1965.

Johnson touched upon civil rights so lightly that I think most Americans missed his comment. He promised a Great Society "to Negro Americans through enforcement of the civil rights laws and elimination of barriers to the right to vote."

There it was, a diamond in the rough. It didn't sparkle or shine, but it was there. And that was all I needed to hear from Lyndon Johnson. I remembered what he had once told me. It was one of the few times he had called me by my given name, a sign that what he had to say was important to me personally. "Robert," he said, "when you can vote, every politician is your friend."

I knew he'd make good on the veiled promise of voting rights legislation. I looked down at Congressman William Dawson, his hair all white now. I couldn't see his face, but I'm sure he was smiling, "I told you his heart is in the right place!"

I had such confidence in Lyndon Johnson at that moment that I felt like shouting to him from the gallery, in the words of Adam Clayton Powell, "Keep the faith, Lyndon!" I knew he'd need it in the battle ahead.

The Democratic side of the Inner Sanctum was filled with southerners the next morning, all hanging on to a thin thread of hope. I heard them say that underneath all the vote-getting and kowtowing to "niggers," Lyndon was still a southern boy, suckled, educated, and politically seasoned in the South. He wouldn't betray them. The 1964 Civil Rights Act, they conceded, had been a piece of shrewd political strategy that had won Lyndon Johnson a huge landslide. Every southerner could be proud of that.

"Look at ol' Lyndon's voting record when he was one of us," Senator Ellender told Senator Russell. "Why, he was against every civil rights bill that ever came up!"

"You're right, Al," Russell said. But I sensed the beginning of a big doubt.

Two weeks after the State of the Union address and a few days before President Johnson's inauguration, I served Perle Mesta's rather small party for two to three hundred Texas and Washington friends of President and Lady Bird Johnson. To help me, I brought twenty-five waiters and waitresses to Mesta's Spring Valley mansion. In terms of power, fame, and money, it was the most impressive Mesta party I ever saw in my twenty years of serving them. Vice-president-elect Hubert Humphrey was there with his wife, Muriel. Most of the important senators and their wives were present. So were Julie Andrews, Carol Burnett, Barbra Streisand, Eva Gabor, and Carol Channing decked in diamonds. Composer Jerry Herman dropped by, as did Broadway director Mike Nichols and comedian Woody Allen. Harry Belafonte sang.

It was another Perle Mesta coup, for on the same night, the American Newspaper Women's Club threw a party for the stars hired to entertain at the inaugural balls later in the week. The club rented buses to pick up the celebrities at their hotels. The only star to come was Johnny Carson. Everyone else was at Mesta's home.

The newspapers the next day said that Alfred Hitchcock had made a cameo appearance at Mesta's as he did in each of his movies, but I was so busy supervising the party that I hadn't noticed him. The mood was as sparkling as the Dom Perignon. And the Texans bubbled the most.

No one there seemed interested in what Lyndon Johnson would actually *do* as president.

Lyndon Johnson wasted no time. Right after his inauguration, he appointed Nicholas Katzenbach, the assistant attorney general under Robert Kennedy, as the new attorney general. Then he told Katzenbach to get busy drafting a voting rights act. I set up a meeting for the new attorney general in S–120 shortly after his appointment but before he was confirmed. The Senate leadership was present: Majority Leader Mike Mansfield, Minority Leader Everett Dirksen, and Assistant Minority Leader Tom Kuchel of California. Missing was the new Senate whip, Russell Long of Louisiana, whom the liberals didn't trust. In his place was the old whip, Vice President Humphrey.

Nicholas Katzenbach sketched the voting rights bill as he then saw it. He told the Senate leaders that it would be directed at six southern states in particular—Louisiana, Alabama, Georgia, Mississippi, South Carolina, and Virginia—as well as thirty-four counties in North Carolina where less than half the people of voting age were registered to vote. Literacy tests, used to prevent blacks from voting, would be suspended in these states. And to make sure that blacks who wanted to register in them could, the Justice Department would appoint federal registrars.

In other states where more than half the blacks of voting age were registered, Katzenbach explained, blacks would be encouraged to complain to the Justice Department if they couldn't register. If there were twenty complaints, the Justice Department would send in federal registrars and poll watchers.

Finally, under the proposed bill, if the Justice Department received complaints that registered blacks were being turned away from the polls or that their votes were not being counted, a federal court would hold up certification of the election until the problem was corrected.

I couldn't believe what I was hearing. I knew the South. I knew the senators from the seven southern states the Justice Department was targeting—from old country lawyer Sam Ervin of North Carolina to gumbo-party host Allen Ellender of Louisiana. Lyndon Johnson's voting rights bill would force them to their knees in public.

Katzenbach went on to tell the Senate leaders that President Johnson supported the bill completely. He described how LBJ had pounded on a white antique table in the Oval Office, almost smashing it, and had said, "I want the goddamnedest, toughest voting rights bill you can come up with!"

A vague sense of urgency hung over Johnson's bill. Martin Luther King had avoided Atlantic City. I'm sure that if he had demonstrated there for a stronger civil rights plank in the Democratic platform or in support of the unofficial Mississippi delegation, he would have turned the convention on its ear. He also would have spoiled Lyndon Johnson's hoedown. I was convinced that Dr. King's silence was his way of saying thank you to Lyndon Johnson for the 1964 Civil Rights Act.

But now that the convention was over and Lyndon Johnson was reelected, Dr. King was not about to stop marching through the South to please LBJ. He had, however, told Johnson that he would keep a low profile until March in order to give him time to write and introduce a voting rights bill into Congress. But no longer. I know that LBJ took Dr. King seriously; nine years earlier as a senator, Johnson had warned Humphrey, Hart, and Douglas about the power of the "nigger" preacher. And early in 1965, I heard him tell Senator Dirksen, "Ev, these niggers are worrying the hell out of me."

I'm not so sure that Katzenbach paid as much attention to Dr. King. Although he spoke about pressure building up, he never referred to Dr. King directly during that important meeting in S–120.

The pressure on Johnson and the voting rights bill began to mount all during February. There were small demonstrations around the country with people carrying signs saying, "Voting Rights Now! Not Later!" Dr. King was upsetting NAACP leaders in Washington like Roy Wilkins and Clarence Mitchell. Both were working closely with Katzenbach to get a bill drafted so Johnson could send it to the Hill. They both told me they were afraid that Dr. King would so upset the president that he would withdraw his support for the bill. After all, they said, deep down Lyndon Johnson was still a southerner.

I continued to set up private meetings for black civil rights leaders on the Hill all during February. On March 5, Dr. King came to Washington to check on the voting rights bill. He met with President Johnson and Attorney General Katzenbach in the Oval Office for an hour and forty minutes. Then he came to the Hill to talk to the House black caucus. I attended a small reception for him that night in room 2145 in the Rayburn building.

Dr. King told us that, although he was satisfied with the thrust of the voting rights bill as outlined by Katzenbach, he would be leading a "voting rights march" from Selma, Alabama, to the steps of the state capitol in Montgomery. Alabama, of course, was one of the states targeted by the voting rights bill. It was one of four states that still had a poll tax for state and local elections. It also had George Wallace for its governor.

Dr. King told us that President Johnson had asked him to delay the march at least until he, Johnson, had sent the voting rights bill to Congress. Dr. King said he had told the president that he would announce the march at a press conference that very day and that he intended to begin the fifty-mile walk on Sunday, March 7.

Black civil rights leaders working closely with Katzenbach were not pleased. Like Johnson, they wanted Dr. King to wait. They feared that the pressure he would create by marching would hurt rather than help the passage of a strong voting rights bill. Roy Wilkins, who opposed the march, told me that President Johnson had asked him personally to talk to Dr. King. Wilkins said Johnson told him, "Roy, you are a leader. Can't you get him to wait a little longer?"

"I can't stop King," Wilkins said he told LBJ. Then Wilkins told me, "What would I look like trying to make him back off?"

George Wallace didn't like the idea either. "Such a march cannot and will not be tolerated," he said publicly.

Governor Wallace and Dr. King had put the senators on the spot, for reporters began hounding them for statements and comments. Unwilling to commit themselves in a no-win situation, they ducked the press as best they could. When reporters started gathering outside the Senate Dining Room, hoping to catch a particular senator, I had to shoo them away.

Neither Dr. King's announcement of a demonstration nor Wallace's threat to stop it made the headlines. The march itself, however, sent a shiver through the country.

CHAPTER

On Sunday, March 7, I was home alone with my three-year-old daughter Wanda Maria. Although we had tried to rebuild our relationship, Modean and I had finally divorced. She kept our home on Capitol Hill, and I moved to suburban Maryland. I flipped on the news. Dr. King had canceled his voting rights march because he didn't want to risk violence, and he had returned to Atlanta. But John Lewis of the Student Non-Violent Coordinating Committee and Dr. King's aide Hosea Williams had refused to be intimidated by Governor Wallace. What I saw on television that Sunday was worse than Magnolia, Texas, in the 1920s.

Williams led 525 blacks from Browns Chapel Methodist Church in Selma to the Alabama River. Two hundred state troopers and volunteers from the Dallas County Sheriff's office, armed with riot guns, pistols, billy clubs, and whips, waited for them at the Edward Pettus Bridge, which opens onto Highway 80, the route to Montgomery, fifty miles away. Loaded down with bedrolls and backpacks, the silent marchers crossed the river two by two. Three dozen possemen sealed the west end of the bridge after them.

Fifty troopers and fifteen possemen, some on horseback, stretched across all four lanes of Highway 80 on the east side of the river. As the last marcher stepped off the bridge, the troopers put on gas masks and held their billy clubs in front of them.

"This is an unlawful assembly," a bullhorn blared. "Your march is not conducive to the public safety. You are ordered to disperse and go back to your church or homes."

"May we have a word with the mayor?" Hosea Williams asked.

"There is no word to be had," the mayor answered.

The bullhorn repeated its message. Williams asked the same question. The mayor repeated his answer. There were several sec-

174

onds of silence as the marchers held their ground. A group of a hundred white bystanders lined the shoulders of the highway.

"Troopers advance!" the bullhorn ordered.

A flying wedge of blue and white uniforms attacked the marchers. It trampled and stomped the first ten to twenty. The bystanders let out a cheer as if it were a bullfight. Sleeping bags, sandwiches, and bodies lay strewn on the road.

The troopers began clubbing the marchers back across the bridge. The mounted posse charged into the fleeing mob, cracking skulls and shoulders and arms. Marchers screamed in pain and fear as they scrambled across the bridge, where more possemen waited with clubs and whips.

There was a loud crack. Tear gas exploded. Marchers began choking and coughing and crying. Four or five women lay gasping on the grassy median strip where the troopers had felled them. They began crawling toward the bridge. The possemen on the west side of the river whipped and clubbed the marchers back to Browns Chapel.

When the tear gas settled, seventeen men and women were rushed to the hospital with fractured skulls, cracked ribs, and broken arms and legs. Scores more needed stitches and first aid. Black leaders kept urging the angry and shocked marchers to be calm and peaceful. Hosea Williams told the press, "I fought in World War II, and I once was captured by the German army. And I want to tell you that the Germans never were as inhuman as the state troopers of Alabama."

President Johnson moved as fast as the Dallas County posse. I got a call from Joe Diamond a little later that day to get a room ready because LBJ was coming to the Hill to meet key congressmen and civil rights leaders. I rushed to the Capitol, opened S–120, and hastily made an urn of coffee.

I was in the hallway when LBJ strode into the Capitol, grim and angry at Governor Wallace. "Get that little sonofabitch George up here and fast," I heard him tell an aide. "We got to put this fire out."

I followed Johnson into S–120. Present were Vice President Humphrey, Attorney General Katzenbach, Senators Jacob Javits and Birch Bayh, among others, and civil rights leaders Roy Wilkins of the NAACP, Whitney Young of the Urban League, and Floyd McKissick of CORE. Johnson told them that a strong voting rights bill would be passed in 1965. He guaranteed it. But the violence in Selma and elsewhere must stop, he warned. It was tearing the nation apart. It could make the passage of the bill more difficult. He asked the civil rights leaders what they could do to stop the violence.

Speaking for the others, Roy Wilkins tossed the sticky ball right back into Johnson's court. "Mr. President," he said, "the situation is so serious right now that only your immediate action can stop the violence. Governor Wallace is digging in and won't budge. Blacks are determined to march, and they won't turn back."

Wilkins was right. Dr. King returned to Selma the next day, Monday, and announced that he would lead a second march on Tuesday. Refusing to rescind his order prohibiting the march, Wallace promised that "all necessary means" would be used to stop it. Federal Judge Frank Johnson ordered Dr. King to wait until he had time to rule on the legality of the governor's injunction. White religious leaders began pouring into Selma. Blacks and whites across the country began marching, picketing, and sitting in. In Washington, they invaded the Justice Department, blaming Johnson and Katzenbach for failing to protect the marchers on Sunday and for not promising federal protection for Tuesday.

The heat on LBJ and his voting rights bill became intense. To federalize the Alabama National Guard or to send in federal marshals would anger the South. Johnson needed all the goodwill he could get in order to move his voting rights bill through Congress quickly before the whole nation exploded. Rather than intervene, Johnson chose to force Wallace to back down.

On Tuesday, March 9, Dr. King crossed the Pettus Bridge. Instead of 525 blacks behind him, there were three thousand blacks and whites, including Emily Taft Douglas, a former congresswoman and the wife of Senator Paul Douglas of Illinois. The posse and troopers were waiting. Another crowd of gawkers, thirsting for blood, lined the shoulders of Highway 80.

"This march will not continue," a bullhorn blared.

The marchers stood in silence. Reporters gathered nearby, some wearing steel helmets. *Life* magazine photographers had gas masks dangling from their belts like scalps. Dr. King spoke up: "We're engaged in an attempt to petition the Governor of Alabama for the right to vote."

The bullhorn threatened. Dr. King asked if the marchers could pray. "You can have your prayer," the bullhorn said, "and then return to your church, if you so desire."

Three thousand people fell to their knees in a silent wave. Dr. Ralph Abernathy led the prayer, asking that the heart of President Johnson be touched to send troops not only to Vietnam but to Alabama as well. Emily Douglas came to the front of the line. The bullhorn spoke again. "Troopers, get off the road," it said.

The marchers let out a victory cheer. But Dr. King waved them around, and they walked back to Browns Chapel in peace. "The reason I didn't advance," Dr. King told the press later, "is because as a nonviolent, I couldn't move people into a potentially violent situation."

I had never seen such control and power in all my life. Dr. King waved his hand, and three thousand people fell to the ground in prayer. Dr. King pointed his finger, and three thousand people turned around as one and walked back across the Alabama River. I thought of Moses leading his people through the Red Sea. And I knew that Lyndon Johnson would respect the "nigger preacher" even more than he already did. It was almost as if Dr. King were sending him a message: "There! I've done my part. Now you do yours."

That night, a gang of white thugs pounced on three white marchers—all clergymen—while they were walking down a street in downtown Selma. They sent James Reeb, a Unitarian minister, to the hospital with a fractured skull.

The next morning, the southern senators showed no sympathy at breakfast in the Inner Sanctum. They laughed at Emily Douglas, who wasn't popular on the Hill. Pushy and outspoken on civil rights, she didn't chum around with the more submissive Senate wives. Bigots called her "the bag lady" because she didn't dress like a *Vogue* model just to please the senators. Strom Thurmond, in particular, disliked her. When Dr. King took his peaceful demonstration north to Chicago and Cicero not long after Selma, Thurmond chuckled in delight. "I wonder what Paul thinks now that they've come right into *his* backyard!"

Not surprisingly, the southern senators blamed Dr. King for the violence in Selma. "The more you give those niggers," they were saying, "the more they want. They got the civil rights bill last year, what else do they want?" It was clear to me that underneath their tough talk, they were worried. The question was no longer how to handle "uppity niggers." Whites had joined Dr. King, and the southerners just couldn't believe it. It had never dawned on them that any white would want to hold hands with blacks over civil rights.

"What's happening?" I heard them grouse. "Now we're getting white Jewish kids involved. What next?"

Senator Eastland, who was especially bitter at Dr. King, spoke up. He told his colleagues that he had complained to J. Edgar Hoover about the long-haired white radicals joining King. He said that Hoover, who had done surveillance on several of the whites, had told him, "I can't agree. Some come from very fine, wealthy families." Eastland bragged that he was working closely with the FBI to get King.

Senator Eastland was serious. Not long after that sad Inner Sanctum breakfast, I brought lunch to Strom Thurmond's office. Eastland was there. "I have something on him," I heard Eastland say about Dr. King. "He'll lose all his credibility with his people."

Several days later, a waiter and I brought a tray of sodas to Eastland's hideaway, S–206. Besides Eastland, Thurmond, and several other senators and staff whom I knew, there were a group of people I didn't recognize. They were all sitting in front of a movie projector. Eastland told an aide to darken the room and start the show, just as I was leaving. I stole a glance at the screen. It was a surveillance film of Dr. King. I was willing to bet my last dollar that the strangers were FBI agents.

Senator Eastland eventually leaked a story to the press about Dr. King allegedly approaching a white woman for sexual favors. The story was so thin, it couldn't stick.

On Thursday, March 11, two small unofficial groups of marchers started off from Selma to Montgomery. Sheriff Jim Clark and his volunteer posse turned them back. In response to their "We Shall Overcome" chant, Clark wore a huge button that said, NEVER. Dr. King applied more pressure that day by calling for nationwide demonstrations for voting rights. They sprang up all over the country.

On Friday, Reverend Mr. Reeb died of a crushed skull. He had never regained consciousness. A dozen civil rights demonstrators mixed with tourists and walked into the White House. They held a sit-in for six hours. President Johnson met with religious leaders, who pleaded with him to send federal marshals to Alabama or to federalize the National Guard. He refused.

On Saturday, fifty men and women lay across Pennsylvania Avenue in front of the White House and snarled traffic. Governor Wallace finally asked President Johnson for a conference. "At any time that is convenient to you," LBJ told him sarcastically.

On Sunday, a week after the first Selma march, Wallace met with President Johnson in the Oval Office for more than three hours. After the conference, the southerners held a reception for the governor on the Hill. I was there. Most of the southern bloc, led by Senator Russell, was there too, as well as a smattering of southern congressmen from the House side.

I had seen Wallace many times, for he frequently met on the Hill with the Alabamans, and I usually set up a room for him. Always polite, he'd smile at me and nod in recognition. But as soon as he opened his mouth during those caucuses, his hatred for blacks and for Dr. King in particular dripped like acid from his lips.

Chomping on a cigar and surrounded by bodyguards with guns on their hips, I heard Wallace tell his southern friends that the president had given him three pieces of advice. He joked about old Lyndon advising *him*, George Wallace, when all Johnson was doing was giving in to the "niggers." Wallace said Lyndon first told him to state publicly that every Alabaman has the right to vote. Second, to state publicly that every Alabaman has the right to demonstrate peacefully. Third, to call a biracial meeting to explore ways for whites and blacks to work together in Alabama.

Wallace laughed. "Who the hell does he think he is?" he said to Senator Russell.

Without offering a word of encouragement, Russell listened to Wallace brag and spout. I sensed that he knew Wallace was wrong but felt that the governor of Alabama was Johnson's problem, not his. Most of the other senators were quiet as well, but the Alabama congressmen kept egging Wallace on. "You're right, George," they'd say. "You tell 'um."

Wallace complained that Johnson wanted him to call up the National Guard to protect Dr. King and the marchers. If he did, Wallace said, Alabama would have to pay them overtime. He said

179

he told Johnson that he had no intention of spending state money to protect Negroes engaged in an illegal action. If Johnson wanted to protect them, then he should federalize the Guard.

"Let big government pay!" Wallace said.

"You're right, George," the Alabamans chimed in.

The scene would have been funny if the subject weren't so serious. Selma had turned into a turf battle, Alabama versus the United States, Wallace versus Johnson. They reminded me of two moose locking antlers in a fight for leadership of the herd. What amazed me was that Wallace really believed he could beat LBJ. Russell knew he couldn't. I could see from his face that he knew Wallace would lose on every score—in the courts, in Washington, in Selma, and in the hearts of most Americans.

The next day, Governor Wallace backed down. Gone were the bragging and bravado I had heard on the Hill. Sounding like a humanitarian, he promised to try to protect the marchers if the court declared the march legal. He said he deplored violence and supported every eligible citizen's right to vote and to demonstrate peacefully.

While Wallace was making his announcement to the press, fifteen thousand people crammed into Lafayette Park across from the White House and spilled into the street, protesting Johnson's failure to federalize the Guard. That night, LBJ addressed a special joint session of Congress to announce his voting rights bill, which he was sending to Congress that week. The pressure on Johnson and Congress was the strongest I had ever seen in my twenty-two years as an observer on the Hill.

I was busy all that day, March 15. Because Johnson was to give an address that evening, the Senate Dining Room would be open for dinner. Late in the afternoon, civil rights leaders began gathering on the Hill. I arranged for them to have conferences in S–138 and S–120. Just before seven that evening, I set up EF–100 for President Johnson and his entourage. The Senate reception party waiting for him there was small, and Johnson had brought with him only a handful of key aides. He looked very grim. He had a quick cup of coffee, a glass of water, and then immediately proceeded to the House Chamber.

I cleaned up the room quickly and rushed to join Clarence Mitchell, Yvonne Price, and Joe Rauh in the staff gallery. The House

Chamber was charged and edgy, almost as if the tension of the nation had seeped into it. When I reached my seat, President Johnson was already standing at the podium. The usual round of applause died suddenly.

When he opened his mouth, Lyndon Johnson was magnificent.

I speak tonight for the dignity of man and the destiny of democracy," Lyndon Johnson said. He was leaning over the podium, his torso almost horizontal to it. "At times, history and fate meet at a single time in a single place to shape a turning point in man's unending search for freedom.

"So it was at Lexington and Concord. So it was a century ago at Appomattox. So it was last week in Selma, Alabama."

The words went through me like a jolt of electricity. I sensed that Johnson himself was making history. I looked over at Lady Bird and her two daughters. Their eyes were fixed on the president. Below me, all 435 members of Congress waited for the next words to drop. No cathedral could have been more hushed.

"There is no cause for pride in what has happened in Selma," Johnson continued. "There is no cause for self-satisfaction in the long denial of the equal rights of millions of Americans. But there *is* cause for hope and for faith in our democracy—in what is happening here tonight.

"For the cries of pain and the hymns and protests of oppressed people have summoned into convocation all the majesty of this great Government. . . . Our mission is at once the oldest and the most basic of this country—to right wrong, to do justice, to serve man."

Pictures flashed across my mind. A boy and a girl in a wagon pulled by mules down a dirt road as evening fell. A white man with a whip on a big horse. A father who wouldn't speak up. A sister crying by the side of the road, hugging her sweater. A boy with two snakes in a bag. An honorably discharged soldier with German POWs on a train in the Shenandoah Valley. A frightened man in a jail cell in Bristol, Tennessee. A letter from the man at the podium saying, "This nigger drives for me." I could hardly control the feelings of rage that shook me.

I watched Congress applauding below. I could see the battle line drawn as clearly as it had been at Lexington and Selma. Some clapped with enthusiasm, and some out of politeness. Others stared at LBJ in stony silence like the marble busts in the hallways.

"Rarely in any time does an issue lay bare the secret heart of America itself," Johnson went on. "Rarely are we met with a challenge, not to our growth or abundance, or our welfare or our security, but rather to the values and the purposes and the meaning of our beloved nation.

"The issue of equal rights for American Negroes is such an issue.

"And should we defeat every enemy, and should we double our wealth and conquer the stars, and still be unequal to this issue, then we will have failed as a people and as a nation.

"For, with a country as with a person, 'What is a man profited, if he shall gain the whole world, and lose his own soul?'

"There is no Negro problem. There is no southern problem. There is no northern problem. There is only an American problem."

I thought of that unnamed woman from Montana who had said the same thing in a letter to Senator Mansfield the previous year. I had cried when I heard him read it to the full Senate Chamber. Tears welled in my eyes now.

"This was the first nation in the history of the world to be founded with a purpose," Johnson said. "The great phrases of that purpose still sound in every American heart, North and South: 'Government by the consent of the governed' . . . 'Give me liberty or give me death.'

"And those are not just clever words, and those are not just empty theories.

"In their name, Americans have fought and died for two centuries, and tonight around the world they stand there as guardians of our liberty risking their lives. . . .

"To deny a man his hopes because of his color or race or his religion or the place of his birth is not only to do injustice, it is to deny America and to dishonor the dead who gave their lives for American freedom.

"Our fathers believed that if this noble view of the rights of man was to flourish it must be rooted in democracy. The most basic right of all was the right to choose your own leaders."

183

I swallowed hard and thought of John F. Kennedy. He had written *Profiles in Courage,* for which he had won a Pulitzer Prize, but he would never have been a chapter in his own book. As dashing and as inspiring as he was, he had never put his political life on the line as Lyndon Johnson was doing before the eyes of the world.

Now I understood why he had looked so grim in his hideaway minutes before he walked to the podium. He was calling the nation a hypocrite. He was standing alone—tall and firm against the South he loved. He was earning the undying anger of his former colleagues. And he was challenging blacks. We had doubted him. We had thought he was playing politics with our hopes and our rights. We never believed he would honor his promises. But here he stood before us, baring himself and speaking the toughest civil rights language of any president in history.

"There is no reason which can excuse the denial of that right," Johnson continued. His voice was soft, but strong and sincere. "There is no duty which weighs more heavily on us than the duty we have to insure that right. Yet the harsh fact is that in many places in this country, men and women are kept from voting simply because they are Negroes. . . . Every device of which human ingenuity is capable has been used to deny this right."

Johnson went on to explain how: Blacks go to register to vote only to be told the registrar is "out." If they persist and eventually find him in, he disqualifies them for making a technical error on their application form, such as not spelling out a middle name. If they make no "errors," the registrar gives them a test that they fail.

I was certain that this was the first time most Americans had ever heard how the South had been disenfranchising blacks. Even I was shocked to be reminded. After all, it was 1965, one hundred years after Abraham Lincoln had proclaimed emancipation.

"Even a college degree cannot be used to prove that he can read and write," Johnson continued. "For the fact is that the only way to pass these barriers is to show white skin."

Johnson went on to explain the provisions of the voting rights bill that he was sending to Congress the next day. Then he challenged the U.S. Congress itself in stinging words, spanking it in public.

"There is no constitutional issue here," he said. "The command of the Constitution is plain. There is no moral issue. It is wrong—

184

deadly wrong—to deny any of your fellow Americans the right to vote in this country.

"There is no issue of state's rights or national rights. There is only the struggle for human rights.

"I have not the slightest doubt what will be your answer. But the last time a President sent a civil rights bill to the Congress, it contained a provision to protect voting rights in Federal elections. That civil rights bill was passed after eight long months of debate. And when that bill came to my desk from the Congress for my signature, the heart of the voting provision had been eliminated.

"*This* time on *this* issue, there must be no delay, or no hesitation, or no compromise with our purpose.

"We cannot—we must not—refuse to protect the right of every American to vote in every election that he may desire to participate in.

"And we ought not, and cannot, and we must not wait another eight months before we get a bill.

"We have already waited a hundred years and more, and the time for waiting is gone. . . .

"Their cause must be our cause, too. Because it's not just Negroes, but really it's all of us who must overcome the crippling legacy of bigotry and injustice. And we *shall* overcome."

My tears flowed. Lyndon Johnson had reached into my soul and touched a part of me that no one had ever touched before. It was exhilarating, overwhelming, frightening. I joined in the applause, clapping till my arms were exhausted and my palms numb.

"Did you hear ol' Lyndon say 'We Shall Overcome'?" Spessard Holland said at breakfast the next morning in the Inner Sanctum. He sat at the long table with seven or eight other southerners. A cloud of gloom hung over them. "He's gone crazy with that nigger talk. You can't trust anything he says. One thing about Truman, you knew where he stood. When that haberdasher opened his mouth, he meant every damn word."

I'd never seen the southern senators looked so whipped. Their slow drawl sounded like a whine, and their depression was worse than when they had lost the cloture vote the previous year. Most were sad, but Strom Thurmond was angry.

"The president betrayed the southern cause and everything that's decent in this country." There was a bitter edge to his voice. "*He's* the one that needs to be overcome. He's let that nigger preacher get to his head. I believe the war has sent him off. It happened to Truman, you know."

James Eastland and John McClellan chimed in.

"I just can't understand why he's so involved in this voting rights bill," Eastland said. "He's creating some real problems trying to appease that nigger preacher. Why, Lyndon sees him more than us. We don't owe that nigger nothing."

"It's a disgrace for the President of the United States to be crawling to the niggers," McClellan said. *Disgrace* was one of McClellan's favorite words when it came to civil rights legislation.

Lister Hill turned to Richard Russell in disbelief. "Dick, tell me something. You trained that boy. You taught him everything he knows. What happened to that boy?"

Russell spoke for them all. "I just don't know, Lister." He shook his head. "I just don't know. If old Sam Houston were alive today, he'd go right down to the White House and spank his pants. That White House has done something to him. He's a turncoat if there ever was one!"

Black leaders, however, were deeply impressed with Lyndon Johnson's speech. "A moment at the summit of the life of our nation," Roy Wilkins called it.

"President Johnson," Dr. King said, "made one of the most eloquent, unequivocal, and passionate pleas for human rights ever made by a president of the United States. He revealed great and amazing understanding of the depth and dimension of the problem of racial injustice. [He was] disarmingly sincere."

To me, the week after Johnson's voting rights speech was the darkest I had ever seen in Washington. I could feel the hurt, anger, and hatred of the southern bloc in every corner of the Senate Dining Room. It was hatred born of humiliation. Lyndon Johnson of Texas had challenged and insulted the sovereignty of the southern states.

It was also hatred born of defeat, for sixty-five senators had cosponsored the voting rights bill introduced by Senator Mansfield on March 17, two days after Johnson's speech to the joint session. The bill was certain to pass and, when it did, it would smash white political supremacy in thousands of counties and small communities throughout the South, where as few as 2 percent of the blacks of voting age were registered. Senators like Holland, Hill, Thurmond, Eastland, and McClellan were convinced that, once registered, southern blacks would do what southern whites had been doing for decades—voting for color instead of ability. In their minds' eye, they saw black sheriffs, judges, county commissioners, and council members taking oaths of office all over the South.

The events during those seven days whirled by me in a blur: Wielding clubs and canes, sheriff's deputies in Montgomery gallop into six hundred demonstrators, injuring seventeen. . . . Federal Judge Frank Johnson finds the Selma-Montgomery march legal and orders Alabama to protect the marchers. . . . Angry and bitter, Wallace asks Johnson to send in U.S. marshals. . . . LBJ refuses, telling Wallace to use the Alabama National Guard. . . . Dr. King calls for the most massive march ever made on a state capitol. . . . Fearing more violence, President Johnson gives in, federalizes the Guard, and sends marshals and FBI agents to Montgomery. . . . Dr. King peacefully leads fifteen thousand blacks and whites into Montgomery, where twenty-five thousand more await him. . . . After the march, members of the Klan gun down Viola Liuzzo, a white woman.

I was standing on the steps of the old Alabama capitol next to Senators Eugene McCarthy of Minnesota and Fred Harris of Oklahoma when Dr. King walked into town. "We Shall Overcome" had never meant more to me than it did at that moment. My heart was bursting with pride, as it had during the March on Washington two years earlier. But unlike Washington, Montgomery made me feel sad for LBJ. By federalizing the Guard, Lyndon Johnson had committed high treason in the eyes of the segregationists. They would neither forget nor forgive. If blacks had paid a heavy price for their right to vote, so had their president.

Back on the Hill, Senators Mansfield and Dirksen threatened to cancel the Senate's Easter vacation if they didn't pass the voting rights bill within a month. The southern bloc didn't stand a chance. Its leader, Richard Russell, was in the hospital. So was Olin Johnston. Lister Hill and Harry Byrd were both nearly seventy-eight years old. It fell upon Allen Ellender to carry the Confederate flag.

Senator Ellender did not hide his racism under a bushel. I heard him say many times in the Inner Sanctum what he later said in public: "The voting rights bill violates the Magna Carta, the Declaration of Independence, the Constitution, and the Bill of Rights. . . . If it is enacted, you could have the governments of many towns and counties in the hands of incompetents. . . . I will talk against the bill as long as God gives me breath."

It was Jacob Javits and the Kennedy brothers, not God, who actually helped Ellender. The Twenty-fourth Amendment had outlawed poll taxes in all federal elections in 1964. But Texas, Virginia, Alabama, and Mississippi still had them in state and local elections, where their constitutionality had never been tested. Javits and Ted and Bobby Kennedy wanted those taxes outlawed in the voting rights bill. Uncertain of the constitutionality of such a ban, however, Mansfield, Dirksen, and Katzenbach didn't want to risk snarling up the voting rights bill in the courts after it was enacted. Although President Johnson supported banning the taxes, he deferred to his attorney general. To the delight of Senator Ellender, the poll tax issue tied up the bill for nearly two months. He didn't have to lead a filibuster.

I saw through the Kennedys. By introducing an amendment to ban the poll taxes, they had grabbed headlines and appeared to be strong civil rights advocates. If their amendment passed, they were heroes. If it failed, they were courageous. Either way, Lyndon Johnson would lose, for his administration fought against it.

After the poll tax amendment was defeated in a very close vote (49 to 45), Mansfield, Dirksen, and Katzenbach worked out a compromise, which Dr. King approved: as soon as the bill passed, the attorney general would have to ask the Supreme Court to rule on the constitutionality of state and local poll taxes. After the Senate adopted the compromise amendment on May 19, Mansfield called for a vote to end debate. For the second time in a row, the Senate voted cloture on a civil rights bill, 70 to 30.

When the Senate passed the final version of the voting rights bill on August 4, 1965, less than five months after he had sent it to Congress, President Johnson couldn't wait. He announced that he would sign the bill the very next day, and he rushed to the Hill to congratulate Mansfield and Dirksen. I hadn't seen LBJ so happy and relaxed in months. He pumped Mansfield's hand, grabbing him at the elbow with his left hand. He slapped him on the back. He bear-hugged him. Then he joined Dirksen in conference room S–207, where I had set up a bar.

The historic signing on August 5, 1965, was another LBJ gala. He chose the Capitol rather than the White House for the enactment, the first president to do so since Herbert Hoover, thirty-two years earlier. He chose to speak to the nation from the Rotunda rather than from the Rose Garden. And instead of the Oval Office, he chose to sign the bill in the President's Room in the Capitol, where Abraham Lincoln had signed a bill 103 years before, freeing slaves impressed into the service of the Confederacy.

Standing on the podium in the Rotunda next to a bust of Abe Lincoln and smiling for what seemed like minutes, Lyndon Johnson once again addressed the nation on voting rights. I stood next to Lincoln. LBJ compressed history and hope into three simple sentences:

"Today is a triumph for freedom as huge as any victory won on any battlefield.

"Today we strike away the last major shackle of those fierce and ancient bonds.

"Today the Negro story and the American story fuse and blend."

There were one hundred of us crammed into the ornate President's Room to witness the signing of the 1965 Voting Rights Act.

Sitting at the table at which President Lincoln had probably signed the Emancipation Proclamation and surrounded by baroque frescoes, gilt-framed mirrors, and madonnalike figures on the ceiling above him, President Johnson enacted the new law. He gave the first pen to Vice President Hubert Humphrey and the second to Senator Everett Dirksen, as the White House photographer clicked away. LBJ was so happy, I thought he might explode.

At the request of the White House, I had set up the hideaway of Minority Leader Tom Kuchel for a private reception for the president and key members of Congress. Immediately after the signing, I started to leave the President's Room so I could open the bar. Johnson called me back.

"Robert!" he bellowed. "Come here and stand at the head of this line. I want to give you something your grandchildren will like."

People began gathering around Johnson like flies to honey. He shoved me in front of him for a final photograph.

Thoughts raced through my mind as I smiled for the White House camera. I remembered long evening hours as a boy talking by the fire with my granduncle, Allen Parker, about his life as a slave. He had spent thirty-seven years in bondage, and when he died in 1935 at the age of 108, his chains were long gone. But he had never enjoyed full citizenship during his seventy-one years of freedom. I wished he could have been there, standing next to me and Lyndon Johnson.

Waiting for the president in Kuchel's hideaway were House and Senate leaders. Missing were many of the southern senators like James Eastland, Lister Hill, Strom Thurmond, and John McClellan, who had boycotted the signing ceremony. A few, like Senator Ellender, had come.

Johnson bounded into the room, walked over to a table, and pounded his fist on it. He surprised everyone present. His words, directed at the southerners who had opposed the voting rights bill, are branded on my memory:

"I know y'all opposed this piece of legislation I just signed. But let me tell you one goddamned thing. I want y'all to be proud to be part of this administration that just freed the niggers. One hundred and three years ago, Abraham Lincoln signed the Emancipation Proclamation. And if you check back in history, you'll see that Lincoln signed the bill because he thought the niggers would go back to Africa. Well, this piece of legislation *really* freed the niggers.

"Old Jim Eastland's been calling me all week about this goddamned bill, asking me how come I'm so hung up on voting rights. I told him, 'Jim, I don't know what the hell you're worried about. It'll take sixteen years to register enough niggers in Mississippi to defeat you. And by that time, you'll be too damn old to run again.'

"Then Jim told me that his niggers don't want to vote—that they were all satisfied—that the communists were coming down there stirring 'um up. He said that his foreman called him the other day and told him there wasn't a nigger in sight in the cotton fields. They were all downtown trying to register, and he didn't have nobody to pick his cotton."

Throughout his speech, Johnson continued to pound the table. His face grew as red as east Texas clay. Then, when he finished lashing his opponents, he rejoined their ranks.

"Now I want to tell you something else," he concluded. "If I were still the senator from the great state of Texas, I would have voted against this goddamn bill, too."

With that, he crashed his fist on the table for the last time. It shook as if it, too, were in awe of LBJ and his passion. It had been quite an hour and a half. President Johnson had spoken eloquently about freedom, hope, and equality. With great dignity, shrouded in history, he had signed the most important piece of civil rights legislation in over a hundred years. And in earthy language, Lyndon Johnson had spoken to his fellow southerners, congratulating those who had had the courage to back his bill while showing empathy for those who hadn't. It was some show. No wonder the southern senators were never sure what to believe about "ol' Lyndon."

Before Johnson returned to the White House, a congressman pulled him to the side, near the bar. "Mr. President," I heard him say, "I'm sorry Mr. Ford wasn't there for the signing, especially since he supported the bill all the way."

Gerald Ford and Lyndon Johnson had been at odds over the war in Vietnam for some time. When Ford, the House minority leader, leaked a story to the press that embarrassed Johnson, LBJ had quipped, "I don't know how the hell Mr. Ford could be giving out information. Hell, he can't even chew gum and walk at the same time." The remark hurt and embarrassed Ford as much as it was intended to.

Johnson didn't seem upset that Ford had boycotted his ceremony. "Hell," Johnson told the congressman, "Ford couldn't find the rotunda anyway."

After a few hugs and slaps on the back, Lyndon Johnson left for the White House. On his way out, he winked at me as if to say, "I just bullshitted the whole world and I got what I want."

Two weeks later, I found a large brown envelope on my desk. I opened it quickly. Inside was a copy of the picture taken after the signing of the voting rights bill, and attached to it was a note saying, "Robert, I want you to have something to show your grandchildren—Lyndon Johnson."

Long after the blood had dried on the Alabama streets, an important Alabama mayor came to visit Senator John Sparkman. The senator brought his constituent to lunch and introduced him to me, as he and most senators did with their guests. Before Sparkman could finish his lunch, the bell rang for a Senate vote. On the way to the floor, Sparkman stopped by my desk.

"Robert, I'm sure I won't get back before the mayor finishes," he said. "Will you sign my name to the check and put the appropriate tip on it?"

Sparkman then leaned over to me so no one could hear. "The mayor is staying in a hotel downtown. Would you get him a cab? And the mayor would like to have a girl for the night. He prefers a colored girl. Can you fix him up?"

"Senator, I don't know any colored girls down here," I said. I was insulted. "But I'll get him a cab."

Sparkman smiled and left. He always smiled when he was embarrassed.

I wasn't surprised at his request, for Sparkman himself liked black women, too. A waitress had approached me one day some time earlier. "Mr. Parker, I wish you would say something to Senator Sparkman about touching me," she complained.

Senator Sparkman's table (number 14) was in her section. I had trained all my waitresses to stand next to the senators when taking their orders. Every time she took Sparkman's, he would rub his hand up and down her leg or stroke her bottom. No one could see him because he kept his hand hidden under the tablecloth. The waitress resented it.

"I'll tell you how to handle this one yourself," I said. "If he touches you again, you look him straight in the face and say, 'Senator, the next time you touch me, it will cost you five hundred dollars!' "

Shortly after I gave her that advice, Senator Sparkman was once again up to his old tricks. The waitress looked him in the eye and gave him the message.

"I can't afford that," Sparkman said.

"Well, you can't afford to lose your hand, either," she said, "because I'm going to bite it off right here in the dining room if you ever touch me again."

Senator Sparkman smiled and never bothered her again.

I told the Alabama mayor that, when he was ready to leave, I'd order a cab.

"In about ten minutes," he said.

I went over to the cabstand near the east steps of the Capitol and talked to the first driver in line. He was black.

"In a few minutes I'll have a very important passenger for you," I told him. "He's a mayor from Alabama. He wants to go to his hotel." Then I grinned and added, "Can you believe he asked me to get him a black girl?"

The cab driver laughed. "You bring that bastard out here," he said. "I got *just* the black bitch for him."

I walked the mayor to the front door and watched him drive off in the cab. Then I went back to work, thinking nothing else about it. Two mornings later I picked up *The Washington Post* at my front door as usual. Over coffee, toast, and jelly, I scanned the front page, then turned to the inside of the paper. A headline caught my eye: ALABAMA MAYOR ROLLED. The story under it described how the mayor had awakened the morning after I put him in the cab, only to find his wallet, pants, underwear, all of his clothes, even his eyeglasses, stolen.

That cab driver sure did have "just the right bitch for him." She had cleaned him out and gotten him into the newspaper—the last place he wanted to be—without getting caught.

193

As funny as the story was, I couldn't laugh. "There goes my job!" I thought. I was uptight all that day. I told my secretary, Judy, to take all calls, that I didn't want to talk to anyone. Out of the corner of my eye, I kept looking for Senator Sparkman, but I didn't see him. A few days after the mayor had been rolled and ridiculed, I bumped into Sparkman in the Senate Dining Room. He didn't say a word about his friend.

Then I laughed. I laughed so hard the tears came to my eyes.

CHAPTER

24

The Civil Rights Act of 1964 and the Voting Rights Act of
1965 had little impact on the Hill itself. When I became
maître d' of the Senate Dining Room in 1963, all restaurant
contracts were going to white firms. Then, in 1966, in an attempt
to give blacks a slice of the federal pie, Senator Javits and Governor
Nelson Rockefeller brought Jackie Robinson, the black who broke
the color bar in organized baseball, to the Hill. With a spray of
white now in his hair, Robinson was at that time a distinguished
executive for Chock Full O'Nuts. Typical of the warped thinking of
politicians, Javits and Rockefeller believed that if they got Robinson
a Senate Dining Room contract, they would be helping blacks. It
never dawned on them that they'd only be granting Robinson a
personal favor while enriching Chock Full O'Nuts, a white-owned
and -managed company. For my part, I was pleased to meet my old
high school idol once again.

The first time Robinson had come to the Hill was in the fall of
1946. He had played the season for the Montreal Royals, a Brooklyn Dodgers' farm club. Branch Rickey, part owner and manager of
the Dodgers, had hand-picked Robinson to make baseball history.
Jackie was playing in the Negro League for the Kansas City Mon-
archs at the time.

"I'm looking for a great colored ballplayer," Rickey had told
him, "but I need more than a great player. I need a man who will
accept insults, take abuse, in a word, carry the flag for his race. I
want a man who has the courage not to fight back."

"If you want to take this gamble," Robinson had told him, "I
promise you there'll be no incidents."

Rickey had hinted all during the 1946 season that he was thinking of signing Robinson up to play for the Dodgers during the next
year. Southern senators were in a dither because major-league ball-

players from their states were complaining. They wouldn't sit in a dugout with a "nigger," they told their lawmakers, no matter how good he was on the field or at home plate. The senators, in turn, began leaning on baseball commissioner Happy Chandler, a former senator from Kentucky, hoping he would order Rickey to hold Robinson in Montreal. Baseball was an all-American sport, the senators argued; it would no longer be American if Negroes broke into the majors.

I'm not sure whether it was Chandler's or Rickey's idea to bring Robinson to the Hill, but they both came with Jackie in tow. Representative Lyndon Johnson had sprung me from the post office to set up and serve an informal cocktail party in a Senate conference room to which Robinson was invited. I was just as excited in 1946, before Robinson had become a legend, as I was twenty years later to meet the great athlete; I had followed his career with passionate interest.

Besides a dozen senators, including Johnson, Bilbo, Johnston, McClellan, and Russell, there were several owners who were opposed to integrating baseball in the room. I remember that Clark Griffith of the Washington Senators and Connie Mack of the Philadelphia Athletics had been especially angry at Rickey for signing Robinson up in the minors, and they were bitter about talk of bringing him into the majors.

The purpose of the party, which never made the press or the history books, was to show the southern senators that Robinson was a bright, articulate man whose command of English was better than theirs. Before Jackie joined the party, I heard several senators venting their feelings. "How can Rickey bring in a nigger? Niggers can't play. They can run but can't hit. They're not smart enough to hit. If we let niggers play, they'll kill baseball. No self-respecting white will go to the ballpark."

Rickey defended Robinson. "He's a very intelligent man," he said, "one of the smartest baseball players I ever met."

When Robinson walked into the room, the nasty talk stopped. He spoke to everyone Rickey or Chandler introduced but accomplished little. No matter how articulate he was in his rapid-fire, high-pitched voice without even a trace of dialect, and no matter how outstanding his record had been the previous season in Montreal, he couldn't convince the bigots that he knew left field from

196

right. In spite of the obvious hostility, however, Robinson kept his promise and remained a perfect gentleman all evening. The following spring, 1947, Rickey signed him up. Robinson and the Dodgers made history.

Now, almost twenty years later, I seated Robinson, Javits, and Rockefeller in the Senate Dining Room. It was one of those moments when I stopped thinking about how far blacks still had to walk to achieve equality and began pondering how far we had come in twenty years. In 1946, the senators had barely tolerated Robinson's shadow on the Capitol's white marble. Now the first black maître d' of the Senate Dining Room was leading him to a table, the guest of a senator and a governor.

After lunch, Robinson and I chatted. "I came here once before," he told me, "back in the 1940s."

"I know," I said. "I served the cocktail party."

We both laughed at how Rickey had had to bring him to the hill to prove that he didn't drool at the mouth. It was a bittersweet laugh.

Robinson got a large coffee contract for his company; Javits and Rockefeller beamed. But a year later, when no one was looking, procurement officer Dan Gary returned the contract to the company that had previously held it for years. There was no competitive bidding, as Senate regulations required. I figured the contract was rigged, but my hands were too full of other problems to worry about kickbacks.

White Senate staff persons were doing everything they could to discriminate against my restaurant workers. Legislative aides, with their college degrees, and secretaries, with their shorthand and typing skills, looked down on waiters and waitresses. That my staff was almost entirely black compounded the problem. I became determined to force the Senate staff to integrate their other activities, such as the credit union and the Senate Staff Club, in much the same way that I had broken the Jim Crow tradition in the Senate staff dining room. As an old high school running back, I knew the best offense was to attack an opponent's strength. I selected the Senate Staff Club as my target. Dan Gary was president.

The Senate Staff Club threw a party every Friday night in the cafeteria of the new Senate office building, the Dirksen Building. There was free beer and food and dancing to live music. None of the Senate Dining Room waiters or waitresses had ever tried to attend. Knowing full well that they were not welcome, they saw no point in stirring up the bigots on the Hill. I agreed with their silence at first, but the more I watched how the Hill operated, the more apparent it became that no one would ever volunteer to make my staff equal. We'd have to fight together for our rights.

I asked five attractive, adventurous waitresses who had complained about being excluded from the Senate Staff Club, if they would be willing to crash the color bar. It wasn't exactly major league baseball, but it was real, and it was close to home. They agreed. Among them were Eloise Washington, Vividell Holmes, and Mary Clark, all of whom still work in the Senate Dining Room. I told them that if they fought for their rights at the door, I would defend those same rights before the Rules Committee.

Dressed in their weekend finery, the five women walked into the Dirksen cafeteria the following Friday night. A Senate staff person at the ID desk turned them away. "Sorry," she said with ice in her voice, "you're not members."

The women gave her five dollars each, the price of club membership. "Sorry," she said, "but you're not Senate staff."

Leaving in dignity and without a fuss, the waitresses reported back to me Monday morning. I immediately made an appointment to see Senator Jordan. "Can you tell me how restaurant employees are classified?" I asked. I was purposely vague.

"Why, hired help, Robert," he drawled, puzzled by the question.

"Not Senate staff?" I asked innocently.

"Yes, Robert, yes. Senate staff." Jordan didn't suspect where I was leading him.

"Does that mean they can join the credit union?"

"Certainly, Robert!"

"And the Senate Staff Club?"

"Of course, Robert!"

"Could you write a letter saying that and address it to Joe Diamond?" I asked.

"Certainly, Robert," Jordan said.

Later, Joe Diamond, manager of the Senate restaurants, showed me Jordan's letter, which stated that from that day on restaurant workers were officially Senate staff personnel. Diamond thought little of the matter, for he didn't realize that I intended to use the letter to integrate the club. The following Friday night, the same five waitresses went to the Senate Staff Club party. The woman who checked IDs had to let them join the club and drink the free beer. We had won.

Diamond's and Gary's reaction was typical. Trying to hide their anger and resentment, they asked, "Why did you go to Senator Jordan? Why didn't you come to us? We would have taken care of it."

Not only was I pleased that I had helped crash another race barrier on the Hill, but I was delighted that I had done it in the Dirksen Building, which had become for me a symbol of discrimination. The Architect of the Capitol had designed another Senate Dining Room there, which served only lunch. The three new white waitresses who worked the Dirksen restaurant made more money in four hours than my staff, many of whom had years of seniority, did in eight. I sensed that the Architect of the Capitol in general and Gary in particular were trying to shut me down.

Competition between the two dining rooms was fierce. The new one was bright and cheery. There were no roaches or mice, no tattered drapes or worn carpets; but neither was there atmosphere or tradition. I suspect I would have lost the battle for survival if it hadn't been for the wives of the senators who supported the changes I had already made and who wanted to see the historic Senate Dining Room returned to the elegance it had once had. They continued to come there for lunch with friends and family. They encouraged their husbands to eat there as well. And they kept hammering at a theme as true as the Constitution: constituents like to brag back home that they ate in the Senate Dining Room in the Capitol, where presidents had lunched, rather than in the Dirksen Building, which looked so much like the other marble boxes dotting the Hill and Constitution Avenue. We survived.

It took a stroke of unfortunate luck and some Johnson-like manipulation to get the Senate Dining Room actually renovated. One of the waitresses whom I had hired was Mildred Smith, a responsible hard worker who always looked as if she needed a good meal. She was sick, but I didn't know it. Back in the days before I won full-time status for the staff, medical examinations for restaurant workers were neither provided nor demanded.

One of my jobs as maître d' was to organize the Inauguration

Day lunch in the Capitol for the president and his party. Every four years, the president-elect, his wife, and his very close friends would gather in EF–100, which was right under the inauguration stand. In the large, elegant room, filled with couches, comfortable chairs, and a long mahogany table, I would serve hot toddies and brandy as well as tea and coffee before and after the inaugural address. The Senate Dining Room kitchen would prepare lunch for about sixty, and my staff would serve it in S–207 after the president's speech on the Capitol steps and before the parade down Pennsylvania Avenue to the White House. Eating with the president and vice president and their families were the Speaker of the House, the majority leader of the Senate, the chief justice of the Supreme Court, who had just sworn in the president, and the ministers who had given the invocations. I selected the menu.

President Richard Nixon was sworn in on January 20, 1969. For his inauguration lunch, I ordered hot beef bouillon, fresh green salad, beef tenderloin roast with wild rice and carrots julienne, and peach cobbler. With President Nixon and his family were, among others, Vice President Spiro Agnew, John and Martha Mitchell, Maurice Stans, and Charles Colson of Watergate fame. I assigned six waiters and three waitresses to serve them. It was a tense time for us because the president's schedule was extremely tight, and we had to seat and serve everyone in an hour. Mildred Smith was one of the waitresses.

Two months after the inaugural lunch, Mildred took deathly ill. She was popular on the Hill, and during her first week at George Washington University Hospital, members of the staff and I visited her every day. One evening, the floor nurse refused to admit us. Mildred Smith has been moved, she told us. She was in the isolation ward. I was both curious and concerned, but I couldn't find out why the hospital had quarantined her.

Soon after her isolation, the hospital released her so she could recuperate at home in North Carolina. Two weeks later, she was dead. A group of dining room staff, including me, drove down to her funeral. Less than two weeks after that, health inspectors from the U.S. Navy paid us a visit. It was the first time since I had joined the restaurant as headwaiter seven years before that I had seen an inspector.

Reporters got wind of the story almost as fast as the dining room staff did. If they hadn't, I would have given it to them. What the press hadn't learned, however, was that Mildred Smith had served every important person at the White House, including President Nixon, during the inauguration lunch. *I* leaked *that* tasty morsel.

The result was stunning. Instead of health reports to the Rules Committee, there was instant lightning from the White House. It may not have been a consolation to Mildred's family, but she hadn't died in vain. Hill bureaucrats moved as fast as our dining room roaches. In a few hours, Mildred Smith had accomplished what I had failed to do in six years.

The Senate Dining Room got a facelift. New floors, rugs, and drapes. Health inspectors tossed out all the old silverware and dishes and junked the antique dishwasher. Every hole was plugged. Every inch of the dining rooms, kitchens, and storage areas was fumigated and painted. The staff got free physicals.

We were almost there.

25

I never would have accomplished what I did in the Senate Dining Room without the support of the senators' wives. Influential southerners like Elizabeth Eastland, Betty Talmadge, Eula McClellan, Katherine Jordan, Margaret Ervin, and Pauline Gore helped me improve the service, menu, and physical appearance of the place. The more liberal wives, like LaDonna Harris, Martha Hartke, Muriel Humphrey, Virginia Tydings, and Marvella Bayh, encouraged me to integrate and to improve staff working conditions.

I continued to serve the parties of some of these wives as a personal favor. I especially enjoyed planning and serving for LaDonna Harris, the outgoing and vivacious wife of Fred Harris of Oklahoma. Mrs. Harris and I had something in common. She was a full-blooded Indian, while I was part-blooded. We became such good friends that whenever she had been out of Washington for a long time, she'd bounce into the Senate Dining Room wearing a beautiful smile and give me a big hug and kiss. She didn't care what people thought. I remember the reaction of one Senate staff person in particular. When he saw her with her arms around me, he pushed away from the table, left his lunch on his plate, and stomped out of the dining room. I heard him mutter, "What a goddamn shame!"

Mrs. Harris threw parties regularly, because she did a lot of lobbying and fund-raising for Native American causes. She frequently entertained diplomats and heads of state and, like all the Senate wives, was concerned about protocol. I would advise her who should sit next to whom. More than the other wives, Mrs. Harris was concerned about serving something different. She was always asking me, "Robert, what did Mrs. So-and-So have for dinner last night?"

I would tell her. That was part of the game. When a hostess warned me not to leak what she served for dinner, I took it as a cue to make sure that her menu was the topic of conversation among "the girls," as Senate wives called themselves, in the Senate Dining Room the next day.

I remember one special dinner party Mrs. Harris gave for an impressive list of guests. After it was over, she told me with mischief in her black eyes, "Robert, just think! By noon tomorrow everybody in the Senate will know I served black bean soup, Buffalo Wellington, spinach soufflé, California salad, and baked Alaska."

"Exactly right," I laughed.

I'll never forget the backyard party I served for Dorothy Gruening, the wife of Senator Ernest Gruening of Alaska. Elderly and charming, but nervous, she tended to be forgetful. One day, Vividell Holmes and I were preparing a special First Lady Lunch sponsored by the senators' wives in the Senate Caucus Room (318) in the Richard Russell Building. "Oh, Robert!" Mrs. Gruening bubbled. "I'm so happy to see you brought Shirley Chisholm to help serve today."

Vividell and I laughed until we cried. Vividell looked nothing like the congresswoman from New York. I still can't believe the naïveté of the otherwise educated Mrs. Gruening. Not only did all blacks look alike, she actually believed that a black congresswoman would leave legislation piled up on her desk for the privilege of serving salad to the First Lady. As word of the gaffe spread during the luncheon, even the wives of the southern senators tittered.

The guest of honor at the Gruenings' backyard party was Senator Joseph Tydings, who, as a Marylander, was proud of Chesapeake Bay seafood. Senator Gruening had bragged to Tydings that bay fish tasted like wet newspaper compared to Alaska freshwater fish. To prove his point, Gruening had 150 pan-ready perch flown in from Juneau for the party. Mrs. Gruening planned to prepare them herself, Alaska style.

While I was mixing drinks in the backyard for the handful of guests who had arrived early, Mrs. Gruening whispered to me almost in tears, "Robert, I forgot the fish. They're still *frozen!* Senator Gruening will be so mad."

Not sure how to defrost and cook fish in an hour and a half

without destroying their delicate flavor, I was willing to try anything. I seasoned the frozen perch as best I could with lemon and
spices. After wrapping them first in tinfoil, then in towels, I placed
them in the empty dishwasher. With my fingers crossed, I turned
on the machine. The idea was to defrost the fish slowly, allowing
the spices to seep in. Then I would help Mrs. Gruening cook them.

When I unwrapped the perch after a half-hour wash, I was
surprised. They were cooked straight through and tasted delicious.
While the guests were still sipping before-dinner cocktails, I gar-
nished fish platters with fresh parsley and lemon wedges and served
the perch as an appetizer.

"The fish are wonderful," guests kept telling Mrs. Gruening.
"How did you prepare them?"

"My secret recipe." Mrs. Gruening beamed.

Naturally, I told the fish story in the Senate Dining Room the
next day. Years later, I heard senators and their wives telling friends
how they had discovered the most unique way to prepare fish: spice
them while still frozen, put them in the dishwasher for a half-hour,
then serve.

Martha Hartke, wife of Vance Hartke of Indiana, was another
Senate wife who liked to entertain. The problem was, she couldn't
cook for big parties. One night, she asked me to serve a party for
fifty. A simple buffet dinner, she said, with steak, baked potatoes,
tossed salad, and corn pudding. When I arrived at her home, the
steaks were already marinating in garlic and butter. She told me she
wanted dinner served promptly at eight-thirty. It was my first party
with her, and I wasn't sure what to expect. Each wife entertains in
a different style.

At six-thirty, Mrs. Hartke rushed into the kitchen while I was
preparing the salad, which I intended to chill before serving.
"Robert!" she said, nearly panicking. "You should have the steaks
on!"

"Mrs. Hartke, it's much too early," I said. I hadn't even lighted
the charcoal yet. "They won't take more than fifteen or twenty minutes. If I put them on too early, they'll turn tough and dry."

"I'll do them myself," she insisted.

That was fine by me. Mrs. Hartke lighted the charcoal grills
and laid out all fifty inch-thick New York strip steaks. Busy with

her guests, she soon forgot about them. So did I. Long before eight-thirty, they were charcoal black.

Mace Brodie, an administrative assistant to the Senate, was a Hartke guest that evening. "Bob," he whispered to me, "I don't know if anyone warned you, but I've never seen Martha make anything without overcooking it."

"Wrong, Mace," I told him. "Martha didn't overcook her steaks. She burned them to a crisp."

Brodie fished two hundred dollars from his wallet and asked me to run out and buy fifty fresh steaks. I served the buffet on time. Only Brodie, I, and Martha's garbage knew the difference.

I especially enjoyed watching the wives of the southern senators. They mirrored the racial attitudes of the Deep South caught in the currents of change. Elizabeth Eastland stood at one extreme, and Nancy Thurmond was at the other.

Like her husband, Mrs. Eastland treated the Senate Dining Room as another Mississippi plantation. She was as sweet about it as he was nasty. She called me one day. "Robert, I have a request," she drawled. "I know *you* will understand it. I'm bringing some of my close friends from Mississippi to lunch next week. I want a good southern menu."

I suggested southern fried chicken smothered in gravy, hash browns, Papa Hill's cornbread, and squash in brown sauce. She approved.

"And, Robert," she said, almost as an afterthought, "I don't want those girls serving us. I want the biggest, blackest waiter you can find. I want him to wear a tuxedo."

I bit my lip to keep from laughing. "How big and how black?" I asked.

"Oh, Robert, you know what I mean. One who's nice and polite."

Indeed I did. A *Gone with the Wind* special.

One of the waiters who worked the Inner Sanctum was as tall as a basketball player and as black as ink—straight from central casting. The only thing he couldn't do was tap-dance. I asked him if he minded putting on a show for Mrs. Eastland. He said he would be delighted. We pitied that old lady, who still saw the world as 1920 Mississippi and who was unaware she was the joke *du jour* of the Senate Dining Room.

I sat Mrs. Eastland and her party of elderly women at a large round table. With a big, black waiter in bow tie and tails, the Mississippi lunch was a great success. The staff enjoyed themselves, and so did Mrs. Eastland. To show her appreciation, she tipped extremely well.

"Robert, I want to thank you so much," she told me in her southern voice, as sweet as a magnolia blossom. "That was just the kind of waiter I wanted. He was so polite and smiled all the time. My guests felt right at home. They really enjoyed him."

Nancy Thurmond, a former Miss South Carolina and the wife of Strom Thurmond, was as young and openminded as Mrs. Eastland was old and closeminded. She ate in the Senate Dining Room regularly and the waitresses loved her. Beautiful and friendly, she was a celebrity in her own right. I detected no racial cynicism behind her radiant smile.

Once she became pregnant, Mrs. Thurmond stopped coming for lunch. We all missed her. Then one noon she returned with a new daughter in her arms. My waitresses kept pestering her to see the baby. Finally, she gave the infant to one to show the rest of the staff. Just at that moment, Strom Thurmond strode into the Senate Dining Room.

"Nancy, where's the baby?" he asked as soon as he sat down.

"The girls have her."

"What girls?"

"The ones who work here."

Senator Thurmond's face became red and blotchy. "You go get my baby from those niggers," he exploded. "I don't want those niggers showin' my chile around."

After the senator left to cast a floor vote, one of my waitresses told Mrs. Thurmond how hurt she felt at her husband's remark, which she had overheard. Nancy got up and put her arms around the woman. "Oh, honey," she said, "why, he didn't mean it the way it sounded."

Touched as I was by Mrs. Thurmond's gesture, I knew the senator meant exactly what he had said. Just a few years earlier, he had blistered Lyndon Johnson for nominating Thurgood Marshall to the Supreme Court. "How can the President of the United States send this illiterate man's name in to be confirmed to the highest court in the land!" I heard him tell his southern cronies.

206

I know Mrs. Thurmond tried to change her husband. And she succeeded to a degree. Several years after she had shown off her baby in the Senate Dining Room, Senator Thurmond brought four black men to lunch. I was shocked. It was the first time he had ever come into the dining room with a black. And here he was actually sitting at the same table with them.

Thurmond anxiously introduced me to his guests. Shortly after I seated them, the bell rang for a Senate vote. On his way to the floor, Thurmond stopped by my desk. "Robert," he said, "would you go over and tell those colored folk just how good I've been to you?"

"I certainly will, Senator," I promised. He was always polite to me.

I walked over to Thurmond's table smiling. "You know what? The senator asked me to tell you black folk how nice he's been to me," I said. "He treats me wonderful. But you niggers are lucky to be here!"

We had a good laugh at Strom Thurmond's expense.

The more I served the senators' wives, the closer I got to them. I soon recognized that being a Senate wife, glamour aside, was an impossible job. Many were lonely to the point of desperation, children and civic duties notwithstanding. I knew wives who hadn't talked to their husbands for days; others who hadn't seen their husbands in weeks; wives who played a poor second to a secretary; wives who were close to breakdowns; and others who drank out of sheer boredom. Hardly a day passed without a wife telling me at lunch, "Robert, I need a drink so badly!" I kept the storeroom well stocked precisely for such requests, for it is illegal to serve alcohol in the Senate Dining Room. Not that anyone ever bothered to check. I'd fix them a Bloody Mary or bring them Scotch or bourbon or brandy in a coffee cup. Many an early evening, I'd have to drive a senator's wife home in her own car while one of my staff followed in mine. I'd drop her off and park the car for her. My staff would take me back to the restaurant.

Most of the time I was caught between a senator, his wife, and his girlfriend. I knew which senators were sleeping with their secretaries, where they were when they sneaked out of town, and with whom they were lunching or dining while their wives were waiting in the Senate Dining Room or at home. I also knew how most of the wives felt, for they confided in me like a friend. They knew that if I wouldn't say what their husbands were doing in their hideaways, I wouldn't tattle on them either.

Much of what I saw was sad and cruel. A secretary would call me up in the Senate Dining Room and say, "Robert, don't tell anyone that the senator is having lunch in his hideaway today."

An hour later, the senator's wife would come for lunch. She'd sit in the reception room or at a table. She'd sip coffee or iced tea, glancing at her watch. Finally, she'd say, "Robert, would you get the senator off the floor and tell him I'm here?" I'd fake a call to the cloakroom. The wife would wait around until two-thirty, then order her lunch and eat alone.

One of the cruelest things I saw involved Ted and Joan Kennedy. Like his brother John Fitzgerald before him, Edward Kennedy was a playboy in the 1960s, and he didn't try to hide the fact. Joan heard about one pleasure trip he was planning and insisted on going with him. Overnight bag in hand, she arrived at the Senate Dining Room promptly at noon. After sitting around for half an hour, she asked me to call her husband's office and say she was waiting.

As I was about to place the call, I spotted Kennedy's top aide, Paul Kirk, in the hallway.

"Mrs. Kennedy's inside waiting for the senator," I told him. "Could you let him know?"

"Oh, my God, no!" Kirk said. "Hell, Robert, he left at eight-thirty this morning. I'll get the office to handle this."

I never did hear how Senator Kennedy bailed himself out. His office eventually sent a staff person to the restaurant to talk to Joan. I saw her leave the dining room around two-thirty, humiliated and close to tears.

Because I was friendly and sympathetic, several frustrated Senate wives flirted with me after a few drinks. One from the Midwest was especially lonely. It was sad to watch her try to cope. She called me up one day and asked me to help her plan a birthday party for her husband. She had invited fourteen VIPs, who presented a puzzling protocol problem. When I arrived at her house after the Senate Dining Room had closed for the day, I found her with a glass in her hand and feeling no pain. After settling on the menu and solving the seating arrangements, she was even more tipsy. She started to flirt.

I wasn't tempted. For one thing, I could never be sure whether she (or any other wife) was trying to entrap me. For another, I had learned never to mix women and work after I got stuck in the attic for three days with Betty sixteen years earlier. I took the invitations of Senate wives as compliments. They trusted me enough to be themselves in front of me. They knew I wouldn't tell anyone what they said or did. Neither would I take advantage of them. In a way, their flirting was more of a game than a serious offer.

I eventually encouraged the midwestern senator's wife to rest on the couch, and when she fell asleep, I left. I never slept with the wife of a senator, even though my bosses Joe Diamond and Louis Hurst would accuse me of doing so.

Not all Senate wives sought comfort in a bottle. Betty Talmadge, for example, coped with her husband's drinking and constant philandering by trying to look at the bright side of life. She loved to tell jokes. Almost every time she came to lunch, she'd buttonhole me at the busiest time to tell me her latest story. I remember the doctor joke the best. It seemed to me to be a commentary on her marriage:

One day a friend went to the doctor for her annual exam. Concerned about cancer because she was getting on in years, she asked him to check her breasts.

"They're fine," he said when he finished. "And as firm as a twenty-year-old's."

The woman drove home on a cloud, undressed, and stood in front of the mirror, admiring her body. Her husband walked in.

"What's going on?" he asked in surprise.

"I have wonderful news, dear," she said. "The doctor gave me a clean bill of health. And do you know what he said? I have the breasts of a twenty-year-old woman!"

"Well, that's great," her husband replied, "but what did he say about that big fat ass of yours?"

"Funny you should ask, dear," she answered sweetly. "He never mentioned a word about *you*!"

Mrs. Talmadge laughed so hard when she told me that story that I thought she would never be able to finish her lunch. It became one of our favorites. All she had to do was to say, "One day a friend went to the doctor," and we'd both start giggling.

I found it touching how Senate wives banded together for support. They called themselves the Red Cross Girls and met in the Red Cross Room (room 51, in the subbasement of the Richard Russell Building) each Tuesday the Senate was in session. There they sewed and knitted baby bibs and booties, scarves, gloves, and sweaters for the Red Cross. Ninety percent of the wives in town on Tuesdays attended. I rented china and silver for the occasion, for Senate wives couldn't stand the greasy-spoon tableware in the Senate Dining Room. My kitchen prepared their lunches, which they paid for and which my staff served.

Southern matriarchs like Elizabeth Eastland and Eula McClellan, wearing Red Cross uniforms and white caps, controlled the club. They reminded me of Confederate women making bandages for their husbands and sons fighting the abolitionist Yankees.

I enjoyed the weekly lunch as much as the Senate wives did. They joked with me, and I found the atmosphere in the Red Cross Room much more relaxed than in the Senate Dining Room. Lighthearted and at ease, the women laughed and gossiped. They were neither Democrats nor Republicans, just Senate wives bound together for at least six years by common ties.

Each year, on the last Tuesday of April, the Red Cross Girls exhibited their work at a First Lady luncheon. I'll never forget the one for Lady Bird Johnson in 1964, five months after the assassination of John F. Kennedy. I led a party of wives, including Elizabeth Eastland, Katherine Jordan, Nancy Cook, Marvella Bayh, and Ellyn Fong, to meet Mrs. Johnson at the street entrance. A Secret Service man had already checked the luncheon room, 318, in the Richard Russell Building and he was standing guard outside the door while the other Senate wives waited inside.

A White House limo pulled up to the curb with a white Secret Service man behind the wheel; a black one rode shotgun next to him. The black agent got out, opened the rear door, and reached in to help the First Lady step onto the sidewalk. Mrs. Eastland was standing near the limo as the senior representative of the wives.

"Move your hand," I heard the First Lady tell the Secret Service man. He pulled his arm out of the car and stood by like a soldier. I looked at his face. It was set in stone. Like husband, like wife, I thought. Lady Bird just needed to show Mrs. Eastland how southern she really was.

In February 1968, Vice President Humphrey asked me to prepare an informal dinner at his home in the Tiber Island Condominium. His guests were Nguyen Cao Ky, vice president of South Vietnam, and Ky's wife. Although I had served many Humphrey office parties on the Hill, I had never prepared dinner in his home.

"Well hello, Robert." Humphrey beamed at the door. He was in shirtsleeves and looked more relaxed than I had ever seen him. "Come on in. Come in, by golly!"

The vice president led me into the kitchen, tossed me an apron, and tied one around himself. "I love to cook," he said, chattering like a magpie. "But you know, I don't get much chance anymore. We're having filet mignon roast. Oh, by the way, I seasoned it and placed it on the rack, but I didn't put garlic on it. I don't care too much for garlic. And we'll have wild rice, green beans amandine, and tossed salad. Oh, Robert, I was hoping you'd whip up one of your delicious crème de menthe parfaits. Now, let me see if I can sell a few martinis."

Humphrey left the kitchen and returned a few minutes later with Ky, who had been meeting all day with Pentagon generals. After introducing the vice president to me, Humphrey mixed martinis and talked about Lyndon Johnson.

"When do you think he'll announce his bid for reelection?" Ky asked.

"Well," Humphrey said, "I had a conversation with the president the other day. He figures that this is just what Bobby Kennedy wants—a head-on confrontation. As the president sees it, in order for him to survive a fight with Kennedy, he's going to need ninety-eight percent of the black vote. He's sure he can't count on that. Since the voting rights bill, he's lost his hold on the South. And his problems with the war certainly don't help."

I continued dicing vegetables at the sink. I knew LBJ was right. He had lost the South. And even though he had pocketed 95 percent of the black vote in 1964 against Goldwater, who had trashed civil rights legislation, it was clear that, given a choice between Johnson and Kennedy in the Democratic primaries, most blacks would run to Kennedy.

"So you see," Humphrey continued, "a confrontation with Kennedy could mean defeat. And the president candidly told me that he would rather smother in horseshit than let any damn Kennedy beat him. So I asked him, 'Mr. President, don't you think blacks would support you after all you've done for them?' "

Humphrey handed Ky a martini and took a sip of his own. He described how a long, sad smile had spread over Johnson's face and how LBJ had said, "Hubie, after all these years, you still don't know a damn thing about niggers. What the hell does a nigger know about loyalty? You do him a favor today, and he forgets you next week!"

Johnson was right again, not about the loyalty of blacks but about that special Kennedy magic. I had talked with Clarence Mitchell about a Johnson-Kennedy showdown not long before Humphrey's dinner. "Well, Bob," Mitchell had said, "I believe the president would beat Bobby Kennedy at the convention."

I knew he wouldn't. I remembered how the delegates had gone wild in 1964 in Atlantic City when Bobby had just *walked* to the microphone to introduce a movie. That kind of emotion still existed. It might even have grown since then. Rightly or wrongly, fairly or unfairly, Lyndon Johnson had lost the black vote, and he was smart enough to realize it.

After he said "nigger," Humphrey realized that I was standing less than six feet away. "Isn't that right, Robert?" he asked me.

I turned. His face was red. "I'm sorry," I said, recognizing that Humphrey really didn't expect an answer, "but I didn't hear the question. Wouldn't you like me to serve a drink to the ladies?"

For days, I thought over the Humphrey-Johnson conversation and concluded that Lyndon Johnson would not run for a second term. I knew Johnson. He might risk defeat over the war in Vietnam, but he would never risk losing to a Kennedy. He couldn't live with that humiliation.

Two weeks after the Ky-Humphrey dinner, I was at a party hosted by Senator Frank Moss of Utah. After all the guests had left,

213

Senator Moss and I got into a light political conversation. "You know what, Senator?" I said. "I don't think my former boss is going to seek reelection."

Moss grinned. "Lyndon Johnson not going to run?" he said. "Oh yes, he will. This war is not going to make him quit. I've known him too long!"

"I'll bet you ten dollars he won't run," I challenged.

"You got a bet, Robert."

For the next couple of weeks, Senator Moss joked with me every time we met about Lyndon Johnson throwing in his political towel. Then, when Johnson announced on March 31 that he wouldn't seek reelection, Moss sought me out.

"Robert, I don't understand." He handed me a ten-dollar bill. "No one ever suspected that Lyndon Johnson wouldn't run. How in the world did you know that?"

I just smiled.

Moss reached into his pocket and handed me a five-hundred-dollar ticket to the Democratic National Fund Raising Dinner, to be held at the Washington Hilton Hotel on April 4, 1968. Looking back, I'm glad I decided to go.

It was a rather warm April evening. The Hilton ballroom was jammed with three thousand happy Democrats. I sat at a table filled with Senate staff. Vice President Humphrey was the keynote speaker; President Johnson was to make a cameo appearance. The bar was open, and it was almost dinnertime. Hubert Humphrey came to the mike and tried to get everyone's attention. I knew something was wrong, for he was scheduled to speak after dinner, not before.

"Ladies and gentlemen . . . ladies and gentlemen . . . please."

The crowd refused to quiet.

"Now, ladies . . . ladies and gentlemen, *please,* could I please have your attention!"

Humphrey wasn't wearing his happy Hubert smile that could melt ice at a hundred feet. The room finally hushed.

"We have just received news over the wire that Dr. King—Martin Luther King—has been shot in Memphis, and we think he's dead!"

The crowd gasped and began buzzing quietly as if it were in a funeral home. Humphrey left the podium but returned a few moments later.

"We have been informed that Dr. King is dead," he said. "Mrs. King has left Georgia for Memphis. We have also been informed that the president will not be joining us. The dinner has been canceled."

It was another of those moments in life that I'll never forget. Four or five hundred Democrats greeted the news of Dr. King's murder with undisguised pleasure. Some smiled. Some shook each other's hand. Some actually clapped. A few said "hurray." I heard comments like, "It's about time. I knew it would happen. It's been long in coming."

I thought of a New Year's Eve party. All we needed were streamers, horns, and funny hats. I was ready to vomit, but I shouldn't have been so shocked. Hatred for Dr. King had mounted on the Hill with each of his marches. In the beginning, he had stayed in the South, far away and safe in Montgomery, Atlanta, Selma, Birmingham. Then he had dared to come to Washington. If that weren't enough, he focused his power like a laser on Congress and got a voting rights bill. After that, he marched north to expose closet bigots. He humiliated the Hill by winning a Nobel Peace Prize. Even worse, he dared to use his popularity and eloquence to criticize the war in Vietnam. Even some black leaders began avoiding him when he did that. I remember Clarence Mitchell, who was talking to Senator Harry F. Byrd, Jr., of West Virginia one day, asking me to open S–120 so he could duck inside after he saw Dr. King walking down a hallway in the Capitol. Mitchell didn't want to be seen with King.

Vice President Humphrey urged the Democrats in the Hilton to return home immediately. He didn't have to say why. The nation had just lost one of its great leaders, and Washington blacks wouldn't be clapping and shouting "hurray."

While most of the partygoers scrambled to get out of the city, fearing for their lives, I drove into the ghetto. I was stunned. I was angry. And I felt like doing what hundreds of other blacks in the nation's capital were doing—venting my rage at the injustice of it all.

I drove down to Fourteenth and U streets, an area of seedy hotels, liquor stores, brothels, and bars. Fires were already burning, and looters were on the move. I drove down H Street in northeast

D.C., a strip of shops and stores just blocks from the Capitol. It looked like Dresden after the Allies had firebombed it. I heard gunshots in the distance. Smoke burned my eyes. Flashing blue and red lights from police cruisers cast strange shadows on faces peering out of doors and windows.

Fear, grief, and rage gripped the capital. I should have been frightened, too, but I wasn't. Pain left no room for fear.

What irony, I thought, as I drove out of the city to my home in Maryland. The apostle of nonviolence had died violently, and the city into which he had led the biggest peace march ever was on fire.

Most senators waited until the morning of Dr. King's funeral before flying down to Atlanta. It was like putting off a visit to the dentist and hoping to spend as little time in the chair as possible. The night before, Majority Leader Mike Mansfield had called President Johnson to ask if the group of some twenty senators and twenty congressmen, plus staffs, could fly down on an air force jet. "I don't give a damn," Johnson had said. "But I don't want all white folks. I don't want no riot down there."

The president had put Mansfield in a bind. Senator Edward Brooke was the only black member of the Senate at the time and, as it happened, he was also the only black legislator still in Washington; all the House blacks had left for Atlanta the night before. So Senator Mansfield asked me to go along. Not only did I want to attend the funeral, I was delighted to travel with the senators themselves. It didn't bother me at all that Mansfield was using me to add a little "color" to the U.S. Congress.

While all seventy-nine of us were climbing onto buses for Andrews Air Force Base shortly after seven on the morning of April 9, Washington was still smoldering. From the Capitol steps, I could see smoke billowing up along H Street. Parts of the city looked like wartime London after an air raid. Still armed with machine guns, the National Guard and federal troops had the Capitol cordoned off. The 7:00 P.M.-to-5:30 A.M. curfew was still in effect. Ten people lay dead, and 909 businesses and 283 houses had been destroyed. To the east, Baltimore was still in flames. Most of Washington had not gotten over the shock of a city gone wild.

I stood outside the bus watching the senators board. Their silence was born more of fear than of respect for Martin Luther King.

They were like soldiers about to go on a death-defying mission deep into enemy territory. "Where's Robert?" I heard someone say on the bus. "Where's Robert?" I would hear that question a lot before the day was over.

Senator Pete Williams stepped off the bus to get me, and as he began nudging me ahead of him, I heard Stan Kimitz bark, "Who do you think you are?"

Kimitz was Senator Mansfield's top aide and the one in charge of seating arrangements. I knew he was biting back the word "nigger," for he was one of the Hill staffers out to get me. "Wait until *all* the senators are on the bus. And what are you doing fraternizing with the senators anyway?"

On any other morning, I could have laughed at Kimitz's thinly disguised racism. But here we were boarding buses at the steps of the Capitol in a city partially burned to the ground because of bigotry, to pay homage to a man who had died preaching equality. And the undercurrent of racial prejudice was so strong, I could feel it tugging at the facade of congressional dignity. On the bus were many of the people who had applauded Dr. King's death at the Hilton. They had no business going to Atlanta, much less taking up precious seats in the Ebenezer Baptist Church, while his devoted followers, who had marched and suffered with King, had to stand outside in the hot sun.

"What hypocrisy," I thought. "And the taxpayers are footing the bill for the whole charade!"

When we landed at Dobbins Air Force Base, just outside Atlanta, buses hauled us to a drop-off point about one mile from the church where the services would begin around ten-thirty. We had been told to walk three abreast down a roped corridor through the fifty thousand people who had come to mourn outside the church. By way of courtesy, Senator Wayne Morse asked Senator Brooke to step off the bus first. It was his way of saying, "Ed, he's your fallen leader more than he's ours, so you've earned the right to be first." Morse and Phil Hart joined him, forming the first trio. Most of the others on the bus were pleased that Brooke got off first, too, but for another reason: They wanted that restless sea of blacks along the street to see that some of our group of important mourners from Washington were black just like them, so if they were going to riot, they should do it on another street.

I was the centerpiece of the fifth threesome, with Senator Williams on my left and Senator Charles Percy of Illinois on my right. Percy had insisted on walking with me, as if I were an African medicine man who would protect him from the angry mob of blacks he expected to find. On the way into Atlanta from Dobbins, he had told me how frightened he was, and he had asked me over and over again if I thought there would be a riot like the one in Washington. I had assured him that black people knew how to mourn their dead heroes and that he had absolutely nothing to worry about.

"Well, Robert, I'll tell you what," he had said. "I want to walk with you all day." And he stuck to me like flypaper. I was glad to oblige. Even though King had caused him a peck of problems when he had dared to walk into Cicero, Illinois, Percy was no bigot.

I jumped off the bus feeling as if I were in charge of this frightened group of white men. A woman in the crowd waved at me and shouted, "Hi, Senator Brooke! Hello, Senator Brooke!" I heard another lady cut her off. "That's not Senator Brooke. He's up yonder. That's Secretary Weaver."

I turned to Percy. "What should I do, Senator?"

"Well, Robert," he said, "it looks like you're going to be Secretary Weaver. You better wave, and wave high."

All during the walk to the church, I was Robert C. Weaver, secretary of the Department of Housing and Urban Development, and the first black in a presidential cabinet. Whenever anyone shouted "Weaver," I would smile and wave like the best of politicians. I must admit that I enjoyed the game immensely, even though I was attending a funeral. When I finally walked into the Ebenezer Baptist Church, I saw the real Secretary Weaver sitting up front next to Vice President Humphrey.

After the church service, we began the 4.3-mile walk to South View Cemetery. The cemetery had been created for Negroes because Atlantans who wouldn't sit next to a black weren't about to be buried next to one, either. I marched thirty to forty feet behind the cherrywood coffin resting on a farm wagon drawn by two Georgia mules. Percy and the other senators were even more frightened during the march than they had been during the brisk walk from the bus to the church. I tried to keep them calm. "Don't worry, Senator," I would say. "There won't be any rioting. Everything will be peaceful."

Atlanta had closed down for the day. Governor Lester Maddox would later call it blackmail, claiming that the city's businesses had received so many phone calls promising firebombs if they stayed open during the funeral that businessmen had had to lock their doors. There were no state or federal troops or city policemen in sight. Maddox had called them all to guard the gold-domed State Capitol, while two thousand National Guardsmen stood by at Dobbins Air Force Base, armed and ready to storm the city. It was almost as if Maddox were sending a message to the congressmen from Washington: "If there's going to be a riot, the crowd can have you white folks. We'll protect the State House."

The situation was tense, the police knew, because no one had been arrested yet for King's assassination, and there were no suspects. To most blacks, it looked like just another police cover-up. I thought how appropriate the song we were singing was: "If I had a hammer . . . I'd hammer out justice."

What justice? I felt certain that the white folks who killed King would get away with it. But I knew that no matter how jittery and angry Atlanta was, there would be no riot during Dr. King's funeral. I had no predictions for the day after, however.

The irony of the peace-loving Dr. King being pulled by mules surrounded by 150,000 to 200,000 people while Lester Maddox, the consummate racist, hid in the State Capitol surrounded by 160 helmeted riot police, was too much for the crowd. The scene raised the ghosts of Selma and Montgomery. The marchers took up King's chant as if he himself were leading it in his powerful baritone voice:

"What do you want?"

"Freedom!"

"When do you want it!"

"Now!"

"What do you want . . ."

During lulls in the singing, as we climbed Atlanta's hills in the eighty-degree heat, I could hear the squeak and groan of the wagon ahead of me and the clippity-clop of the mules on the street. I thought of my sister Robbie. I always think of Robbie when I hear wagons pulled by mules or horses. It's a sound that haunts me. Her life had been wasted. She had been a human sacrifice to a white man's desire.

I thought of my father and how deeply he still hurt from not having defended his daughter. How he had carried that burden for thirty-five years, and how the pain had never gone away. How no one—neither his children nor his friends—could get him to talk about the old days. He just grew as still as a cottonfield early in the morning, or else he got up and walked away.

I thought of how I had not and could not forgive him in my heart for saying "Yes, suh!" My refusal to forgive hurt him as much as what had been done to his daughter.

And I thought of Martin Luther King himself. To me it looked like another wasted death of yet another black man, for I had no inkling at that time of how powerful he would become in death. And as I walked behind the mules that were pulling his corpse covered with lilies and white carnations, I was not sure that he had accomplished anything, or that anything would ever change. I know it's almost heresy to say it, but that's the way I felt on that confusing and stirring spring day in 1968, and I suspect that millions of other blacks felt the same but can't admit it.

It was stifling in Atlanta that April afternoon (at least a hundred people would be overcome with heat exhaustion before the day was over), and none of us from Washington had eaten or drunk since seven that morning. The senators were wilting. I broke line and asked a white woman, who was standing at her fence watching the cortege march by, for a bottle of water. She fetched a large mayonnaise jar from her kitchen, and I filled it at the garden tap and after I drank passed it along to the senators. It was quite a sight— U.S. senators marching at a black man's funeral in the Deep South, surrounded by mostly black folks, drinking water—not martinis, mind you—from a mayonnaise jar, and happy to have that.

Senator Claiborne Pell, who was walking next to a little black lady, was the last one to get the jar. "I'd give anything for a drink of that water," I heard her tell him. He gave the bottle to her instead of drinking the last drop himself. Another irony on a day full of surprises.

The senators were still tense and nervous at King's gravesite, which was set on a grassy slope. And as soon as his coffin was lowered into the mausoleum of Georgia marble, they scampered onto the buses waiting to take us to the Officers' Club at Dobbins as quickly as seemed senatorial. There sandwiches were piled high, and it seemed to me that all the liquor bottles in the U.S. Air Force were lined up along the bar. What a sight. Never had I seen so many congressmen drink so much so fast. They were so happy to get out of that "nigger preacher's" funeral alive and to be safe in the bosom of the air force, where no lynch mob could get them, that, like mules back in the barn after a burning day, they nearly watered themselves to death.

"Come now, Robert!" Senator Percy said to me. We were sitting at a table in the club with six or seven senators. "Weren't you scared?"

"To be honest, Senator," I said, "I was. But not of blacks rioting. I was afraid that those ignorant whites lining the sidewalks would retaliate because so many of you important white folks came to Dr. King's funeral. That's the only thing I was worried about."

I kept my eye on Senator Williams, who had one of the worst drinking problems on the Hill back then; I fully expected that I'd have to drive him home after we landed in Washington, and put him to bed, as I had done so often in the past. When we got back to Washington, Stan Kimitz invited Senator Williams, his aide Joe Black, and me up to his office for a few nightcaps. After Kimitz locked up for the night, I did drive the senator to his home near the wharf, just off Maine Avenue, in his small Mercedes sports car, and I tucked him in.

So it was that I said good-bye to the greatest leader blacks have ever known. I began the day with racial insults. I continued it as a nursemaid to a bunch of frightened congressmen whom King, powerful even in death, had drawn to his graveside even though most of them wouldn't grant him an interview in his lifetime. And I ended it by putting one of them to bed in a stupor.

Once again I remembered LBJ's remark to those who were predicting that Dr. King would pass like a rainshower: "Ain't nothing in this world as powerful as a nigger preacher."

In the summer of 1970, not long after Mildred Smith died and the Senate Dining Room was renovated, H. Rap Brown, one of the most militant black activists of the civil rights movement, visited the Hill. Although I approved of his goals, I took exception to his methods, and I resented his attempt to stir up trouble in my backyard. At stake were seven years of progress that I had made by chipping away at indifference and racism.

H. Rap Brown and I wanted the same things for Senate Dining Room workers: better wages and full-time jobs with health benefits, annual leave, life insurance, civil service ratings, and retirement pensions. The problem, as I saw it, was that Brown was more interested in embarrassing the Senate than in helping my staff.

One afternoon several days after he had arrived on the Hill, Brown called a meeting of all Senate restaurant workers in the corridor outside the Rules Committee hearing room in the Richard Russell Building. I and most of my staff of 208 attended. Brown wanted the group to present a list of demands to the Rules Committee itself, but the committee's chief counsel, Hugh Alexander, wouldn't even talk to us, much less allow us inside the door. I wasn't surprised. Alexander had no love for me.

Brown used Alexander's refusal to negotiate as an excuse to call a strike for the following noon. It was another serious mistake. The strike would make the evening news, as Brown planned, but the workers who walked out would lose their jobs. Nothing would change, and I said so.

It was not easy to stand my ground against Rap Brown. I know that I must have sounded as if I were afraid to anger the senators who had gotten me my job and who liked me. But I remembered how Branch Rickey had told Jackie Robinson that he not only needed a good Negro ballplayer but one who could swallow insults without fighting back. That was the only way to integrate baseball.

For my part, I was convinced that the only way to win concessions for my staff was quietly, one step at a time. That afternoon in the Richard Russell Building with Rap Brown screaming "strike," I was concerned about the daily life as well as the civil rights of my staff of two hundred men and women whose faces and families I knew. I was unwilling to sacrifice them just to embarrass the Senate. Like Robinson, I was willing to swallow insults to get results.

Rap Brown was angry.

"Strike," he yelled at me.

"No," I said.

"It's the only way."

"Not here," I said. "It won't work."

"You're an Uncle Tom," Brown shouted.

"The hell with you," I said right back. "You're doing nothing but causing problems here."

Brown slugged me in the jaw. The Capitol Police grabbed him and led him out of the building and off the Capitol grounds. They eventually barred him from the Hill. I was angry and humiliated, and I felt totally misunderstood. Only years later did I recognize that Brown had been baiting me, hoping that I would strike him back so that we would make the front pages together. He would be the courageous civil rights activist and I the Uncle Tom.

When Senator James Allen of Alabama, who had replaced Robert Byrd of West Virginia as chairman of the subcommittee on restaurants, heard about the pending strike, he threatened to fire any waiter or waitress who honored it. Unlike Byrd, Allen was the worst kind of redneck. Insulated by a hand-picked staff cut from the same bolt of cloth as he, he was inexperienced and unapproachable. Since I had never served his parties, I did not know him personally as I had Byrd. When I wanted to offer a suggestion to improve the restaurant or to complain, I had to go through one of his staff. They cut me off at the pass. Therefore, I took Allen's threat seriously.

To make sure that opposing the strike was my best bet, I sought the advice of several influential senators. Ed Brooke of Massachusetts, who was committed to civil rights, told me, "Robert, don't strike. Allen will fire all of you. You can't fight a gun with a stick. Keep pounding on the Rules Committee just the way you are."

Walter Mondale, Birch Bayh, and Stuart Symington told me the same thing. Ted Kennedy said that Senate restaurant workers had always been treated like slaves. Theoretically, they should strike to make their point, he said, but they'd never win. Spoken like a true politician.

The next morning, I consulted my staff. I was against a strike, I told them. I had talked to several senators, and they all agreed. Those who strike will lose their jobs while gaining nothing for those who don't. If you want to walk out, I told them, I will not stand in your way. Neither will I support you.

To a person, the staff decided to work. Just before noon, about fifty of the 135 cafeteria workers from the Russell and Dirksen buildings picketed in the parking lot below the east Capitol steps. While the television cameras rolled, Senator Allen addressed them. "If you don't get back to work by two o'clock," he warned, "you'll all be fired."

The strike lasted two hours. The cafeteria workers went back to their tables, and no one got fired except Gerald Quinn, the black leader of the strike. Brown had totally miscalculated. He hadn't embarrassed Allen. The folks back in Alabama loved watching their senator stand up to a bunch of "uppity niggers." And with nothing to gain or lose, the other senators declined to interfere in Allen's little problem. A typical day on the Hill.

Rap Brown called a meeting for all four hundred Senate restaurant and cafeteria workers that evening in a union office building in northwest Washington. I hadn't planned on attending, but some of the more militant members of my staff urged me to join them. They wanted to see what Rap Brown had in mind next.

Brown wanted to form a union on the Hill. I sat in silence and listened to the passionate speeches promising the two hundred waiters and waitresses who attended that the Senate would be brought to its knees. I knew Brown could never do it. Not only wouldn't the Senate tolerate a union, but individual senators would find a way to retaliate. I had seen it happen often. Knowing that the spotlight would shine on them only for a few weeks, they would give an inch. As soon as the front line moved to other battlefields, they would take five inches back.

My staff urged me to speak up. I did. "I'm against a union," I said. "It won't work on the Hill. The Senate will never allow one. We'll gain nothing and lose everything."

Brown did not get a union in 1970. And today, even after repeated attempts to organize, there still isn't one.

A few days after Brown left Washington in defeat, CBS correspondent Roger Mudd asked me if any of the Senate dining rooms would remain open while the Senate was on recess during the next two weeks. I told him that all the restaurants would be closed, including the press dining room, by order of the Architect of the Capitol. Syndicated columnist Sarah McClendon overheard the conversation. The next day, her column quoted me as saying that while the senators were on vacation at the taxpayers' expense, the Senate Dining Room staff would be on leave without pay. She was right, of course, but I had never said it.

Bill Cochran, Senator Allen's staff director, called me. "Why the hell did you open your big mouth?" he yelled. I tried to explain that I had never made the statement.

"In the future keep your mouth shut," he warned.

I became more determined than ever to get what I wanted for my staff. It took two years, and I had to embarrass Allen to get action. Unlike Rap Brown, I used inside pressure. I knew that senators respond more easily to that. It was a lesson I had learned from Lyndon Johnson.

I wrote Allen a strong letter asking for full-time jobs for Senate Dining Room workers, and I told him why. "During the Thanksgiving and Christmas seasons and at a time when all of us are looking for extra money," I wrote, "our restaurant employees are either applying for welfare or are lined up at the credit union seeking personal loans. When they do take out these loans to cover their basic family needs of food, shelter and clothing, they must spread the payments over the following year, when the cycle is repeated again.

"More than two-thirds of our employees are self-supporting heads of households. This is no accident. These people are handpicked for their ability to handle responsibility.

"Some of the employees, unable to secure loans and unwilling to go on relief, search for other employment. These individuals have been specially trained at government expense to work in, what some consider to be, the most prestigious dining facilities in Washington. When these well-qualified individuals move on to more stable employment, the efficiency and effectiveness of our restaurant operation suffers.

"Aside from the personal hardship that our present policy imposes on these employees, there is a question of fairness involved. To my knowledge, the restaurant employees are the only workers on Capitol Hill to be singled out for this debilitating treatment. . . .

"Our Senate is held in high esteem the world over as an inspiration to those who believe in equal treatment and personal dignity under the law. I would not want, and I know you would not want, any appearance that would unnecessarily taint the integrity of the Senate."

I sent the letter to Allen in October 1972, one month before Congress was to adjourn and eleven years after I had first become headwaiter. It was my last shot. I made a hundred copies of the letter and placed them on a table during my morning restaurant meeting. "This is what I've done for you," I told my staff, hinting that I would be delighted if they passed out the copies to senators and their wives. The staff snapped them up while I sat back waiting for the fireworks. I didn't have to sit long.

The liberal crowd—Kennedy, Mondale, Morse, Brooke, Humphrey, McGovern—expressed shock that restaurant workers right under the Capitol dome were being forced onto the welfare rolls for part of the year. (I smiled, for the system was only a hundred years old.) They pressured Senator Allen. Before Congress adjourned, my staff got full-time jobs and eventually most of the benefits that go with steady work.

Allen himself didn't seem upset by my pressure tactic, but his staff sure was. Cochran tongue-lashed me over the phone as if he owned me. "Why did you embarrass the senator and the subcommittee like that?" he demanded.

"Look, Bill," I said. I took special pleasure in calling him by his first name, an experience young blacks today could never appreciate. "I didn't tell them to pass out those letters."

"Well, keep this call to your goddamn self," he said, somewhat appeased. "Don't tell anyone I chewed you out."

I won. I had the last laugh.

* * *

I certainly didn't spend all my time as maître d' fighting the Architect of the Capitol and the Rules Committee. Most of the time, I enjoyed my job and had a lot of fun doing it. The day I was elected 101st senator stands out in my mind.

Senator Talmadge and Kentucky Senator Marlow Cook got into a heated debate over lunch in the Inner Sanctum one day in the summer of 1967. The issue was vintage Hill: Which state produced better hams, Georgia or Kentucky?

"Well, Marlow," I heard Talmadge tell Cook, "ain't but one way to settle this argument, and that's for you to bring one of your little ol' Kentucky hams here, and for me to bring one of my good ol' Georgia hams. We'll get Robert to have them cooked and served. And we'll let our colleagues taste them."

With the pride of Kentucky at stake, Cook agreed. The contest was on. It came as no surprise to me when the simple test didn't turn out the way Talmadge had planned it. Parker's Law: If it's simple, the Hill will make it complicated.

Word spread through the Senate like news of a pay raise that Georgia and Kentucky were locked in a ham-tasting battle. Soon there were forty slabs of pork hanging in the kitchen, each labeled with a senator's name, his home state, and a note that generally read, "Robert, please enter me into the ham contest." The Washington press corps, eager for a summer event, picked up the story, and the wire services sent it around the world.

Talmadge's challenge turned out to be more than a ham contest. President Johnson had just redeemed a promise he had made to black leaders by appointing Thurgood Marshall to the Supreme Court, the first black to sit on the bench. Marshall was a good choice, for it was he who had argued and won *Brown* v. *The Board of Education* before the court, forcing public school desegregation ten years earlier. Marshall's appointment did not sit well with racists around the country, and for some, news of the ham judging must have been the last straw. I remember a letter from a woman in Pine Bluff, Arkansas, who had read about the ham contest in her local paper. "I was most surprised to see that our 'turncoat President' has now appointed a nigger in our Capitol to judge hams!" she wrote. "I doubt if you have ever heard of our ham here in Arkansas that is called razorback." She ended her offensive letter with, "Nigger, I know it's not your fault." To her, there wasn't much difference between choosing me to judge hams and choosing Justice Marshall to judge the law. We were both black.

I set a date for the ham cooking and tasting. Some of the senators sent me their favorite recipes with instructions to follow them to the quarter teaspoon. On the momentous day itself, a few Senate wives insisted on being in the kitchen to supervise their state hams. It was quite a day.

There was wall-to-wall sliced ham piled on tables in the kitchen, Senate Dining Room, and public corridor. My staff and I collared everyone we could to taste a piece—senators, lunch guests, Senate staff, Capitol Police, and tourists. I knew how the day would end even before it began. Although the senators were pleased to supply hams (it was good promotion back home), no one wanted to judge them. It was a no-win situation, which every politician tries to avoid. The burden fell on me, as I knew it would.

During lunchtime on Ham Day, I got a call from Wisconsin Senator Gaylord Nelson's personal secretary. The senator was at home, she said, and had heard about the contest on the radio. He was upset because Wisconsin hadn't entered a ham. No one had told him about the contest. How was he going to explain this to his constituents?

Naturally, it was all my fault. I should have sent a letter to each senator, announcing the contest and setting the rules!

I explained to Nelson's secretary that there was no official contest, despite the news stories, but just a little competition between a Georgia ham and a Kentucky ham that had turned into—well, a contest. She said *she* understood, but she doubted that Nelson would.

An hour later, a waitress knocked at my door. "Mr. Parker," she said, "the TV man wants you."

I went to see what it was all about. When I walked into the Senate Dining Room, television lights nearly blinded me. I covered my eyes with my hands for a moment. Once I got used to the light, I found myself standing next to CBS correspondent George Herman.

"Robert," he said, pushing a microphone under my nose, "the senators want you to judge the hams represented here today. Tell us, which state has the best one?"

228

I knew I had to find a way out fast. Herman's question was far from facetious. My answer would literally affect the pork economy of the states that had submitted hams. I could see the national ad campaign in a flash before my eyes: "Judged to be the best ham by the U.S. Senate." I could also see the hate mail piling up in front of my office door. Bags of it. I thanked God for Gaylord Nelson.

"I don't feel I can give a fair answer at this time," I told Herman while the cameras were rolling. "There are still senators who want to enter this contest. I am very sorry, but I can't truthfully answer now."

That evening, I flipped on Walter Cronkite, as I usually did. Deep into the broadcast I heard him say, "There was a contest today in Washington, D.C., at the Capitol." I couldn't believe it. Of all the things I had done on the Hill, I was about to make national television over forty hams. "A different kind of contest," Cronkite continued. "We will now go to George Herman in Washington. George!"

The senators couldn't wait to shake my hand the next day. I had talked through both sides of my mouth, just like them. Senator Percy, in particular, was so proud of me that he bestowed on me the honorary title, "101st Senator."

It didn't stop there. Senator Harry Byrd, Jr., of Virginia had been out of the country for several weeks before and after Ham Day. Virginia had been unrepresented. "Robert," Byrd complained as soon as he got back, "I have a whole bunch of letters from my constituents wanting to know how there could have been a ham contest in the Capitol without a Virginia ham. And they wanted to know why I didn't enter one. Why, our hams are world famous. We have Smithfield hams, Virginia hams, sugar-cured hams, hickory-smoked hams. How come you didn't let my office know about the contest?"

Senator Jordan wasn't exactly pleased either. "Robert, how come I knew nothing about that ham contest in the Senate Dining Room?" he complained. "Here I make policies for the restaurant, and I didn't know a thing about it. Why, everybody knows North Carolina makes the best ham and pork sausages in the United States!"

Soon after George Herman made Ham Day famous, the hate

229

mail started in earnest. There were piles, all directed at the "nigger" who presumed to judge hams and at the senators who had put him in charge. By that time, I was so sick of ham, I made a firm resolution never to eat another slice as long as I lived.

CHAPTER

* 28 *

On the airplane back to Washington after Lyndon Johnson's funeral in January 1973, I realized how much trouble I was in. LBJ could not protect me from the grave, and the list of my enemies on the Hill was long. I thought about all the toes I had crushed in thirteen years.

From my first day as headwaiter, I had refused to say, "Yes, sir!" every time restaurant managers spoke. I had made friends with most of the senators and their wives, when other staff couldn't. I had reported Robert Sontag for stealing. I had taken Marie German's job, becoming the first black maître d' in the history of the Senate Dining Room. I was the only person on the Hill with a key to every hideaway in the Capitol. Circling around restaurant managers, I had gone time and again directly to Senator Jordan, the Rules Committee, and its subcommittee on restaurants. I had set up meetings for black civil rights leaders in private rooms without asking. I had gotten Senators Javits, Williams, and others to use their influence to increase staff wages. I had integrated the restaurant staff and the staff dining room. I had helped crash the color barrier in the Senate Staff Club. I had written a letter to Senator Jordan, embarrassing the Rules Committee into improving restaurant working conditions. I had traveled all over the country with senators while my bosses stayed home. And I had been on national television when they couldn't even get reporters to talk to them.

On the plane back home, I thought about the last conversation I had had with Lyndon Johnson. It was during the dedication of the Johnson Library in Austin, Texas, in 1971. With a special invitation in hand—none of my bosses had received one—I flew to Austin on a chartered plane filled with VIPs. I cornered LBJ in the vestibule of the library and talked with him for seven or eight minutes. Dressed in cowboy boots and a Western shirt, open at the neck, he looked relaxed and happy. I told him so.

Although he seemed very proud of what he had done for civil rights, I could tell that he was still hurt because blacks had flocked to Bobby Kennedy. In all the years I knew and worked for him, LBJ was never as kind and considerate to me as he was in Austin that day.

"How you gettin' along?" he asked.

"The pressure is building up," I said.

"Robert," he said, "the longer you're on the Hill and the higher you climb, the greater the pressure gets. Let me tell you somethin'. As long as you're there, never buy a big Cadillac and park it on the Hill." He grinned from ear to ear. "And for hell's sake, Robert, keep your damn name out of the papers. You'll be all right."

Although I had laughed at Johnson's advice in Austin, I wasn't smiling on my trip back to Washington after his funeral. I had never taken his advice seriously. Although I didn't have a Cadillac, I did drive a big blue Lincoln Continental, and I did park it on the Hill. On weekends, I moonlighted as headwaiter at the Watergate Hotel restaurant. My new wife, Jane Gormillion, held a responsible job on the House side of the Hill. With the help of Senator Williams, I had bought a home in the exclusive Tantallon Estates in suburban Maryland. And I had broken the color bar at the Tantallon Country Club, which at the time had no blacks or Jews. As a friend of mine put it, I was "a nigger that got too close."

Senator Lloyd Bentsen's promise to watch out for me didn't make me feel any more secure. Not long after Lyndon Johnson had given up the White House and retired to his ranch, Bentsen, a fresh-man Texan on the Hill, had met me in the Senate Dining Room. "I understand you're a Texan," he had said.

"Born and raised in Texas," I told him.

"Well, don't you worry none, I'll take care of you now that Lyndon's not around," he had bragged.

I knew there was no way Bentsen would or could save me from the lynch mob that would now be watching my every move. It took a piece of gum during the Watergate hearings to break the camel's back.

One afternoon late in the fall of 1973, about eight months after LBJ had died, Pauline Gore stopped at my desk in the Senate Dining

Room on her way back from the ladies' room to her table. She was embarrassed and peeved. When her guest had crossed her legs, brushing the underside of Senator Milton Young's table (number 4), her dress had got stuck on gum. Both women had gone to the ladies' room to try to get it off.

"Robert," Mrs. Gore complained, "this table is loaded with gum."

"Thank you," I said. "I'll get all the tables scraped."

Since no one had ever complained about gum in my twelve years as headwaiter and maître d', I had never turned the tables over to check. Later that day, I asked Joe Diamond's permission to have two busboys clean the tables the following Saturday when the restaurant was closed. Diamond had to authorize their overtime, and he did.

On Saturday morning, the busboys and I went to work. One began removing all the china and silverware from the twenty-one tables in the restaurant (they were set for Monday morning breakfast), while the other busboy and I turned over a table to see how much gum was there. The table happened to be Stuart Symington's (number 17).

As we flipped it, I saw a little brown box three inches long and one and a half inches wide attached to the bottom of the table where the two sides of the frame met. I knew it was a bug, and it didn't look new. The busboy working with me couldn't see it from his angle of vision.

"My God, look at the gum under this table," I said. "Let's turn it back over again."

After we righted Symington's table, I crawled under four more nearby: Sam Ervin's, Milton Young's, Lloyd Bentsen's, and Scoop Jackson's. Each had the same kind of bug in the same corner, protected by the tabletop and the frame so it could not be easily seen or brushed loose. Then I walked clear to the other end of the Dining Room to the table under the portrait of George Washington. It was the table Hugh Scott of Pennsylvania liked. I got on my hands and knees.

Another bug.

"Put the cloths and dishes back on all the tables," I told the busboys.

"Why, Mr. Parker?" I knew they were disappointed because they wanted the overtime.

"This'll take longer than I thought," I said. "I'll have to talk to Mr. Diamond."

After they left, I closed the restaurant and went home. For the rest of the weekend, I stewed over what I should do. I wasn't totally surprised that the Senate Dining Room was bugged. Ever since Sam Ervin had called the Senate Select Committee on Presidential Campaign Activities into session in May—a few months before I found the bugs—it seemed like everyone on the Hill was complaining that his or her phone was tapped. Many weren't joking.

If Lyndon Johnson was still on the Hill, I thought, I could go to him. Not only would he handle it while protecting me, he would know how to use the information to his advantage. With him gone, however, my choices were clear. Their consequences were not.

One: I could keep my mouth shut. Who knew how long the bugs had been there or who put them there? It could have been President Nixon's "plumbers." Or maybe J. Edgar Hoover. Perhaps the Secret Service. Maybe even Lyndon Johnson himself. I had to assume that the bugs worked on Saturdays. If someone was listening or recording, it wouldn't be hard to figure out why I had decided to forget scraping gum. I could be in danger. To protect myself, I had to tell someone. But whom?

Two: I could go to Senator Bentsen, whose table was bugged and who had "adopted" me, or to Senator Jordan, who was ultimately responsible for the Dining Room. But I knew that to tell either would be a mistake. Neither senator would bother to look under a restaurant table. He would tell a staff person to check. It would be a week or a month before anyone took the time to look into my "story." By then, the bugs would have vanished. Robert Parker would be accused of lying or would be branded as a whistle-blower.

Three: I could leak the story to the media. They would have a picnic with it in the middle of the Watergate hearings. The story would make headlines. And it wouldn't take restaurant managers and the staff in the office of the Architect of the Capitol and the Rules Committee long to figure out where the leak came from.

Four: I could lay the problem on Joe Diamond's desk. As restaurant manager, he was always telling me to come to him with restaurant problems instead of taking them directly to the committee or subcommittee.

I chose number four.

The first thing Monday morning, I caught Joe Diamond in his office, which may have been bugged as well. "Mr. Diamond," I said, "I didn't finish cleaning the gum from under the tables because I found something. I don't know what it is, but I think you ought to know about it. I'll show it to you after closing."

I could see from Diamond's face that he didn't have a clue as to what I was talking about. Around four-thirty that afternoon, I took him into the Dining Room and locked the door after me. I cleared off Stu Symington's table and asked Diamond to help me flip it. I could see that he was getting impatient.

There it was.

"My God *almighty*," Diamond said. "Is this what I think it is? You mean *every* table has one of these?"

"All six that I checked." I pointed out the ones I had crawled under.

"Let me tell you something," Diamond said when he finally got his tongue back. "This is one thing you better keep your mouth shut about. It will blow the lid off the Capitol if it gets out. Forget you ever saw it. Did anyone else see it?"

"No," I said. "I'm positively sure."

"I'll report this to Senator Jordan myself," he said.

Sometime later that fall, I looked under the tables and found all the bugs gone.

Looking back, telling Diamond may not have been the best thing. Although I never told anyone else about the bugs, I'm sure he did. I sensed that he and his assistant, Louis Hurst, as well as staff in the Architect of the Capitol's office and on the Rules Committee and on its subcommittee on restaurants, all knew that I knew something I wasn't supposed to. I may have become a little paranoid, but I sensed they were watching me even more closely, just waiting for me to make a mistake.

They thought I did several months later on April 30, 1974.

29

On the morning of April 30, I set up an early breakfast in
S–120 for nineteen constituents of Senator Frank Church
of Idaho. The Reverend William Van Deusen, an official of
the Lutheran Church, had coordinated the group. After the meal,
Van Deusen couldn't find me to pay the bill. Since a bus was waiting
outside to shuttle his group to the White House for a special tour,
he left without paying.

When I checked the room later and saw that Van Deusen had
already left, I did what I usually did under those circumstances. I
added a six-dollar tip to the thirty-eight-dollar bill, signed it "Frank
Church by Robert Parker," and gave it to the Senate Dining Room
cashier. The forty-four dollars would be charged to Senator Church's
account. The tip was more than 15 percent, but the two waitresses
had worked so hard serving nineteen people that I thought they
deserved at least three dollars each.

Reverend William Van Deusen returned to the Hill later that
morning with thirty-eight dollars. "You forgot the tip," I reminded
him. "Six dollars."

"I'm short on cash," Van Deusen said. "Can I pay by personal
check?"

"Of course," I said.

Van Deusen's request was routine. He made out a check to the
"Senate Restaurant" for exactly forty-four dollars. I took it to the
cashier, initialed it OK—RCP, indicating that Robert Curtis Parker
had approved it, and asked her to scratch "Frank Church by Robert
Parker" from the original bill. She forgot to do it.

Ten days later, on May 10, Louis Hurst called me from his
office in the Richard Russell Building. "Robert," he said, "I have a
complaint from Senator Church's office. They want to see you in

the Architect's office about it. I'll be by in a few minutes and go down there with you."

"Okay," I said. "I'll be waiting."

The office of the Architect of the Capitol, George White, is just down the hall from the Senate Dining Room. William Raines, assistant to White's executive assistant, was waiting for me. I sat down.

"Robert," Raines began, "we have a complaint here. On April 30, you had a breakfast for nineteen people in S–120. They paid you their thirty-eight-dollar bill in cash, yet you signed the check to Senator Church and added a six-dollar tip to it. Why, if they already paid you cash?"

During any given week while the Senate was in session, I set up as many as thirty special breakfasts, lunches, dinners, and parties. Although I couldn't remember Senator Church's in particular, I wasn't surprised that there was some confusion about the bill. There often was. But I was angry that Raines seemed to be accusing me of stealing a measly thirty-eight dollars and that Hurst hadn't told me what the problem was before he called me onto the carpet. All I would have had to do was to check my log and refresh my memory.

I smelled a setup, and I could almost hear Hurst, who sat smirking next to me, thinking, "We got you now, you sonofabitch!"

"What are you trying to say?" I yelled at Raines. "That I pocketed thirty-eight dollars? I don't want to hear that shit!"

"Robert, you don't have to get all upset," Raines said. "We're just trying to straighten something out."

"Let me go look at my log," I said. "Until then, I don't even want to talk about it."

After I read my log notes for April 30, my conversation with Van Deusen came back. I phoned him immediately, explaining the discrepancy. I reminded him that he had offered me thirty-eight dollars in cash, but that since the total bill was actually forty-four dollars, he had paid by personal check.

"You're absolutely right, Robert," Van Deusen said. "You know, a Mr. Hurst has been calling down here asking me about this. But I forgot about the check and told him I had paid you in cash."

I could only imagine how Hurst's blood must have quickened when he thought he had caught me with my hand in the till.

"Mr. Van Deusen," I asked, "would you be kind enough to send me a copy of that canceled check as soon as it comes in?"

When the original canceled check arrived in the mail with a note from Van Deusen about a week later, I made a copy and tossed it onto Raines's desk. "There!" I said with a hint of triumph. "Here's the check. If there's still a discrepancy, it's a bookkeeping error."

I thought that was the end of the forty-four dollars. But when Raines suggested a few days later that if I quit, he would drop the whole matter and make sure I received full retirement, I knew I was in for real trouble.

"Why in the hell should I resign?" I said. "I haven't done anything."

Louis Hurst dropped by my office for a visit not long after Raines's offer. "Robert," he said, "Hugh Alexander has informed me that he is putting you on administrative leave with pay while this complaint is being investigated."

"Investigated?" I was really hot. Hugh Alexander was chief counsel to Senator Allen's subcommittee on restaurants. I didn't think he had the authority to place me on leave without the approval of Allen or the subcommittee. "What do you mean, being investigated? I gave Raines the goddamn check. What's the problem *now*?"

"I don't know, Robert," Hurst said innocently. But he did know. I found out many months later that when Hurst couldn't make the first charge, of taking cash from Van Deusen and then billing Senator Church, stick, he accused me of cashing the minister's check and pocketing the forty-four dollars. And even later, I found out that an audit of the Senate Dining Room books showed no cash shortage for that day.

But I didn't know those two facts on May 23, when Alexander placed me on leave. My happy world simply fell apart. I couldn't believe Senator Allen would allow such a drastic step without explaining the charges against me and without giving me a hearing to defend myself. I made an appointment to see him. "Don't worry, Robert," he promised, "I assure you that you'll have a hearing."

I also saw Senator Marlow Cook of Kentucky, another member of the subcommittee on restaurants and a former judge. Cook assured me that it was unconstitutional to fire me without a hearing. He would speak to Senator Allen on my behalf, he said. And I called Senator Williams, the third member of the subcommittee, several mornings in a row. A woman answered his home phone. When I told her who I was, she said the senator wasn't there. Then one morning she told me not to call again because Senator Williams didn't want to talk to me.

I was crushed. After all the times I had driven Pete Williams home and put him to bed so he wouldn't crack up his shiny Mercedes or get mugged walking from his car to his door, he wouldn't even talk to me.

I spoke to Senators Symington, Brooke, Mondale, and Javits, among others. They all expressed shock that I had been fired, promising to talk to Senator Allen on my behalf. Senator Mondale said he'd take my case to the Senate floor and call for a vote to grant me a hearing. A group of senators signed a petition and sent it to Allen. I felt I was using the right approach for the Hill: quiet diplomacy; pressure from within.

I waited. Nothing happened. I waited. No one would tell me why I had been placed on leave or when and how I would be able to defend myself. Senator Brooke, in particular, advised me not to make the issue racial, even if it was. "If you do," he warned, "there isn't one senator here who will stand up for you."

I knew Brooke was right, and I had never intended to charge "racism" for a lot of reasons. I didn't want to embarrass the senators, for I was convinced that it wasn't Allen or any other senator who was out to get me, but staffers like Hurst, Gary, and Alexander. I remembered what Lyndon Johnson had often told me: "Chief, the worst thing around here is a troublemaker." If I blew the whistle on racism, I knew I would lose everything—my reputation, my job, and, above all, my friends. The most important thing to me was to clear my name and get back the job and people I loved. I was upset, not because I was being discriminated against as a black man, but because my rights as a person had been violated.

I waited two months. When nothing happened, I hired Alexander Hewes, a Washington attorney who had worked for Senator Leverett Saltonstall of Massachusetts at one time and whom I had known for years. Hewes helped me evaluate my options.

One: I could sue the members of the Rules Committee, charging them with violating my Fifth Amendment rights. In the suit, I could plead for a list of the charges against me and a hearing to meet my accusers face to face. If I won the suit, probably I would be setting a precedent. No one had successfully challenged the Senate's practice of firing staff without a hearing.

Two: I could bring the story to the media and create pressure on Senator Allen, as well as on Senator Howard Cannon of Nevada, who had succeeded Everett Jordan as chairman of the Rules Committee. It would be the kind of David-versus-Goliath summer story that Washington loves. If I chose that option, however, I would certainly have my day in the newspapers, but I'd never get my hearing. Senators, as Hewes and I both knew, would resent that tactic. They would wait until the ink on the newsprint was dry, then leave me swinging in the wind. I would also lose what friends I had left on the Hill.

Three: I could continue to work on Senator Allen privately in the hope that he would make good his promise and grant me a hearing.

I chose option three. Whatever I had accomplished in my life so far, I had done quietly and politically. Confrontation had always been my last resort, not my first. If I couldn't persuade the senators to give me a hearing to defend myself, then, and only then, would I sue them, because they would have left me no choice.

Hewes sent Senator Allen two letters during that summer of 1974 asking for a hearing. Allen answered neither. He was up for re-election and apparently didn't have time for Robert Parker.

While Allen was home in Alabama campaigning, I was living in hell. I couldn't eat or sleep. I became so depressed, I couldn't even cut the grass. I developed a bleeding ulcer. I blacked out several times. I spent two weeks in the hospital suffering from exhaustion. When I was released, my doctor placed me on tranquilizers.

Unable to accept the fact that no one was defending me or fighting for me, and not understanding why, I waited some more.

I used to lie awake at night reciting in my mind the list of senators for whom I had done favors. I couldn't understand why they wouldn't stand up for me when I needed them. Besides Brooke, Cannon, Hruska, Montoya, Pell, and Williams, there was:

—The senator from the Northeast whom I remembered meeting in a Capitol hallway one day. He seemed worried. "Is there something wrong, Senator?" I had asked.

"Yes, Robert," he said. "Have a cup of coffee with me and I'll tell you."

We sat at a table in the Senate Dining Room. "I think you can help me," he said. "But Robert, you have to keep it to yourself."

"I promise," I said.

The senator told me that he suspected his daughter was dating a black college student who lived in a rather dangerous neighborhood and that they both were experimenting with dope. He was concerned about his daughter and nervous about a scandal if the press got a whiff of the story. He couldn't confront his daughter with his suspicions because it would look as if he was prying into her personal life. He showed me her picture and gave me an address on T Street, asking me to check it out for him.

A father myself with a college-age son, I could understand the senator's concern for his daughter's welfare and his fear of losing her confidence if she caught him meddling in her life. I agreed to help.

I knocked at the door of the northwest Washington rowhouse and talked my way inside. There was a party going on and the senator's daughter was there smoking grass. If she was doing anything else, I couldn't tell. I reported back to the senator, who quietly handled the matter.

When I needed his help, the senator from the Northeast gave me the same tired answer I had been hearing all over the Hill. "I'll talk to Senator Allen," he said.

—Senator Russell Long, whose drinking problem at least equaled that of Senator Pete Williams. I remembered the day I found him sitting on a couch in the Senate reception room next to the cloakroom. His legislative aide John McConall was with him. Long was so drunk that his aide had to lead him out of the chamber.

I knew Senator Long's hideaway S–154 better than anyone, for I had been stocking it with liquor and snacks for years. I knew he always kept two or three suits hanging in his closet for such emergencies. To save Long from further embarrassment, I ran to his hideaway and brought a suit to McConall, who guided the senator into the men's room and changed his clothes.

When I needed him, Senator Long was as silent as a Louisiana sunset.

—The senator from the Midwest who was having a torrid affair with the married executive secretary of another senator from the

Midwest. At the senator's request, I would stock his hideaway not far from the Senate Dining Room with drinks, cheese, and fresh shrimp.

The senator's lover used to visit him between seven and eight o'clock in the evening when the Capitol was usually as quiet and eerie as a graveyard. She didn't like to walk down the hallway to his hideaway because the security guards would see where she was going. To protect the senator's reputation, I would unlock the door to the Senate Dining Room so she could take a shortcut to the hideaway through the restaurant and out the back door without being seen.

The morning after, the senator's hideaway would always be a mess. Senate maids would have to straighten the room up and my waitresses would have to collect the dirty dishes. They would find lipstick all over the couch.

"What's this, Mr. Parker?" they would say, then laugh.

I would tell them just to clean up and mind their own business.

When I needed his help, that senator, too, was nowhere to be found.

On September 3, four months after Hugh Alexander had placed me on leave, the dam burst. Austin Scott, a black reporter with *The Washington Post,* broke my story with the headline SENATE MAÎTRE D' PLACED ON PAID LEAVE. In his article, Scott pointed out that Senator Allen had failed to answer my letters and that no one would spell out the charges against me.

Scott quoted Alexander as saying that he himself didn't know the specifics of the allegations against me and that the subcommittee had borrowed a full-time investigator from Senator Scoop Jackson's Permanent Subcommittee on Investigations to check me out. He was the same man who conducted the background investigation of vice-presidential candidate Nelson Rockefeller.

That was the first I had heard of a hired gun. It sounded like a hunting expedition, and I still didn't know what Hurst, Gary, and Alexander were looking for. I suspected that they were going to audit the Senate Dining Room records in the hope of finding something else to pin on me. They had crawled out on a limb for forty-four dollars and, when I refused to be bullied into quitting because they couldn't make their charge stick, they were too proud to climb back down the tree.

Scott went on to suggest that the reason I had been placed on leave was that I had fought for black restaurant workers on the Senate side of the Hill. He quoted Michael MacPherson, a black aide to Congressman William Clay of Missouri, as saying, "The Bob Parker case is indicative of the racism that still permeates the U.S. Congress. . . . The methods used to date indicate that Bob Parker is not guilty of anything other than maybe irritating a U.S. senator and lobbying for benefits for employees under his jurisdiction."

Scott had reared the ugly head of "racism" that, Senator Brooke and I had both agreed, would frighten away my supporters. As it turned out, the allegation of racism accomplished what my letters to Allen had not. The senator stepped off the campaign trail to rush back to Washington. Alex Hewes had no trouble getting an appointment to see him.

Allen was so angry that he told Hewes he was going to fire me. "If I'm wrong," he said, "then so be it."

Two weeks later, on September 15, *The Washington Star News* ran a piece saying that Robert Parker had been referred to the Justice Department for criminal investigation. The story was based entirely on an interview with one man: Senator Allen's press secretary, Fred Eiland. "The criminal aspect of the Parker matter has been turned over to the Department of Justice and is out of the Senate's hands," Eiland told *Star* reporter Ymelda Dixon.

I still didn't know what the charges were, but I assumed it had something to do with Reverend William Van Deusen's forty-four dollars. I later learned that the subcommittee had indeed sent my case to the Justice Department, but that it had found "the case" against me to be without merit and had dropped it without an investigation. Unfortunately, that fact never got printed.

Press allegations of racism and crime succeeded in scaring my supporters on the Hill into silence. No senator, not even Brooke, felt he could stand up for me in public under the circumstances.

Four days after the *Star* story, Senator Allen formally fired me. Capitol Architect George White's letter of dismissal offered no explanation. He said my termination was the "unanimous" decision of the subcommittee. I later learned that Senators Cook and Williams had washed their hands of my case, telling Allen to handle me as he saw fit.

Without a job or health and retirement benefits, I went to

Hewes and told him that I had no choice but to take the U.S. Senate to court. Realizing I couldn't afford his legal fees, Hewes recommended my case to the American Civil Liberties Union. The ACLU asked Thomas Matthews, an attorney with the firm of Wald, Harkrader, and Ross, to take me on *pro bono*. Working closely with Hewes, Matthews filed a suit in the U.S. District Court for the District of Columbia against George White and each member of the Rules Committee: James Allen, Howard Cannon, Marlow Cook, Harrison Williams, Claiborne Pell, Hugh Scott, Robert Byrd, Robert Griffin, and Mark Hatfield.

The terms of my lawsuit were simple. I asked for a list of the charges against me and a hearing to defend myself. During the hearing, I asked to be represented by counsel, to meet my accusers face to face, and to cross-examine them. Finally, I asked to be paid $9,500 in back salary and benefits as well as reasonable attorney fees.

My case rested on my Fifth Amendment right "to life, liberty and the pursuit of happiness." Fired from the "most exclusive restaurant" in town and branded a crook, I couldn't get a job anywhere. No one wanted to hire a maître d' or headwaiter under investigation by the Department of Justice. I argued that by denying me a hearing, the defendants had deprived me of my right to "liberty."

As sick, angry, and hurt as I was, I decided to give the senators one last chance. Matthews wrote a letter to each member of the committee saying that if the committee would grant me a hearing, I would withdraw my suit. In December 1974, eight months after I was placed on leave and four months after I was fired, counsel for the Rules Committee said the senators had unanimously voted to deny me a hearing.

From the time I was fired in September 1974 until Judge Oliver Gasch rendered his decision in June 1975, pressure, anger, and hurt drove to me to the brink of a breakdown. They got to my family as well. My daughter Wanda Maria and Jane's two children, Daria and Tracy, were taunted at school. Women in Jane's social clubs avoided her. Her job on the Hill was in jeopardy. I became impossible to live with. I couldn't blame her when she finally walked out on me.

In June 1975, thirteen months after Alexander had placed me

on leave, Judge Oliver Gasch ruled that my dismissal had been a violation of my Fifth Amendment rights. He found that I was entitled to back wages, legal expenses, and a list of the charges against me. And he granted me a hearing—not a private one behind closed Senate doors to be presided over by a senator, but a public one to be presided over by a neutral judge.

I had won. I got everything I had asked for. I believe I set a legal precedent doing it. And I had done it in my own way. Words can't express how happy I felt the day my attorney called me with the news. I cried like a baby.

I was not surprised when the attorneys for the Architect of the Capitol, for whom I legally worked, asked me to settle quietly without a public hearing. On the stand, I would have aired much of what I have written in this book. They didn't want that, and in fact neither did I. For one thing, I truly felt that I had already won and I saw nothing to be gained by an emotional public hearing. For another, I was so exhausted physically and emotionally that I didn't think I had the strength to hang out thirteen years of dirty linen.

The U.S. Senate agreed to drop all charges against me, give me full retirement benefits, pay me back salary, and give me fifteen thousand dollars in damages. Matthews encouraged me to accept. I did.

It was a chilly December day in 1975 when my attorney called me to say that the agreement with the Architect of the Capitol was ready for my signature and that the signing would be in George White's office.

"I'll go with you," he suggested.

I put on my best dark three-piece suit and splashed my favorite after-shave lotion on my face. I eased into my Lincoln Continental. My emotions ran the gamut from bitterness to relief to satisfaction. I wanted to get it over with, to say my painful good-bye to the Hill I still loved.

I pulled into the east parking lot near the door I had entered almost every day for thirteen years as headwaiter and maître d'. I had lost my parking privilege, but the Capitol Policeman on duty knew me and let me park there anyway.

I looked up the steps leading into the Rotunda, the steps Adam

Clayton Powell had walked up so proudly on his first day on the Hill. I thought about how the bigots had lynched him in the end.

The guards on duty inside the Capitol nodded and smiled at me as if to say, "Keep the faith, baby."

I walked down the hallway to the Architect of the Capitol's office, glancing at the marble and bronze statues along the way. Powell was still not among them. He always knew he wouldn't be. I passed through the Rotunda, where I had stood next to the bier of John F. Kennedy and where I had heard Lyndon Johnson call for civil rights and justice for blacks.

When I reached George White's door, my attorney sheepishly asked me to wait outside. He didn't have the heart to say why.

I waited. On that December day, it seemed as if I had spent my whole life waiting: For my father to get even with Mr. Yawn. For a civil rights bill with teeth. For equality for my Senate Dining Room staff. For my friends to step forward to defend me. For the court to grant me a hearing. For a piece of paper that restored my name. For justice.

My attorney returned a few moments later with Russell Pettibone, White's attorney. "There's a problem," my attorney said. "They don't want you in the office. You'll have to sign out here."

The flood of anger made my hands shake and all the insults and injustices I had suffered in my lifetime flashed across my mind. I took the agreement, placed it against the wall, and wrote "Robert C. Parker" with all the pride I could muster. As soon as I signed, pity and sadness washed my anger away.

Pity for all the ignorant people who live with hatred in their hearts. And sadness for all those who will follow me and suffer because of it.

I turned my back on Capitol Hill and drove home.

EPILOGUE

Senator James Allen, Joe Diamond, and Dan Gary died of heart attacks not long after I settled with the Architect of the Capitol. Before Senator Allen died, however, I wrote to explain my feelings. "There is nothing in the record or my past association with you to suggest that your decisions and actions were based on anything other than the facts—as they had been described to you," I said. "I have never believed, nor is there any evidence to suggest, that you were guided by personal malice toward me or racial prejudice. For my part, I am not bitter. . . .

"After considerable thought on the matter, I reluctantly concluded that I did not want to return to the payroll of the Architect of the Capitol. It would have required my facing some of the same attitudes that led up to my difficulty in the first place. . . .

"I did not wish to put my family through any more than they had already suffered as a result of this experience. A hearing would not have repaid them for the abuse, embarrassment, and anxiety injected into their lives as a direct result of the public blemish on my reputation and my inability to find permanent employment during the period this matter remained unresolved. The settlement did not accomplish that either. However, it did bring an end to the turmoil in our lives and has enabled me to make a fresh start with a clear conscience and reputation."

I meant those words when I wrote them, and my feelings have not changed since. Allen replied: "I am sorry that things worked out as they did because our relations in the work of the Senate restaurant facility were always friendly and cordial.

"As to the final termination of the matter, I was glad to see an amicable agreement reached and I hope that you will be able to draw a measure of comfort and satisfaction from the settlement and written agreement that was executed."

Senator Marlow Cook, the minority member of the Subcommittee on Restaurants, lost his bid for reelection. He practices law in Washington and I met him several times in the Republican Club on Capitol Hill where I worked briefly after my settlement with the Senate. He was very cordial.

Senator Harrison "Pete" Williams, the third member of the subcommittee, was stung by Abscam and is in jail as of this writing. Although I am still deeply hurt that he did not defend my right to have a Senate hearing, my strongest feeling for him is pity. I had sat with him many an evening before Abscam and listened to him talk about everything from Nixon to Nigeria as he drank himself under the table. I had never known him to be crooked or corrupt. Just weak.

I went to Williams's Abscam trial in New York still trying to figure out why he had abandoned me. After his conviction, but before he went to jail, the Senate Ethics Committee reviewed his case. Unlike me, Williams had the opportunity to hear the charges against him and to defend himself. I wrote to him in August 1981 during his hearing. "Your colleagues are now giving you an opportunity to tell your story to the Ethics Committee," I said. "I am proud to see you being given the due process of law.

"I was, however, painfully reminded of the day (September 27, 1975) when the late Senator James Allen wrote to the members of the subcommittee of which you were a member, on my behalf, concerning vague charges against me, and the decision to retain or release me from my job. . . .

"I will now quote him: 'If any committee member wishes the subcommittee to reconsider a hearing before Mr. Parker's discharge, I am sure they will advise me at the next meeting of the committee. . . .'

"You denied me due process of the law. May God bless you, Senator Williams. We were always friends and I shall continue to pray for you."

Signing his letter "Pete," Williams answered: "I thank you for your good wishes and prayers. Your support means a great deal to me during this trying time."

After I settled with the Architect of the Capitol, Senator Walter Mondale wrote me a letter I will always cherish. People who don't know the Hill do not understand how difficult it is to stand up to it. Mondale understood. "My heartiest congratulations on the result of the suit," he said. "It took guts to see it through, and I'm very proud of you for doing so. I wouldn't have expected anything else."

George White is still the Architect of the Capitol. I met him in the Republican Club a few months after we settled. "Robert," he said, "I'm very sorry all this had to happen. I only went by what the staff said and it proved wrong."

Robert Sontag, my first boss in the Senate Dining Room, is dead and Louis Hurst no longer works there. But the three women who broke the color bar in the Senate Staff Club—Vividell Holmes, Eloise Washington, and Mary Clark—still do. Vividell is the Senate Dining Room hostess.

Sad to say, many of the benefits I won for the Senate Dining Room staff have been revoked and the restaurant is again becoming "the last plantation." Conditions in the House Dining Room are even worse.

I frequently meet House and Senate black staff who tell me that racism is far from dead on the Hill. Many white staff have the same prejudice and hatred for blacks they had when I worked there. The only thing that has changed is how they express these feelings; they're stated more subtly now. Unfortunately, like Senator Keating in the 1940s, President Reagan has his head in the sand about what really goes on under the Capitol dome. His administration reflects the same ignorance.

Not demanding back my job as maître d' was one of the smartest things I've ever done. Under the pressure of working in the Senate Dining Room, I had developed an ulcer, a heart problem, and high blood pressure. Had I returned to work there, I'm sure the backbiting and the pressure not to make a mistake would have ruined my health completely.

Since 1975, I've bumped into many former senators on the street, in restaurants, or at parties—George Smathers, Walter Mondale, Ed Brooke, Stuart Symington, Frank Moss, Hugh Scott, to name a few. They show me the greatest respect and our conversation is usually the same:

"What are you doing these days, Robert?" they ask.

"Still writing my book," I say.

"Make sure you give me a copy," they say.

In 1980, I managed the Senate hospitality rooms at both the Republican and Democratic conventions. Albert Nellum, a Jesse Jackson campaign coordinator, asked me to serve the hospitality room of the Rainbow Coalition at the 1984 Democratic Convention in San Francisco. Although I had made up my mind that 1980 would be my last convention, I was proud to accept the invitation. I had served every Democratic Convention since 1944 and I never thought I'd see the day when a black man would run for president. I knew, of course, that Jackson had no chance of being nominated, but winning was not the issue. I don't believe a black will ever be elected president in this century because society could not survive the shock. But I would not be surprised if a black man became vice president.

My first wife, Modean, is dead. My second wife, Jane, still works on the Hill. And my three children are doing well. Barbara Ann, the oldest, attended Howard University in Washington and did graduate work at Wayne State in Detroit. She has two children—Don and Ken—and works for the government.

Edwin graduated from the University of Utah with a B.A. in economics. Living in Washington with his wife, Deb, and daughter, Knia, Eddie is a sales representative for a large computer company. It's the kind of job that would never have been open to me in 1943. Wanda Maria is a student at Temple University in Philadelphia.

My father died in the summer of 1984 at the age of ninety-four. I was hoping he'd live to see this book in print. Twelve years earlier I was finally able to forgive him for not protecting Robbie from Mr. Yawn. After the Democratic Convention in Miami (which I served), I drove with Wanda Maria to Houston where he was still living. I had not spoken to him since I had left Magnolia for Wichita Falls as a teenager. I'll never forget that trip:

I pulled off the freeway at Huntsville, Texas, to buy ice for the cooler and fruit for Wanda Maria. When I was a youngster, Huntsville had always given me the creeps. It was there, in the federal penitentiary, that black men were sent to the electric chair for allegedly killing white folks. The town still sent shivers through me more than thirty years later. As I pulled off the expressway, I saw a Texas Ranger on a motorcycle waiting at the side of the road for speeders. I stopped and asked him for directions to a supermarket.

The Ranger pointed me in the right direction. I thanked him and, as I pulled away in my Lincoln Continental, he noticed my Washington license plate, which read, "U.S. Senate Staff." He apparently didn't see "Staff," for he pulled alongside the car and gave me a hand signal to follow him.

Flashing his lights but not turning on his siren, he escorted me to the supermarket. I suspected that he thought I was Senator Ed Brooke. A lot of people—white and black—had confused us in the hallways of the Capitol. We had basically the same build, hair style, and round face. Brooke, however, was lighter skinned than I was and didn't weigh quite as much.

Leaving my car air conditioner running, I went inside to make my purchase. When I stepped back out into the summer heat, close to fifty white people were waiting for me. They began thrusting pieces of paper at me shouting, "Senator Brooke, will you autograph this?"

"I'm not Senator Brooke!" I kept saying.

"Yes you are!"

I looked at Wanda Maria. She had her face to the car window and was laughing so hard that tears were rolling down her cheeks. Concerned that there might be a scene, the Ranger seemed pleased when I pushed my way back into the car without hanging around to sign autographs. He turned his red light on and escorted me back to the expressway. I left him waving good-bye at the side of the road.

Wanda Maria and I laughed all the way to Houston. "You should be ashamed of yourself," she kidded. "You told them you were Senator Brooke."

"No I didn't," I insisted. But to this day, she still thinks I was playing senator.

My father was so happy to see me he kept asking why I had stayed away so long. "I've been very busy" was all I could say.

It was a lame excuse, but I knew he didn't want to talk about Robbie and Magnolia. By 1972, I had come to realize that when he did not stand up to Mr. Yawn, he had done what he had to. He did not have a real choice.

I think deep down my father knew why I had stayed away and why I had come back. We didn't have to talk about it. Ours was one of those father-son conversations where no words are spoken, but a lot is said.

My father died in a home in Redwood City outside San Francisco just after the 1984 Democratic Convention. It was as if he were saying, "Robert's in town. It's a good time to go." I like to remember him the way he looked when I arrived from Huntsville— pleased and happy that I had come home. All seven of my father's children gathered at his funeral to say good-bye: Stella Loggins, Richard Parker, Elvi Barbour, Velton Parker, Margetta Robinson, Ruth Singleton, and me.

After my father's funeral, my fiancée Beverly Jones-Hogan and I drove to Lake Tahoe where we were married. Beverly and her two children, Twanda and Travis, are my new family. I feel like I am starting life over again and have never been happier.

I also feel very fortunate. In my years on the Hill and after I left, I have witnessed important historical events and traveled extensively. I have met hundreds of famous (and infamous) people from presidents to movie stars to duchesses to world champion athletes. I have worked side by side with fine lawmakers imbued with strong moral values. Perhaps my selective memory has not given them enough credit here, but I feel privileged having known them. Through the years, there have been good times as well as bad. And I would not trade any of them.

I believe that everything I have experienced in my life has been woven into the person I am—a man who believes that the future will be better than the past because today is better than yesterday. I can picket the South African Embassy knowing that, as bad as conditions for blacks are in that troubled country, that too shall pass. If a Texan like LBJ could sign into law the most sweeping civil rights legislation of the century and bring racists to their knees with, as he would put it, "that goddamned voting rights bill," then one can hope that even the government of South Africa will abolish apartheid. When I listen to South African politicians argue against giving blacks the right to vote, it's as if I'm back in the Inner Sanc-

252

tum in 1965 listening to the whining of McClellan, Hill, Holland, Thurmond and Ellender.

I think often of those days, and especially of LBJ. I still love him sometimes and hate him at other times. I believe that he pushed civil rights legislation through Congress for two pragmatic reasons. He deeply loved this country and was convinced that if blacks were denied their rights, racism would destroy it. Unity was more important to him than the South's love for him.

I also believe that, like every president, Lyndon Johnson wanted to be remembered as a great leader. Civil rights legislation was his ticket into history.

Was he a bigot or a humanitarian at heart? The answer—as contradictory as the man himself—depends on the time, the day, and the circumstances.

The changes and progress in this country since my childhood on a sharecropper's farm in east Texas are startling. Today, it's a pleasure to drive through the South where most people are polite to me and to other blacks. I know I owe that respect to farsighted politicians like Lyndon Johnson, uncompromising prophets like Martin Luther King, and thousands of civil rights marchers whose names no one even remembers now.

That is not to say that all blacks are treated with fairness today or that racism no longer exists. Hate groups, both black and white, are active again across the nation. Blacks have not made great economic gains in spite of civil rights victories. To win economic security is the task of the future for black Americans.

I have heard it said that young blacks are taking the gains of the 1960s for granted. They should be aware of how hard-fought those gains were. I want my grandchildren to be secure in the knowledge that they have the right to go as far as their abilities will take them. Because they do not have to fight for their basic human rights and freedoms as my generation did, they can pour their energy and creativity into providing for their families and making even greater contributions to the growth and development of this country on all levels—financial, religious, political, and cultural.

When I came to Washington in 1943, I set a goal for myself that perhaps few people today can understand—to survive as a man no matter how much hatred or how many insults I had to suffer. I not only survived, but I prospered and enjoyed my life. The hatred others showed toward me and the pain it has caused have not turned me into a bitter man. I consider that refusal to hate to be my personal victory over the ugliness and evil of racism.

INDEX

* Index *